Ghosts in the Machine

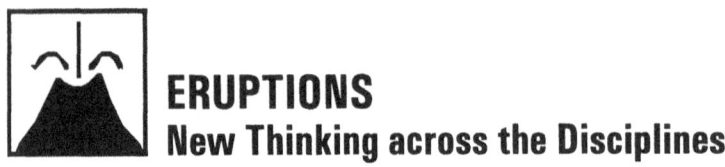

ERUPTIONS
New Thinking across the Disciplines

Erica McWilliam
General Editor

Vol. 10

PETER LANG
New York • Washington, D.C./Baltimore • Bern
Frankfurt am Main • Berlin • Brussels • Vienna • Oxford

Ghosts in the Machine

Women's Voices in Research with Technology

EDITED BY
**Nicola Yelland
and Andee Rubin**

PETER LANG
New York • Washington, D.C./Baltimore • Bern
Frankfurt am Main • Berlin • Brussels • Vienna • Oxford

Library of Congress Cataloging-in-Publication Data

Ghosts in the machine: women's voices in research
with technology / Nicola Yelland and Andee Rubin, editors.
p. cm. — (Eruptions; vol. 10)
Includes bibliographical references and index.
1. Women in technology. 2. Research, Industrial.
I. Yelland, Nicola. II. Rubin, Andee. III. Series.
T36 .G46 607'.2—dc21 2001046279
ISBN 0-8204-4911-3
ISSN 1091-8590

Die Deutsche Bibliothek-CIP-Einheitsaufnahme

Ghosts in the machine: women's voices in research
with technology / ed. by: Nicola Yelland and Andee Rubin.
—New York; Washington, D.C./Baltimore; Bern;
Frankfurt am Main; Berlin; Brussels; Vienna; Oxford: Lang.
(Eruptions; Vol. 10)
ISBN 0-8204-4911-3

Cover design by Dutton & Sherman Design

© 2002 Peter Lang Publishing, Inc., New York

All rights reserved.
Reprint or reproduction, even partially, in all forms such as microfilm,
xerography, microfiche, microcard, and offset strictly prohibited.

Dedication

In memory of Jan Hawkins and in
honor of the women we love,
Tamsyn, Caja and Liz.

Table of Contents

List of Figures ix
List of Tables xi
Foreword xiii
Preface xvii

Part One
The Gendering of Technology 1

Chapter 1
The Gendering of Information Technology 3
Karen Littleton & Celia Hoyles

Chapter 2
Imagining Less-Gendered Game Worlds 33
Katie McMillan Culp & Margaret Honey

Chapter 3
Who's Afraid of a Mouse?—Grrrls, Information
Technology and Educational Pleasures 55
Elizabeth Bullen & Jane Kenway

Chapter 4
The Feminization of Technology 71
Cornelia Brunner & Dorothy Bennett

Chapter 5
Women Artists and Their Relations to Technologies 97
Zoë Sofia

Part Two
New Ways of Learning with Technology in Schools and Communities 117

Chapter 6
Learning by Design: Environments that
Support Girls' Learning with Technology 119
Laurie D. Edwards

Chapter 7
Shades of Gray: Creating a Vision
of Girls and Computers 139
Nicola Yelland

Chapter 8
"I Always Get Stuck with the Books":
Creating Space for Girls to Access Technology
in a Software Design Project 167
*Cynthia Carter Ching, Yasmin B. Kafai
& Sue K. Marshall*

Chapter 9
Tia and the Virtual Expert 191
Michele Evard

Chapter 10
E-GEMS: A Project on Computer Games,
Mathematics and Gender 209
*Maria Klawe, Kori Inkpen, Eileen Phillips, Rena Upitis
& Andee Rubin*

List of Contributors 229
Index 235

Figures

Figure 1.1:	The original *Pong* game	18
Figure 1.2:	Changing the appearance of the paddles and ball	20
Figure 1.3:	Going *Underwater* with sharks and fish	21
Figure 1.4:	The final *Underwater* game with two scores	22
Figure 1.5:	The boys' simulated *Cricket* game	23
Figure 4.1:	One girl's image of the Internet	74
Figure 4.2:	One boy's image of the Internet	75
Figure 7.1:	*Missing Measures*: House	146
Figure 7.2:	Levels of performance in *Missing Measures*	148
Figure 7.3:	Year 3 project: Castle	149
Figure 7.4a:	A sailor by Alice and Alyssa (Year 3)	150
Figure 7.4b:	A sailor by Alice and Alyssa (Year 3)	151
Figure 7.4c:	A sailor by Alice and Alyssa (Year 3)	152
Figure 7.5:	*Sunken Ships*	153
Figure 7.6:	*Rectangles*	155
Figure 7.7:	*Cakes*	156
Figure 8.1:	A constellation page from Team 3's final product	173
Figure 8.2:	Girls from different teams examining software designs	181

| Figure 10.1: | Example of a "cloze" passage screen | 217 |
| Figure 10.2: | *Fibonnaci* game | 220 |

Tables

Table 1.1:	Survey of information and communications technology in schools	15
Table 4.1:	What boys and girls care about	85
Table 6.1:	Original and pre-designed *LEGO/Logo* projects	127
Table 8.1:	Composition of all groups	172
Table 8.2:	Activity classification	176
Table 9.1:	Tia's main game phases. Sessions are numbered from the first day of the Game Design project. The online system became available during session 4.	198

Foreword

I remember visiting an elementary school in the Silicon Valley that was "experimenting with microcomputers" in the early 1980's. The school's only computers were located in the media center, and when I arrived I was struck by the number of students literally a dozen or so, "working" at the two computers that were available. But even more striking was the group of 6th grade boys who were either at the keyboard, or right up front, doing everything they could to be involved. Compared to them, the girls in this 6th grade class held back or were muscled out by their male peers who appeared to be so much more adept with technology than they were.

Twenty years later, we see a different scene. There are now equal numbers of boys and girls engaged at computers, writing, solving problems, preparing multimedia presentations, conducting research on-line, and pursuing their personal interests. Schools' investment in technology over the past decade has increased access and use of technology in many ways. In the United States, most schools now have Internet access; in some schools, all classrooms are wired; and in a few but growing number of schools, there is a computer for every student. Parallel developments are occurring in many other countries as well, as government leaders seek to bring their educational systems into the twenty-first century, stepping up efforts to increase students' information literacy and technical skills and seeking to increase the pool of information age workers on the assumption that technological advances are key to economic growth and development.

But even with this seemingly ubiquitous presence of technology, access to technology is not universal. The ways in which computers are used, the skill with which they are used and the roles they play in people's lives differ dramatically from one community to another. The digital divide between rich and poor communities, schools and households is well documented. And there continue to be significant differences between genders particularly in terms of girls' and boys' approaches to computing and their different preferences for the kinds of activities they pursue with technology. While differences themselves are not necessarily a problem, there is much to be concerned about, for one, the low rate of female participation in mathematics, physics, computer science, engineering and technology courses in high school and in post-secondary institutions.

As technology advances continue to stretch our imagination and provide improvements in tools for learning and communication, it is critical that we make sure that all of society can participate and benefit, and that all have an opportunity to influence, and even design the next generation of tools and applications. This collection of research appears at a pivotal time. Now is the time to better understand the "gendering of technology" and to push the frontier of knowledge on new ways to learn with technology so that girls and boys, women and men, all have opportunities to engage with and master new bodies of content.

The editor and authors of the chapters that follow provide a unique and important description of what is known about how girls and women approach technology and provide important insights on how we better match interests and needs. Because they are all women, the authors approach technology as advocates for women, with a well-trained eye for the unique contributions women can make and the context they need to fulfill their potential. In the first half of the book, the authors set forth a research-based world view that attempts to describe women's uses of technology, not as a deficient approach in comparison to men, but as a different one, with its own strengths and perspectives. In the second section of the book, the authors offer examples of ways to rethink, revise and develop new ways of learning with technology. What changes occur in our educational experiences, both with and about technology, when we use a different lens to view the role of technology in women's lives and the role of women in the ongoing life of technology? In the best case, education can provide the leverage for women to expand their interests and be drawn into computer science, mathematics, and engineering, software design... arenas where "new technology" is created. These chapters suggest how important it is for women to make their voices heard in technology design, so that patterns of design and use that currently favor male voices can expand to include broader segments of society.

What will the future hold? The Web will continue to bring massive amounts of information to a growing number of people, almost anywhere

Foreword

in the world. "Smart" devices and appliances will proliferate and will be interconnected. New interfaces will augment reality, facilitate group and shared experiences, and expand visualization and simulation. Users of technology will become more sophisticated and invent applications never dreamed of by the designers. Will these advances in capability be matched by improvements in education and a blossoming of learning and creativity? Will we succeed in expanding not only the community of users of technology but also the community of designers, engineers and developers of technology? The future is up to us, and we have much to learn from the researchers and authors in this book and the rich studies and explorations they describe. We must answer their call for continuing research, education and action.

Linda Roberts
Founding Director, Office of Educational Technology
U.S. Department of Education

Preface

This book grew out of Nicola's sabbatical at TERC, the educational research and development organization where I work. During the year, she attempted (and generally succeeded) to meet with everyone who had done any research on the complicated relationships between women and technology. She traveled extensively and, in her characteristically enthusiastic and open-hearted way, met everyone I knew in the field and many I had heard of but not talked to personally. She returned to my office at TERC one day near the end of her stay and announced to me "I've met so many women doing great research on women and technology, we should compile a book!" It wasn't a question but a declaration, and so I joined the effort.

This book was thus international from its inception, and now includes authors from four countries on three continents. Yet since the number of women doing research in this area is relatively small, almost every author knew most of the others, and working on the book became somewhat of a community project. On the other hand, a few new faces (at least to me) are included, and we hope that for every reader, there are some new introductions and unexpected insights in the chapters that follow.

While we were compiling the book, there were many reminders that, while we were all women who "took on" technology readily, the gender issues are far from resolved. The most startling example of this fact for me happened one day while I was watching a TV documentary on the origins of the Internet (much of which took place at Bolt Beranek and Newman, where I once worked). The show went on for over an hour but there wasn't a single woman mentioned, much less pictured. It was also obvious from the beginning that gender was not a topic that was going to be addressed in the documentary. The disparity was just *there*, un-recognized and unanalyzed, much as it is today in too many cases.

The chapters in this book are organized into two broad sections. The chapters in the first part focus generally on the relationship between women and technology. They define and dissect what a female or feminist attitude toward technology might be. The chapters in the second part explore the implications of this work for learning, both in and out of school. Interestingly, in addition to documenting and analyzing women's lack of participation with technologies, several of the chapters question the "ideal" image of a person who enthusiastically embraces technologies. One of the purposes of this book was to begin the construction of alternative images of who these people might be.

The first part begins with an examination by Littleton and Hoyles of the ways in which school curriculum, assessment, activities and images of success shape students' views of information technology. They describe a home computer activity that involves designing and building computer games, that creates a different context and varying expectations about the use of computers.

The chapter by Culp and Honey analyzes the role that gender plays in shaping the desires, needs, and motivations that drive individuals' engagement with technology, using a psychoanalytic backdrop. They reject what they call the "false choice" in technology design between "gender" and "no gender" and explore what it might mean for a game environment to be "less gendered."

Bullen and Kenway interrogate the notion of cyberfeminism and argue that new conceptualizations are needed, since existing views do not accommodate the ways in which technologies and consumption can connect with gender, generation issues, pleasure and identity. Their chapter explores the ways in which girls and young women can interact with the new information technologies and suggests that educators need to consider the culture of the current generation in order to provide meaningful educational experiences that incorporate the use of new technologies.

Brunner and Bennett describe the results of several related studies that together delineate a contrast between feminine and masculine perspectives on technology. They then offer several examples of the ways in which women's values can shape the use and design of new technologies in ways that are currently virtually nonexistent.

Sofia's chapter is a foray into a world of women visual artists which is seldom described in the same book as educational technology. She explores the layers and dynamics of women artists' relationship to the digital media they use. One of the interesting perspectives she notes is that, in contrast to students or workers, artists elect to involve themselves with computers and digital media not because they have to in any way, but as a tool for creative and expressive activity. Her chapter has important ramifications for the use of new technologies for women in educational, vocational and social contexts.

The second part of the book turns its focus to learning, in school and out of school contexts. All of these chapters suggest images of educational technology that differ substantially from a simple use of a tool for a prescribed task and in the process consider the social setting of technology for learning as important as the machines themselves.

Edwards' chapter describes a vacation project which involved girls in upper elementary school through early high school in hands-on design and programming activities in an attempt to enhance their interest and self-confidence in science, mathematics, and technology. It was based on a view of science and technology as "messy" exploratory disciplines, whose practice includes both planned and fortuitous actions—an image not always associated with computers.

Yelland's chapter contends that we need to move beyond describing school performances and applications with computers in terms of behaviors that are traditionally associated with male characteristics. She describes a study in which girls and boys used computers in a variety of ways that were not dependent on gender and suggests that all students are afforded new and dynamic ways of learning in some technological environments.

The chapter by Ching, Kafai, and Marshall explicitly addresses the role of learning in a design environment. They explore a particular mixed-gender classroom setting, in which they found that they needed to create new spaces that they characterized as being cognitive, physical, and social to provide opportunities for girls to gain technology access.

Evard describes the online system she created that became a Virtual Expert for a classroom, transforming the students from a collection of individuals into an entity that served as a resident expert for the group. To provide a finer-grained analysis of the transformative power of such a system, she follows one particular student taking advantage of the Virtual Expert to help her classmates and developing a different view of her own communication in the process.

Finally, Klawe, Inkpen, Phillips, Upitis, and Rubin return us to the broader gendered world of technology in an examination of computer games. They explore them as they exist and as they might be designed. They describe the design of a computer game specifically responsive to girls' preferences, the general principles that emerged from research with the resulting prototype, and where these new findings might lead us.

The authors in the book have been fortunate in that, through some combination of aptitude, effort, and serendipity, they have each succeeded in harnessing technology for their own purposes. They have appropriated the machines for their own use and as an object for research. We have all recognized the benefits of bringing women and technology together. Women's voices have been ghosts in the machine. Women's presence in research and activities with the new technologies have been important and paramount to the successes that have been documented yet often remain ethereal and cast in the shadows. We wanted to initiate and extend the conversations out into the light. We also wanted to highlight that the dance is yet to come. This book is an invitation to the dance.

Andee Rubin
Technical Education Research Center (TERC)

Part One

The Gendering of Technology

Chapter 1

The Gendering
of Information Technology

Karen Littleton & Celia Hoyles

Introduction

Recent years have seen a massive expansion of computer technology in schools. This is the case throughout the world, as well as in the United Kingdom, the context of this chapter. The scale of the expansion of computer provision in the United Kingdom is highlighted by Gill (1996), who drew on Department for Education and Employment (DfEE) statistics to show the increased computer provision within the compulsory school sector. As Gill reported, in United Kingdom secondary schools in 1985, there were 60 students for every computer, as compared to 10 students for every computer in 1994 (DfEE, 1995). Over the same period, the total expenditure on information technology in secondary schools alone rose from £9.8 million to £86.9 million. In primary and special schools the picture was much the same with 56% of teaching staff in primary schools using computers at least twice a week (DfEE, 1995). A more recent survey investigating computer provision in the United Kingdom in March 1999 indicated a continuing upwards trend in provision and access. Expenditure on computer equipment has increased, particularly in the primary sector, from £49 million in 1998 to £105 million in 1999. The average number of computers per school has risen from 13 to 16, which has resulted in a decrease in the ratio of students per computer from 18 in 1998 to 13 in 1999 (DfEE, 1999). In the current political climate, where the government is promoting the development and use of a National Grid for Learning (NGfL) to "Connect the Learning Society" (DfEE, 1997), this trend of increased computer provision and usage is set to continue and even to accelerate. The NGfL was launched as part of a rolling program of investment totaling more than £1.6 billion up to 2002 which underpinned Government targets for information and communication technologies (ICT) in education and lifelong learning. These targets included: teachers being confident and competent to use ICT for teaching; all schools, colleges and universities being connected to the NGfL with about 75% of teachers and 50% of students having their own email address and most school leavers acquiring a good understanding of ICT.

Against this backdrop of burgeoning computer use, the idea that computers could influence "the shape of minds to come" has considerable currency, and much is being written about the potential of the computer to offer new educational environments, new learning and new ways to learn (Crook, 1994, 1996; Scrimshaw, 1993; Littleton & Light, 1999). Government ministers, in fact, match the earlier rhetoric of Papert (Papert, 1980) and that of educational researchers (Hoyles, 1985; Noss, 1997) and now talk of a knowledge revolution (Wills, 2000). However, hand in hand with enthusiasm for computer use in the classroom is a growing awareness that the social and educational effects of the technology could be divisive (e.g., Laboratory of Comparative Human Cognition, 1989; Light & Littleton, 1999). Computer technology can open access to a range of abstract disciplines such as mathematics and science by making them more manipulable and engaging, but it can also enhance pre-existing patterns of social inequality and widen the gap between the "haves and the have nots." Different digital under-classes are emerging who are denied access to computers at home, either through cost, attitude, or lack of information. We will argue that this exclusion can be exacerbated by the very nature of the computer activities that are offered in schools.

Clearly issues of class and poverty are relevant to any discussion of exclusion from computer use, but in this chapter our focus is on gender. A growing body of research has revealed that males and females differ in terms of their expressed enthusiasm for, their access to, and participation in computer-related activities (e.g., Brosnan, 1999; Littleton, 1996; Littleton & Bannert, 1999; Light, 1997). There are now serious claims that the increasing deployment of computers in school could place girls at a disadvantage relative to boys, unless more attention is paid to *how* computers are used and how *computer expertise* is judged (e.g., DES, 1989; Evans & Hall, 1988; Hoyles, 1988; Littleton, Light, Joiner, Messer & Barnes, 1998).

Let us consider a situation where males have consistently outperformed females over time in a particular educational discipline. Often, this difference is hardly noticed at first, but gradually over time people may become aware of this inequity and make attempts to resolve it by curriculum intervention. Lewis (1996) has suggested that it is possible to distinguish stages of curriculum intervention as follows: noticing the absence of females, changing females so as to improve their participation, to finally, re-thinking the discipline itself. We will adapt this framework to help structure our discussion of female involvement in information technology (IT) and to provide an analytical framework for tracing the developing relationship of females to IT. Our claim is that within IT we have potentially more opportunity than in other domains, such as mathematics, to reach the third stage of curriculum intervention: building a gender-inclusive curriculum. School mathematics has a long history, and its content is remarkably consistent across different countries, making the discipline hard to re-conceptualize and change. IT is different: it is new, ill defined and still in a state of rapid transition. As there are few entrenched positions about curriculum content to circumvent, it would seem possible that the meaning of IT activities could be shaped to encourage the girls to engage in the work. But to achieve this goal we need to clarify the nature and extent of the problem of female participation in IT. We do this by tracing out the three stages of curriculum intervention in relation to IT.

Stage 1: Noticing the absence of females

Women have long made valuable contributions to "the development and application of computers" (see Lockheed, 1985, p. 117), and computer technology has never been the exclusive preserve of men. However, young women and girls became increasingly "absent" from the domain of computing throughout the 1980's and early 90's. As a result, many researchers attempted to assess the level of girls' participation in IT and IT-related activities (see Sutton, 1991 for a review). There is a significant amount of research on the issue of gender differences in computer-related behavior; while there is much diversity in the studies and results, some clear trends have emerged.

First, during the early years there appears to be little difference between girls and boys in how they see computers, their liking for computer technology, or their involvement in computer-based activities (Brosnan, 1999; Williams & Ogletree, 1992; Bergin, Ford & Hess, 1993; Landerholm, 1994). As they grow older, however, girls' engagement with IT begins to decline (e.g., Lage, 1991), and data spanning the full age range of compulsory schooling indicate that in general computers are used more by boys and male teachers than by girls and female teachers (e.g., Bannert & Arbinger, 1996; Durndell, Glissov & Siann, 1995; Kaye, 1992; Millard, 1997; Podmore, 1991; Straker, 1989).

Computer use in school. During the primary school years, research has shown that boys tend to dominate computer and teacher resources in class time, monopolize machines during free-periods and take over the newest software or the most powerful machines (Carmichael, Burnett, Higginson, Moore & Pollard, 1986). The results of this study would still seem to be relevant today. When small groups of girls and boys work together on computer-based activities, boys are inclined to dominate the discussion and joint-activity (e.g., Keogh, Barnes, Joiner & Littleton, 2000; Barbieri & Light, 1992). It is perhaps not surprising therefore that many girls become hesitant computer users in their junior school years (e.g., Somekh, 1988).

During compulsory secondary education the low levels of female participation in IT and IT-related activities have become increasingly evident, as the relative numbers of girls and boys entered for public examinations in computer studies and computer science testify. In the United Kingdom at least, there is marked gender bias in the numbers of girls and boys being examined in these subjects (Hughes, 1990; Culley, 1993), and the gap has become more pronounced over time as the proportion of girls studying computer science has declined (Buckley & Smith, 1991). In higher education, applications by girls to study computer science at university in the United Kingdom dropped by 50% between 1978 and 1988. A similar trend is noted in the distribution of acceptances into computer science courses (Hoyles, 1988; Dain, 1991; Newton & Beck, 1993), where, for example, the proportion of female student admissions reached an all-time low of 11% in 1987. While these figures have improved a little, 18% in 1995, 20% in 1997 and 19% in 1999, there are still relatively few female computer science undergraduates in the United Kingdom[1].

We recognize that focusing on public examinations and university entry provides only a partial indicator of the absence of females from school IT use. There are, however, other factors concerning the deployment of IT in the secondary school which also suggest that girls can become "disenfranchised" users of computer technology. For example, in co-educational schools, boys dominate computer activities (National Curriculum Council, 1990) with the result that girls obtain less time on the machines than boys. Further, when girls do work on computers, they typically receive less assistance from the teachers (Culley, 1988; 1993). In this way boys are the key players in classroom-based computer-activities. The problem is exacerbated as additionally they are the major users outside the classroom and constitute over 90% of the regular participants in optional computing clubs (Culley, 1988; 1993) which turns our attention to computer use in the home.

Computer use in the home. In addition to the disparities in school, gender disparities in home computer use have long been noted (Culley, 1988, 1993; Evans & Hall, 1988; Hoyles, 1988; National Curriculum Council, 1990; Busch, 1995; Bannert & Arbinger, 1996). Parents are more likely to encourage boys than girls to use computers (e.g., Hoyles, 1988), and parents more frequently buy computers for boys than for girls (Mohamedali, Messer & Fletcher, 1987; National Curriculum Council, 1990; Robertson, Calder, Fung, Jones, & O'Shea, 1995). Many parents still "regard computers as a male rather than a female or common domain" (Busch, 1995, p. 155).

Boys make more use of computers in the home than girls (Doornekamp, 1993; Fife-Schaw, Breakwell, Lee & Spencer, 1986; Lockheed, 1985; Robertson, Calder, Fung, Jones & O'Shea, 1995) and, while this is primarily for games, a point we shall return to later, gender differences in use are reported in all home computer activities (Martin, 1991). These differences in home experience seem likely to impact on children's response to computers at school, an impact likely to grow as computer game playing becomes more sophisticated. As the National Curriculum Council (1990, p. B5) noted: "Boys often see computing as an interesting hobby and so become familiar with the technology and use the jargon which is discouraging to those unfamiliar with it." Thus "boys are far more likely to enter into formal schooling culturally and practically positioned to accept and be motivated by computers" (Beynon, 1993, p. 167). It has also been noted that because of their lack of experience of computers within the home, girls are more likely to perceive themselves as lacking expertise, and this, in turn, contributes to their relative passivity in the computing classroom (Crawford, Groundwater-Smith & Millan, 1989). Familiarity with computers breeds confidence, and confidence breeds more engagement and more familiarity with the machines. The spiral continues. But, if girls and young women are "absent" from the domain of computing, what are their attitudes towards computer technology?

Attitudes towards computer use. There are conflicting results related to gender-related differences in attitude toward computers. The confusion arises first and foremost because "computer" and "computer use" are ill-defined. But additionally there are diverse ways in which attitudes towards computers have been defined and measured. For example, Kaye (1992) identified at least fourteen different approaches to attitude measurement: "with respect to acceptance, affect, cognitions, comfort, confidence, courses, interest, liking, locus of control, motivation, programing, training, case scenarios and stereotypes" (p. 278). It is perhaps not surprising given this profusion of diverse measures, that gender differences favoring males with regard to interest in computers, appreciation of the utility or necessity of computers and confidence in using computers have been reported in some studies but not in others (see Sutton, 1991 and Kaye, 1992 for reviews). Thus, while some data from the entire age range of compulsory schooling do reveal that girls are less positive about computer use than boys (e.g., Martin, 1991; Todman & Dick, 1993; Shashaani, 1993, 1994), we must be cautious in interpreting these findings, particularly as once exposure to and prior experience with computers is controlled, gender differences in attitudes in many studies either shrink or disappear. For example, one of the earliest studies in this field demonstrated that gender did not explain any additional variance in attitudes towards computers after computer experience and mathematics anxiety had been entered into the regression equation (Gressard & Lloyd, 1987), whilst another showed that there were no differences in computer anxiety once effects due to computer access were controlled (Campbell, 1989). Other studies on attitudes and experience have also found that more experience is associated with lower anxiety and more positive attitudes (e.g., Colley, Gale & Harris, 1994; Martinez & Mead, 1988; Sutton, 1991; Williams, Ogletree, Woodburn & Raffeld, 1993; Dyck & Smither, 1994; Maurer, 1994).

There is research that has found that even where girls and boys express equally positive attitudes, both believe that boys like and use computers more than girls (e.g., Hughes, Brackenridge & MacLeod, 1987). However, while some studies have concluded that both boys and girls see the use of the computer as an activity that is somehow more "appropriate" for boys than for girls (e.g., Wilder, Mackie & Cooper, 1985; Brosnan, 1999) and that in schools the computer tends to be regarded as a "machine for men and boys" (EOC, 1983), this is not always the case. Sutton (1991), for example, reviewed a large number of studies that had explored students' attitudes towards the computer "as a male domain". The students in these studies ranged from first graders to high school students in Canada, the United Kingdom and the United States, and the overwhelming finding was that males held more stereotyped views than females. This finding supports the contention that males are more susceptible to sex-role stereotypes than females (Durndell, Glissov & Siann, 1995; Fletcher-Finn and Suddendorf, 1996; Shashanni, 1993). So despite the rather weak theoretical discourse in the computer attitude literature, it does appear that while girls and young women may appear to be "absent" from the domain of computer use, many may in fact be rather positively disposed towards computer technology.

Computing ability. At this juncture it is worthwhile mentioning that what is not at issue here is girls' ability to engage with computer technology. Girls are frequently observed to be competent, skilful and successful computer users (Eastman & Krendl, 1987; Finlayson, 1984; Issroff, 1994; Light & Colbourn, 1987; Linn, 1985; Yelland, 1998; Webb 1984). However, what is equally clear is that many girls do not voluntarily choose to participate in computing and computer-related activities (Wood, 1998). This finding resonates with everyday experience, where men are seen to manage the computer companies, dominate the computer services industry and control all aspects of leading-edge development in digital technologies. The question remains as to how best to foster girls' participation in computing. The answer to this question depends on how the problem is conceptualized but clearly moves us to stage 2 of our framework.

Stage 2: Changing female participation in IT activities

One approach to fostering women and girls' engagement with IT is to focus specifically on girls and women in terms of educational efforts and curriculum intervention. By implication the problem is defined as a "problem of the female sex" and the relationship between males and IT is defined (more or less implicitly) as an ideal which girls should emulate. The problem is located with "the girls" rather than with the "culture of computing." Stage two initiatives for fostering female engagement with computer technology revolve round strategies such as the presentation of positive role models and the organizational provision of "girls only" computer sessions.

Women role models. The need for positive female role models is frequently emphasized in any discussion of poor female participation in computer activity. Newton and Beck (1993) stressed the need for images of women working with computers that portray them as competent participants rather than as "decorative sexual objects or as silly brainless creatures, incapable of understanding anything about computing" (Newton & Beck, 1993, p. 143). They also argued that it is important to promote women with good communication skills who are already working in computing and can talk with conviction and enthusiasm about their work (Newton & Beck, 1993). Others, for example, Reinen and Plomp (1993) have emphasized the role that female teachers would play as positive role models for young girls. The potential value of this kind of role model has been recognized by female teachers: "wherever we teach we need the confidence to act as role models for our students and sometimes our colleagues in the use of computers for writing..." (Beer, 1994, p. 28). However, Reinen and Plomp used data derived from a large international study involving twenty-one countries to demonstrate that such positive role models are typically few and far between. Female teachers are often less-confident computer users than their male colleagues and hold a low regard for their skills and knowledge. This finding was confirmed in a study which concluded that male teachers had a higher degree of self-confidence in their knowledge about computer technology than female teachers (Hansen, 1993).

Mixed gender groups and computer use. Observations of male dominance, as described earlier in the chapter, have led some researchers to conclude that girls' lack of engagement with computer-based activities may, at least in part, stem from their often unsatisfactory experiences of computer use in the classroom. At the same time positive engagement with computers has been noted among students in girls-only schools. These twin observations have prompted enthusiasm in some quarters for segregating girls from boys for computer classes. The hope is that girls in girls-only groups will be less inhibited and will learn more. However, while experimental research has sometimes indicated that girls are particularly disadvantaged by working with boys (e.g., Underwood, McCaffrey & Underwood, 1990), this is by no means always the case (e.g., Hughes, Brackenridge, Bibby & Greenhough, 1988; Littleton, Light, Joiner, Messer & Barnes, 1992).

The effectiveness of single-gender groupings for IT is still a matter of debate. Some, for example, Willis and Kenway (1986), point to potential problems with such a course of action and argue that teachers are likely to regard the girls' classes as of lower interest and ability than the boys' groups and consequently have lower expectations of them:

> Separating out girls from boys (boys from girls) will not, in itself, change the perceptions of the teachers and administrators in the schools, any more than it will automatically change the attitudes of the students themselves. (Willis & Kenway, 1986, p. 145)

So while the strategy of segregating boys and girls for computer-based work holds the superficial appeal of side-stepping potential male domination over resources both physical and human, it is not a long-term solution and could result in attention being diverted away from the fundamental issue of curriculum reform. Willis and Kenway maintain that if schools are to consider adopting single-sex classes, they must ensure that this organizational change is not a substitute for scrutiny of curriculum content, teaching methodologies and assessment practices, all stage three concerns. In any event, any decision to implement changes to the gender structure of classes within a school necessitates sensitivity to the children's socio-emotional experience of separation and segregation and ultimately careful management of the transition back to mixed-sex teaching (Kruse, 1996).

Culley (1993), mindful of the comments of Willis and Kenway, is tentative about advocating segregation as an effective intervention strategy for lesson-based computer work. She sees the need for teachers to develop an understanding of classroom dynamics and the ways in which boys may come to dominate the computer classroom. Classroom management strategies, she argues, need to involve girls more centrally and students must be made aware of the likely patterns of gender interaction. Culley does, however, believe that there is a strong case to be made for ensuring that girls have access to free-time use of computers in girls-only settings, where they can tinker in a supportive environment. She adds that any girls-only sessions should be supervised by teachers who are both competent in computing and sensitive to gender issues (Culley, 1993, p. 156).

Research in more experimental settings has underlined the importance of careful design of tasks and pedagogy. In a study of the factors associated with learning mathematics in groups with computers, great care was taken in designing activities that exploited the interactions between pairs of children at the computer in ways that were integrated with learning goals and with off-computer group discussion (Hoyles, Healy & Pozzi, 1994). The research used a multi-site case study design in six schools involving eight groups of six mixed-sex, mixed-ability students undertaking three different tasks using computers. Quantitative analysis of learning measures indicated positive learning gains as a result of the group work for all children with no differences across gender and ability. The findings along with the qualitative analysis of the process data also pointed to characteristics of activities that were advantageous for learning and unlikely to lead to male dominance: these were balanced co-construction at the computer combined with structured co-ordination of different perspectives off the computer. It was also found that this type of task activity was unlikely to take place when the task was driven by technology rather than learning goals or when the collaborative work was disrupted by prior antagonism between group participants. In both of these circumstances, the groups invariably split along gender lines (see also Healy, Pozzi & Hoyles, 1995).

The potential problems associated with such a reduction in opportunities for interaction between boys and girls have also been noted in more recent experimental work conducted by Light, Littleton, Bale, Messer & Joiner (in press) (see also Light, & Littleton, 1999). They reported that gender differences in performance in mixed gender groupings did occur but only when the children worked alongside one another without opportunities for interaction. When the group actually collaborated, the gender polarization did not seem to occur.

Collaborative working with IT. The use of the computer is often regarded as a solitary and isolating activity involving mastery of a machine. There is evidence that girls find this mode of computer use alienating, particularly when coupled with competition (Hoyles, 1988). This way of working contrasts with the more collaborative project work encouraged in the constructionist tradition, where students help each other to build and debug their programs and models (Papert, 1998). Under these conditions, girls appear to be just as enthusiastic as boys in their response to computers (e.g., Hawkins, 1984; Hattie & Fitzgerald, 1988; Hoyles, Sutherland & Healy, 1991). The study mentioned earlier on group work with computers supports this position.

A similar picture emerges from a range of classroom accounts (e.g., Burke, Edwards, Jeffries, Jones, Miln, Montgomery, Perkins, Seager & Wright, 1988) which together stress the importance of a collaborative mode of working for girls' effective use of computers. Indeed, Pryor (1995) argues that by establishing and nurturing collaborative groups, teachers can create a classroom culture that is liberating for both girls and boys. There are of course thorny issues concerning what makes for appropriate pedagogy (Head, 1996); effective working partnerships (Light & Littleton, 1994); how to promote successfully an ethos of collaboration (Watson, 1997; Underwood & Underwood, 1999; Littleton, 1999); and what is valued as success by the teacher (Hoyles, 1988). Carmichael, Burnett, Higginson, Moore & Pollard (1986) found that boys enjoyed working speedily to achieve the challenges set, but that girls' interest declined as their more careful efforts were not acknowledged: "Boys get commended for things that girls can do, but we complete it half an hour later and it doesn't matter then" (Moore, 1986, p. 7). This leads us naturally to the discussion of what IT actually is. Is it about domination over hardware and software, is it about speed of response or is it more concerned with sharing information, building systems collaboratively and interacting with the technology in pursuit of learning goals?

Stage 3: Challenging the dominant paradigm of IT use in schools

The interventions described under stage 2 provide a basis for action to combat the gendering of IT, since they begin to question what the computer is and what computer activity should involve and start to problematize the prevailing culture surrounding computer use. We distinguish two foci that require attention in order to achieve more equality of access and performance. These foci relate to epistemological pluralism and the embedding of the technology in the curriculum.

Epistemological pluralism. In her discussion of computer programming, Turkle argued that many girls and women find the experience of computer use uncongenial because it imposes upon them a "top-down," formal-analytical method of working (Turkle, 1984a; 1984b; Turkle & Papert, 1990). Bringing females into the computer culture required taking a critical look at the social construction of the computer and the ways made available to control computer activities: "we must recognize that that which can be characterized as male mastery is not the only kind of mastery" (Turkle, 1984a).

Computer programming according to Turkle is often conceptualized as masculine, abstract, mathematical and only for the "techies." Clearly this is the case in some high-level languages such as PASCAL. But with some languages and with some activities, it need not be conceived in this way. Programming can be bottom-up, flexible and intuitive, even convivial (Kirkup, 1992). This was the case in the 80's when Turkle identified the need for epistemological pluralism even when children were engaged with text-based symbolic languages. Now computer technology can exploit multiple representations (including the visual alongside the symbolic) and diverse modalities of interaction, including direct manipulation, speech, and even gesture (Ainsworth, Wood & O'Malley, 1998; Noss, Healy & Hoyles, 1997). Systems effectively can allow children to choose the tools they need to solve problems and build their own solutions iteratively through a process of learning from feedback. Epistemological pluralism is at the beginning of the twenty-first century an even more realistic goal that could be exploited to the advantage for females.

Embedding technology in the curriculum. The constructionist vision of computer use presupposes that IT is an integral part of classroom life with the computer regarded as a potentially powerful tool to be used as and when appropriate—one tool among many. If technology is embedded in ongoing classroom activities, the danger that it is seen merely as an adjunct to them is avoided (Healy & Hoyles, 1999). Children need to develop a form of computer literacy that enables them to make informed decisions about what IT can and cannot do for them. They need to know when it is useful to use a spreadsheet or calculator, how to interpret the output from a database and how to search for information on the Web. Once computers are separated from work in subject domains, the male computer lab culture can all too easily emerge.

This takes us to the latest and potentially most pervasive use of IT in schools—namely, interacting with the Web. Government figures in England again show a dramatic increase in Internet access as shown in Table 1.1.

Table1.1: Survey of information and communications technology in schools

	Primary		Secondary	
	1998	1999	1998	1999
Schools with access to the Internet	17	62	83	93
Schools with ISDN or higher connectivity		58		70
Teachers using the Internet		51		87
Students using the Internet		29		63
Teachers with personal email addresses	2	15	9	32
Students with personal email addresses		4	3	12

Source: HMSO, 1999.

As the Web becomes ubiquitous, the computer is rendered more and more invisible. However new skills are needed in this new context—not the constructionist skills of building from feedback but the skills of sifting and interpreting information. As Baylis (in the RSA report "Redefining Work," 1998) suggested:

> There will be no premium to be gained from the acquisition of information for (in the future) people will have easy access to quantities of information beyond our present ability to grasp. What will be important is the development of critical skills (in all senses) to use information and to evaluate it. (Baylis, 1998)

Challenging the paradigm. We have argued that challenging the paradigm of computer use in schools is central to developing a more gender-inclusive view of IT, and this means that attention must be paid to 1) epistemological pluralism and model building, 2) the embedding of the technology in ongoing classroom activity to pursue learning goals and 3) the fostering of collaborative social interactions around the technology. Yet evidence suggests that these criteria are rarely satisfied.

It is rare to find a constructionist approach to learning which focuses on learning from feedback in today's classrooms. What does make it into the classroom is more often sophisticated technology used to "deliver knowledge" such as that deployed in Integrated Learning Systems (ILSs). The learning paradigm underlying ILS is one where the student is seen as deficient and in need of remediation achieved by the presentation of sequences of tasks devised on the basis of the student's learning history. Student responses provide data that determine the nature of future work, a model of learning reminiscent of programmed learning in the 60's and 70's.

Turning to the second and third criteria, computer use still tends to be isolated from other classroom activities, separated physically in specialized laboratories with specialized teachers. Emphasis all too often is simply on the interaction *with* the computer. Yet the image of computer use is changing, more so in out of school contexts than in the schools. Increasingly people are using computers as part of their everyday life to obtain information from the Web, to buy goods, and to email their friends, and children are in the forefront of this revolution. Papert (1996a, 1996b) has, rather controversially, argued that schools will eventually wither away as students take charge of their own learning. But if the stimulus for change comes from the home, are females less likely to be excluded from computer use than before? There is every chance that the same patterns of exclusion will be maintained with females reluctant to engage in computer activities. As the boundary between these two worlds of IT-use at school and home becomes more blurred, it seems appropriate to consider the dominant culture of home computer use, namely the computer game.

The prevailing paradigm at home: Computer games

For many children, their early experience of computer use occurs within the home and often involves playing computer games. Boys have considerably more experience of computer games than girls (Subrahmanyam & Greenfield, 1994; Yates & Littleton, 1999), and they tend to be more enthusiastic game players. Female gamers seem to be few and far between. This is no doubt at least in part accounted for by the male-oriented nature of most computer games, which depict violence and portray women as sex objects (Stutz, 1996; Provenzo, 1991; Dietz, 1998). The plea for "girl friendly" computer gaming software has been made frequently (see Sutton, 1991). Yet it is difficult to characterize what constitutes "girl friendly" software. We know that the metaphors used in the presentation of a game exert a powerful effect on girls' engagement with and conceptualization of it (Littleton, Light, Joiner, Messer & Barnes, 1998), but we also know that the simple substitution of female characters for male characters is not sufficient to ensure girl's engagement (Joiner, Messer, Littleton & Light, 1996). The huge computer game industry has recognized a potential market for girls, and this has been at least partly filled by a new wave of hugely successful games—some of which still seem to be basically sex stereotyped (Barbie™ in the Shopping Mall) while others more gender-neutral involving narrative and strategic approaches (Purple Moon). Cassell and Jenkins (1998) present an excellent summary of the evolution of these games.

From game player at home to game builder at school. Can another approach be taken that fosters girls' engagement with games without prejudging their taste in games and their styles of game-playing? One possibility is to change children's role with respect to games.

Current computer games typically cast children in the role of game-player, playing according to rules programmed by someone else, a situation which, however motivating, sets strong boundaries around what might be learned. Children's fascination with computer games is almost entirely at the level of interface. That is, manipulation of the game objects is fun, expressive and engaging. But for the most part, the interface is all there is: the level below the interface is the preserve of the programmers and designers, not the user. A way to make computer game playing constructionist and to open a window on learning is to place children in the role of producers as well as consumers of games. This is the aim of an ongoing study, the Playground Project[2] (Hoyles & Noss, 1999) which is building on the work of Papert (1998), Kafai (1995), Harel (1988), Klawe and Phillips (1995), and Rubin (1995) and finding ways for children to change or build games to suit their own purposes. Playground is developing two platforms on which children can create and play their own games: an animation based computer programming language, *ToonTalk*

(Kahn 1999), and a new, concurrent object-oriented version of *Logo*.

To illustrate our approach and how it illuminates issues of gender, we will briefly describe how two girls and then two boys changed a simple computer game so it fit more closely with what they wanted to play. We describe these case studies to illustrate the potential of this constructionist approach to computer use in school and how it *is* possible for students themselves to shape the prevailing computer culture rather than be shaped by it.

The Playground team wrote a very simple *Pong* game in *ToonTalk*. This original *Pong* game was a two-player game, where one player controlled the top paddle using the keys SHIFT and CTRL to move the paddle left and right, and the other used the mouse to move the bottom paddle left and right (see Figure 1.1). The ball bounced around and the players had to try to hit it with their paddles. The score (bottom right-hand corner) increased by 10 points whenever the top paddle hit the ball but did not change when the bottom paddle hit the ball.

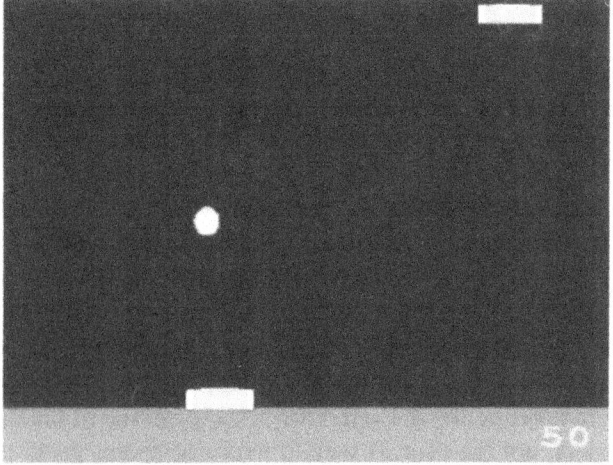

Figure 1.1: The original *Pong* game

We gave the *Pong* game to one pair of 7-year-old girls and one pair of boys of the same age. The children were asked to play the game and to change it if they wanted to make it more enjoyable for themselves and their friends. To change the game the children had to have a certain level of familiarity with programming in *ToonTalk*, and all the children had been working with *ToonTalk* in an after-school computer club for about

The Gendering of Information Technology

three months. They were therefore relatively familiar with the metaphor and the simple tools available. First we describe the work of the two girls.

The girls' case study: From Pong to Underwater. At first the two girls, Harriet (H) and Roberta (R), simply treated *Pong* like a sport: as they put it, "it's like tennis". As they played, they soon worked out that the score was changed by the top paddle. They thought the game was rather boring, so the interviewer (I) asked if the girls wanted to change the game, which took us to the first phase of game evolution.

> I: How can you change the game?
> H: Could have two scores, one for bottom one for top.
> H: Make it more colorful... it's a bit dark.
> H: You could have... like the paddle as a fish.
> R: I've got an idea: Bammer hits the thing down and hits the ball.

Out of these ideas, they first implemented the change in background color, making it light blue. This is trivial in *ToonTalk*, achieved by hitting the space bar. They decided to make the paddles look like Bammer, a special animated mouse in the *ToonTalk* world, so we asked:

> I: How will you get Bammer to behave like the paddle?
> H&R: I know, you stick the paddle on the back.

The two girls were referring to a general method for exchanging behaviors in *ToonTalk*. On the back of any picture are its behaviors. The girls knew that if you flip over a new picture, flip over the paddle, and put the paddle on the back of the picture, then the picture will inherit the paddle's behaviors. Next they changed the ball to look like a bird.

> I: That's horrid! [i.e. the bird is being hit by a hammer!]
> H&R: No, no, it's flying up and down, up and down, it's OK.

This change was achieved in the same way as the change of appearance of the paddle. They also changed the color of the background at the bottom to yellow (see Figure 1.2).

The changes in color stimulated more ideas, and seemed to support the girls' inclination to build an *Underwater* narrative. They were full of ideas as to what the screen could signify and were willing to suspend conventions of reality, and indulge in make-believe play.

> H: I know... that's like the sea and he's [Bammer] running down into it! Cos that's like there's a hill and there's sand going down.
> R: There's a problem! He's walking on... the water!
> H: It doesn't matter.

The girls found this game far more compelling because they had made it. They also became less concerned about scoring. We only encouraged them to implement the (simple) picture changes at this point. (This indicates the importance of the interactions with a more capable or experienced other (such as a teacher) who is able to judge what is possible as well as desirable in computer interactions at a particular time and for a particular group of children.) It was clear that Harriet and Roberta needed extra playground elements for their *Underwater* world, such as pictures of fish and sounds. We developed these resources for them and stored them in libraries to be accessed later.

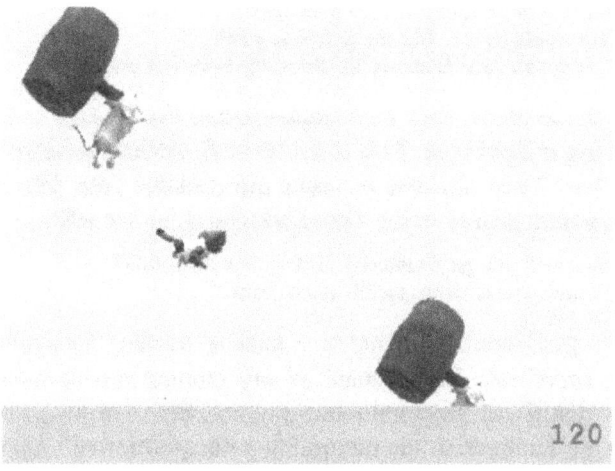

Figure 1.2: Changing the appearance of the paddles and ball

In the next session, we gave Harriet and Roberta new pictures of fish, and they picked out the shark picture for the paddles. Roberta wanted to have lots of fish bouncing up and down, an idea she had developed from observing the boys who had made multiple balls for their game.

H: But if the fish reach the top or bottom, then they make another fish?
R: And also they take away from your score.

This latter suggestion required a different sort of transformation incorporating a penalty scheme in addition to the scoring one. In fact, the girls simply changed the paddles to sharks, now an easy maneuver, as they had already changed the paddle to be Bammer. The girls were changing the appearance of the game and programming at what we

The Gendering of Information Technology

termed "the picture level." They simply put the paddle on the back of the shark picture. They also changed the ball to a fish by putting the "ball with all its behaviors" on the back of a fish, and then copying it many times with a *ToonTalk* tool which copies objects and all their inherited behaviors. Their game now looked like Figure 1.3.

Once Harriet and Roberta played with the shark and the fish, they immediately wanted to make more changes, changes in the rules of the game as well as its appearance.

R: The sharks are the paddles. And if one of those hits the sharks.
H: Any of them?
R: It goes like this [R chomps].
H: No, it doesn't.
I: That's what you want?
H: This is what we want.
R: We really want to make more of the balls and when it comes they go [chomp], and if you press a button, it spurts out again.

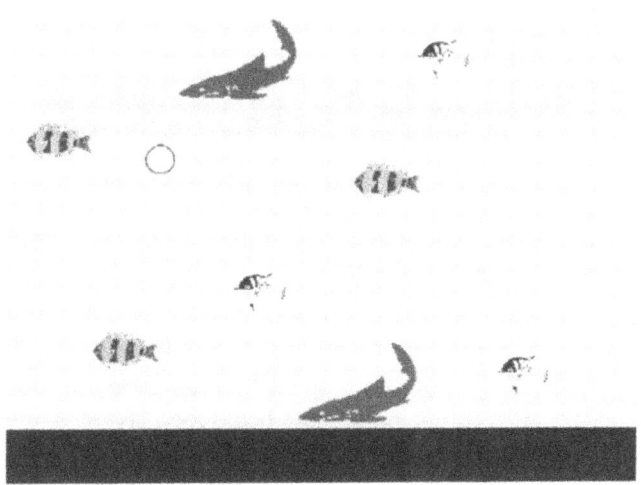

Figure 1.3: Going *Underwater* with sharks and fish

Thus, the girls wanted a new sound that would be played whenever the shark hit the fish. This was rather harder to manage: they needed to get further into the system. Next, the girls tried to build a game that was more realistic by changing another rule: every time a fish hit a shark, instead of bouncing off, it would be eaten. This idea made the pair think of a new way to win the game; you win if the shark you control eats the most fish!

It is not appropriate here to illustrate all of the phases of their game evolution, but, in summary, they involved: changing the setting of the game, changing the paddles to sharks and the ball to a fish and then making lots of fish, making the shark eat the fish, and then finally having two scores, (one for each shark) rather than one to make a competitive game. After help with this final phase, their game looked like Figure 1.4.

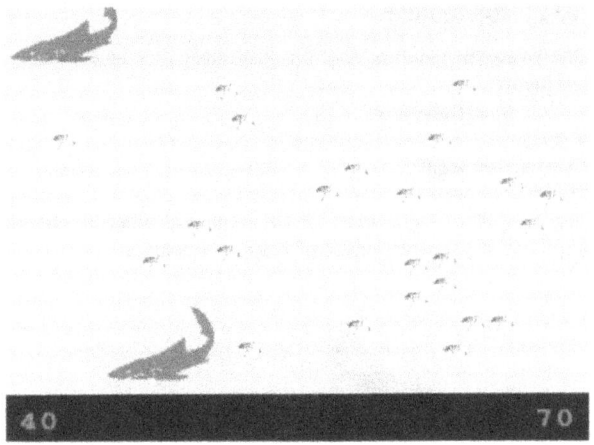

Figure 1.4: The final *Underwater* game with two scores

The boys' case study: Simulating Football and Cricket. We also gave *Pong* to two boys, Rashid and David, who despite the fact that they didn't always agree, played together fairly successfully. Initially they came up with few ideas as to what they wanted to change in the game. They added cars and rockets but did not come up with a new game. Rather, they *accumulated* different pictures, noises and behaviors. David wanted to make a *Cricket* game, so Rashid explained how he would like it:

R: There's a man and he has a bat if the number... you can move the man with the hand if you go near a number you have to hit it with the bat....

Both boys talked about the *Cricket* game as if it was a real *Cricket* game. They did not appear to appreciate what could or could not be implemented or how the game could be improved as it was on a computer. We helped them design a cricket pitch, gave them a picture of a cricketer and stumps and a working ball (see Figure 1.5).

When we asked them asked how to play the game, again Rashid wanted to simulate the real game of cricket:

R: I want a bowler ... I want it like cricket.
R: Put that wicket at the front and a ball comes along and that man hits it, and if it hits the wicket he's out and if it goes over the wicket he's not out ...He hits it, and if he hits the wicket he's out.

At this point Rashid turned to make a *Football* game, and again the boys only referred to actions apparent in a real football game including the characters, team names and football rules. They did not talk about a computer version of a football game, nor did they at any time suggest that anything in their game could or should be different from reality. They even gave their football teams authentic names, Arsenal and Watford.

Figure 1.5: The boys' simulated *Cricket* game

As we knew the boys had played many computer games, we found it surprising that they were not ready to suspend reality and come up with new ideas for a computer game. But while talking about building games and during design, they were simply not willing to move away from reality and make up their own—to play with the rules.

The two case studies serve to illustrate what we could anticipate from our review of the literature, namely, that boys and girls have different interests when interacting with computers. The children changed the games in ways they liked, clearly making activities that were part of their culture and that they wanted to play and share. It is our view that either game evolution could be potentially productive for learning. What is crucial though is that one style is not imposed on all children.

Conclusions

In this chapter we have traced the development of females' participation in IT in school. We have argued that girls' disengagement from computer work may be compounded by the computer-based activities with which they are required to engage. Technologies inevitably arise in the context of existing social relations and for this reason are likely to result in the reproduction, even the magnification, of these forms of relationships. We are aware of the danger of creating digital under-classes and must guard against this in terms of gender. The same technologies can open up possibilities for the transformation of social relations if we seek out and create the conditions for achieving such a transformation. As technology and access to it change dramatically, we have pointed to the danger of schools still imposing a style of IT use which not only disadvantages girls but may be fundamentally at odds with computer use and interactions at home. Clearly for IT to be useful for all children in schools, it must encourage diversity in interaction and models of learning, to expand rather than constrain horizons. The way IT is defined in school in terms of curriculum, assessment, activities and images of success will fundamentally shape students' views of the meaning of education.

At the same time, children are creating their own definitions of computer use, largely in the context of computer games, which all too often can suffer from gender stereotyping. We have suggested one way to avoid this. It capitalizes on the potential of computer games for learning by allowing children to some extent to design, build and modify their own computer games. It is possible that in this process the image of the computer game will change for the benefit of all children. We presented two case studies that serve to illustrate this potential of allowing children to build their own games, to define the culture in which they can play, and to define how they might conceptualize the potential of ICT and shape it according to their needs.

This takes us to our final comment in thinking about computer culture. We feel it is necessary to challenge some of our own assumptions and expectations concerning children's relationship with computers. All too often it is assumed that a high level of enthusiasm for computers is unquestionably a good thing. This is the implicit assumption underpinning the design of many of the computer attitude scales referred to earlier in the chapter. Yet from in-depth interviewing of girls and boys about their use of computers, it is clear that when asked about their use of computers, children often talk about the penalties associated with being too enthusiastic a user—you risk being characterized as a "boff," a "geek" or a "jonah" (loner) (Littleton, Artis & Oosterwegel, in preparation). As researchers, we often study girls' and boys' engagement with computer technology without recognizing the way in which our own interpretations of the children's behavior could be open to alternative readings. A striking paper by Elkjaer (1992) represents a good case in point. The author presents a detailed analysis of boys' dominance and extensive use of computer technology and offers a full interpretation of this as behavior born of insecurity rather than confidence. In doing this the author illustrates that through our tendency to characterize boys' relationship with computer technology as positive and unproblematic, we may be failing to acknowledge and address the problematic facets of the male relationship with computer technology. Challenging the paradigm will thus involve being continually open to alternative readings of research findings and constantly questioning the basis of our own analyses and interpretations.

References

Ainsworth, S., Wood, D. & O'Malley, C. (1998). There's more than one way to solve a problem: Evaluating a learning environment to support the development of children's multiplication skills. *Learning and Instruction, 8* (2), 141–157.

Bannert, M. & Arbinger, R. (1996). Gender related differences in the exposure to and use of computers. *European Journal of Psychology of Education, 11,* 269–82.

Barbieri, M. S. & Light, P. (1992). Interaction, gender and performance on a computer-based problem solving task. *Learning and Instruction, 2,* 199–213.

Baylis, V. (1998). *Redefining work.* London: Royal Society for the Arts.

Beer, A. (1994). Writing, computers and gender. *English Quarterly, 26* (2), 21–29.

Bergin, D. A., Ford, M. E. & Hess, R. D. (1993). Patterns of motivation and social behavior associated with microcomputer use of young children. *Journal of Educational Psychology, 85,* 437–45.

Beynon, J. (1993). Computers, dominant boys and invisible girls: Or Hannah, it's not a toaster, it's a computer! In J. Beynon & H. Mackay (eds.), *Computers into classrooms. More questions than answers* (pp. 160–189). London: Falmer Press.

Brosnan, M. (1999). A new methodology, and old story? Gender differences in the "draw-a-computer-user" test. *European Journal of Psychology of Education, XIV* (3), 375–385.

Buckley, P. & Smith, B. (1991). Opting out of technology: A study of girls' GCSE choices. In G. Lovegrove & B. Segal (eds.), *Women into computing: Selected papers 1988-1990.* Heidelberg: Springer-Verlag.

Burke, J., Edwards, J., Jeffries, J., Jones, K., Miln, J., Montgomery, M., Perkins, B., Seager, A. & Wright, H. (1988). My mum uses a computer, too! In C. Hoyles (ed.), *Girls and computers* (pp. 13–30). London: University of London, Institute of Education, Bedford Way Papers, No. 34.

Busch, T. (1995). Gender differences in self-efficacy and attitudes towards computers. *Journal of Educational Computing Research, 12* (2), 147–158.

Campbell, N. (1989). Computer anxiety of rural middle and secondary school students. *Journal of Educational Computing Research, 5,* 213–222.

Carmichael, H., Burnett, J., Higginson,W., Moore, B. & Pollard, P. (1986). *Computers, children and classrooms: A multisite evaluation of the creative use of microcomputers by elementary school children.* Ontario, Canada: Queen's Printer.

Cassell, J. & Jenkins H. (eds.), (1998). *From Barbie to Mortal Kombat. Gender and computer games.* Cambridge, MA: The MIT Press.

Clements, D.H. & Sarama, J. (1995). Design of a Logo environment for elementary geometry. *Journal of Mathematical Behavior, 14,* 381–398.

Colley, A., Gale, M. & Harris, T. (1994). Effects of gender role identity and experience on computer attitude components. *Journal of Educational Computing Research, 10* (2), 129–137.

Crawford, K., Groundwater-Smith, S. & Millan, M. (1989). *Gender and the evolution of computer literacy.* School of Teaching and Curriculum Studies, University of Sydney, Australia.

Crook, C. (1994). *Computers and the collaborative experience of learning.* London: Routledge.

Crook, C. (1996). Schools of the future. In T. Gill (ed.), *Electronic children: How children are responding to the information revolution* (pp. 75–88). London: National Children's Bureau.

Culley, L. (1988). Girls, boys and computers. *Educational Studies, 14,* 3–8.

Culley, L. (1993). Gender equity and computing in secondary schools: Issues and strategies for teachers. In J. Beynon & H. Mackay (eds.), *Computers into classrooms. More questions than answers* (pp. 147–159). London, Washington: Falmer Press.

Dain, J. (1991). Women and computing: Some responses to falling numbers in higher education. *Women's Studies International Forum, 14* (3), 217–225.

Department for Education and Employment. (1995). *Statistical Bulletin: Survey of information technology in schools.* Department for Education and Employment.

Department for Education and Employment. (1997). *Connecting the learning society: The national grid for learning.* Department for Education and Employment.

Department for Education and Employment. (1999). *Survey of information and communication technology in schools.* Department for Education and Employment.

DES (1999). *Information technology from 5 to 16.* London: HMSO.

Dietz, T. L. (1998). An examination of violence and gender role portrayals in videogames: Implications for gender socialisation and aggressive behaviour. *Sex Roles, 38* 425–442.

Doornekamp, B. (1993). Students valuation of the use of computers in education. *Computers in Education, 21* (1/2) 103–113.

Durndell, A., Glissov, P. & Siann, G. (1995). Gender and computing: Persisting differences. *Educational Research, 37* (3), 219–227.

Dyck, J. & Smither, J. (1994). Age differences in computer anxiety: The role of computer experience, gender and education. *Journal of Educational Computing Research, 10* (3), 239–248.

Eastman, S. & Krendl, K. (1987). Computers and gender: Differential effects of electronic search on students' achievement and attitudes. *Journal of Research and Development in Education, 20* (3), 41–48.

Elkjaer, B. (1992). Girls and information technology in Denmark, An account of a socially constructed problem. *Gender and Education, 1* (1–2), 25–40.

Equal Opportunities Commission (1983). *Information technology in schools*. Manchester: EOC.
European Union ESPRIT/Experimental Schools Program. (Project #29329). The Playground Project.
Evans, A. & Hall, W. (1988). Computer education and gender inequality. *National Union of Teachers' Education Review, 2* (1), Spring.
Fife-Schaw, C., Breakwell, G., Lee, T. & Spencer, J. (1986). Patterns of teenage computer usage. *Journal of Computer Assisted Learning, 2,* 152–161.
Finlayson, H. (1984). The transfer of mathematical problem solving skills from LOGO experience. *Research Paper Number 238*. Department of Artificial Intelligence, University of Edinburgh.
Fletcher-Finn, C.M. & Suddendorf, T. (1996). Computer attitudes, gender and exploratory behaviour: A developmental study. *Journal of Educational Computer Research, 15* (4), 369–392.
Gill, T. (1996). Conclusions. In T. Gill (ed.), *Electronic children: How children are responding to the information revolution* (pp. 100–106). London: National Children's Bureau.
Gressard, C. & Lloyd, B. (1987). An investigation of the effects of math anxiety and sex on computer attitudes. *School Science and Mathematics, 87* (2), 125–135.
Hansen, K. (1993). Teachers' choices of content and context in computer education courses. *Computers in Education, 21* (1/2), 17–23.
Harel, I. (1988). Software design for learning: Children's constructions of meanings for fractions and Logo programming. Unpublished doctoral dissertation. Cambridge MA: MIT Laboratory.
Hattie, J. & Fitzgerald, D. (1988). Sex differences in attitudes, achievement and use of computers. *Australian Journal of Education, 31* (1), 3–26.
Hawkins, J. (1984). Computers and girls: Rethinking the issue. *Technical Report 24*, New York, Bank Street College of Education.
Head, J. (1996). Gender identity and cognitive style. In P. Murphy & C. Gipps (eds.), *Equity in the classroom: Towards effective pedagogy for girls and boys* (pp. 59–69). Brighton: Falmer Press.
Healy, L. & Hoyles, C. (1999). Visual and symbolic reasoning in mathematics: Making connections with computers? *Mathematical Thinking and Learning, 1* (1), 59–84.
Healy, L., Pozzi, S. & Hoyles, C. (1995). Making sense of groups, computers and mathematics. *Cognition and Instruction, 13* (4), 505–523.
Hess, R. (1985). Gender differences in enrolment in computer camps and classes. *Sex Roles*, 13 (3/4), 193–203.
Hoyles, C. (1985). Developing a context for Logo in school mathematics. *Journal of Mathematical Behaviour, 4* (2).
Hoyles, C. (1985). Culture and Computers in the Mathematics Classroom. Inaugural Lecture. Institute of Education: University of London.
Hoyles, C. (ed.). (1988). *Girls and computers*. London: University of London, Institute of Education, Bedford Way Papers, No. 34.
Hoyles, C., Healy, L. & Pozzi, S., (1994). Groupwork with computers: An overview of findings. *Journal of Computer Assisted Learning*, 10, 202–215.

Hoyles, C., Morgan, C. & Woodhouse, G. (eds.). (1999). *Re-thinking the mathematics curriculum*. London: Falmer Press.
Hoyles, C. & Noss, R. (1999). Playing with (and without) words. *Proceedings of Eurologo 1999 Conference*, Sofia: Bulgaria, 18–30.
Hoyles, C., Sutherland, R. & Healy, L. (1991). Children talking in computer environments: New insights on the role of discussion in mathematics learning. In K. Durkin & B. Shire (eds.), *Language in mathematical education: Research and practice* (pp. 162–175). Milton Keynes: Open University Press.
Hughes, M. (1990). Children's computation. In R. Grieve & M. Hughes (eds.), *Understanding children: Essays in honour of Margaret Donaldson* (pp. 121–139). Oxford: Basil Blackwell.
Hughes, M., Brackenridge, A., Bibby, A. & Greenhough, P. (1988). Girls, boys and turtles: Gender effects in young children's learning with Logo. In C. Hoyles (ed.), *Girls and Computers* (pp. 31–39). London, Institute of Education, Bedford Way Papers, 34.
Hughes, M., Brackenridge, A. & MacLeod, H. (1987). Children's ideas about computers. In J. Rutkowska & C. Crook (eds.), *Computers, cognition and development* (pp. 9–34). London: Wiley.
Issroff, K. (1994). Gender and cognitive and affective aspects of co-operative learning. In H. Foot, C. Howe, A. Anderson, A. Tolmie & D. Warden (eds.), *Group and interactive learning* (pp. 67–79). Southampton, Boston: Computational Mechanics.
Joiner, R., Messer, D., Littleton, K. & Light, P. (1996). Gender, computer experience and computer-based problem solving. *Computers and Education, 26* (1–3), 179–187.
Kafai, Y. (1995). *Minds in play: Computer game design as a context for children's learning*. N.J.: Lawrence Erlbaum Associates
Kahn, K. (1999). Helping children learn hard things: Computer programming with familiar objects and activities. In A. Druin (ed.), *The design of children's technology* (pp. 223–241). San Francisco: Morgan Kaufman Publishers Inc.
Kaput, J. & Roschelle, J. (1999). The mathematics of change and variation from a millennial perspective: New content, new context. In C. Hoyles, C. Morgan & G. Woodhouse (eds.), *Re-thinking the mathematics curriculum* (pp. 155–170) London: Falmer Press.
Kaye, R. (1992). An analysis of methods used to examine gender differences in computer-related behaviour. *Journal of Educational Computing Research, 8* (3), 277–290.
Keogh, T., Barnes, P., Joiner, R. & Littleton, K. (2000). Gender, pair composition and computer versus paper presentations of an English language task. *Educational Psychology, 20* (1), 33–43.
Kirkup, G. (1992). The social construction of computers. In G. Kirkup & S. Keller (eds.), *Inventing women: Science, gender and technology* (pp. 267–281). Oxford: Polity Press.
Klawe, M. & Phillips, E. (1995). A classroom study: Electronic games engage children as researchers. *Proceedings of Computer Support for Collaborative Learning '95 (CSCL)* Bloomington, Indiana.
Kruse, A.M. (1996). Single-sex settings: Pedagogies for girls and boys in Danish schools. In P. Murphy & C. Gipps (eds.), *Equity in the classroom: Towards effective pedagogy for girls and boys* (pp. 173–191). Brighton: Falmer Press.

Laboratory of Comparative Human Cognition (1989). Kids and computers: A positive vision of the future. *Harvard Educational Review, 59* (1), 73–86.
Lage, E. (1991). Boys, girls, and microcomputing. *European Journal of Psychology of Education, 6,* 29–44.
Landerholm, E. (1994). Computers in the kindergarten. *Early Child Development and Care, 101,* 13–22.
Lewis, S. (1996). Intervention programs in science and engineering education: From secondary schools to universities. In P. Murphy & C. Gipps (eds.), *Equity in the classroom: Towards effective pedagogy for girls and boys* (pp. 192–213). London: Falmer Press & UNESCO publishing.
Light, P. (1997). Computers for learning: Psychological perspectives. *Journal of Child Psychology and Psychiatry, 38* (5), 497–504.
Light, P. & Colbourn, C. (1987). The role of social processes in children's microcomputer use. In W. Kent & R. Lewis (eds.), *Computer assisted learning in the social sciences and humanities.* Oxford: Basil Blackwell.
Light, P. & Littleton, K. (1994). Cognitive approaches to groupwork. In P. Kutnick & C. Rogers (eds.), *Groups in schools* (pp. 87–103). London: Cassell.
Light, P. & Littleton, K. (1999). *Social processes in children's learning.* Cambridge: Cambridge University Press.
Light, P., Littleton, K., Bale, S., Messer, D. & Joiner, R. (in press). Gender and social comparison effects in computer based problem solving. *Learning and Instruction.*
Linn, M. C. (1985). Fostering equitable consequences from computer learning environments. *Sex Roles, 13,* 229–240.
Littleton, K. (1996). Girls and information technology. In P. Murphy & C. Gipps (eds.), *Equity in the classroom: Towards effective pedagogy for girls and boys* (pp. 81–96). Brighton: Falmer Press.
Littleton, K. (1999). Productivity through interaction: An overview. In K. Littleton & P. Light (eds.), *Learning with computers: Analysing productive interaction* (pp. 179–193). London: Routledge.
Littleton, K., Artis, J. & Oosterwegel, A. (in prep.). Boffs, Geeks and Jonah's: Children talk about computers.
Littleton, K. & Bannert, M. (1999). Situating differences: The case of gender and computer technology. In J. Bliss, R. Saljo, & P. Light (eds.), *Learning sites: Social and technological resources for learning* (pp. 171–182). New York: Pergamon.
Littleton, K. & Light, P. (eds.). (1999). *Learning with computers: Analysing productive interaction.* London: Routledge.
Littleton, K., Light, P., Joiner, R., Messer, D. & Barnes, P. (1992). Pairing and gender effects on children's computer-based learning. *European Journal of Psychology of Education, 7,* 311–24.
Littleton, K., Light, P., Joiner, R., Messer, D. & Barnes, P. (1998). Gender and software effects in children's computer-based problem solving. *Educational Psychology, 18,* 327–340.
Lockheed, M. (1985). Women, girls and computers: A first look at the evidence. *Sex Roles, 13* (3/4), 115–122.

Martin, R. (1991). School children's attitudes towards computers as a function of gender, course subjects and availability of home computers, *Journal of Computer Assisted Learning, 7,* 187–94.
Martinez, M. & Mead, N. (1988). *Computer competence: The first national assessment (Technical Report No. 17–CC–01).* Princeton, NJ: National Assessment of Educational Progress & Educational Testing Service.
Maurer, M. (1994). Computer anxiety correlates and what they tell us: A literature review. *Computers in Human Behaviour, 10* (3), 239–248.
Millard, E. (1997, September). *New technologies, old inequalities: Variations found in the use of computers by students at home with implications for the school curriculum.* Paper presented at the British Educational Research Association Annual Conference, University of York, England.
Mohamedali, M., Messer, D. & Fletcher, B. (1987). Factors affecting micro-computer use and programming ability of secondary school children. *Journal of Computer Assisted Learning, 3,* 224–239.
Moore, B. (1986). *Equity in Education.* Ontario, Canada: Ministry of Education.
National Curriculum Council (1990). *Non-statutory guidance for information technology capability.* London: Department of Education and Science
Newton, P. & Beck, E. (1993). Computing: An ideal occupation for women? In J. Beynon & H. Mackay (eds.), *Computers into classrooms. More questions than answers* (pp. 130–146). London, Washington: Falmer Press.
Noss, R. (1997). New Cultures, New Numeracies. Inaugural Lecture. Institute of Education: University of London.
Noss, R., Healy, L. & Hoyles, C. (1997). The construction of mathematical meanings: Connecting the visual with the symbolic. *Educational Studies in Mathematics, 33,* 203–233.
Noss, R. & Hoyles, C. (1996). *Windows on mathematical meanings: Learning cultures and computers.* Dordrecht: Kluwer.
Okebukola, P. & Woda, A. (1993). The gender factor in computer anxiety and interest among some Australian high school students. *Educational Research, 35* (2), 181–189.
Papert, S. (1980). *Mindstorms: Children, computers and powerful ideas.* Brighton: The Harvester Press.
Papert, S. (1996a). *The connected family: Bridging the digital generation gap.* Atlanta, GA: Longstreet Press.
Papert, S. (1996b). *The children's machine: Rethinking school in the age of the computer.* Hemel Hempstead: Harvester Wheatsheaf.
Papert, S. (1998). Does easy do it? Children, games, and learning. *Game Developer,* June, 77–78.
Podmore, V. (1991). 4–year–olds, 6–year-olds, and microcomputers: A study of perceptions and social behaviours. *Journal of Applied Developmental Psychology, 12,* 87–101.
Pozzi, S., Healy, L. & Hoyles, C. (1993). Learning and interaction in groups with computers: When do ability and gender matter? *Social Development, 2* (3), 223–241.
Provenzo, E. (1991). *Video Kids: Making Sense of Nintendo.* Cambridge, Massachusetts: Harvard University Press.
Pryor, J. (1995). Gender issues in groupwork: A case study involving work with com-

puters. *British Educational Research Journal, 21* (3), 277–288.
Reinen, I. & Plomp, T. (1993). Some gender issues in educational computer use: Results of an international comparative survey. *Computers in Education, 20* (4), 353–365.
Robertson, I., Calder, J., Fung, P., Jones, A. & O'Shea, T. (1995). Computer attitudes in an English secondary school. *Computers and Education, 24,* 73–81.
Rubin, A. (1995). *Through the Glass Wall: Computer Games for Mathematical Empowerment.* Cambridge, Massachusetts: TERC.
Scrimshaw, P. (ed.). (1993). *Language, classrooms and computers.* London: Routledge.
Shashaani, L. (1993). Gender-biased differences in attitudes toward computers. *Computers in Education, 20* (2), 169–181.
Shashaani, L. (1994). Gender differences in computer experiences and its influence on computer attitudes. *Journal of Educational Computing Research, 11* (4), 347–367.
Somekh, B. (1988, September). *Micro-reflections.* Paper presented at the British Educational Research Association symposium on I.T./Education, University of East Anglia, England.
Stasz, C., Shavelson, R. & Stasz, C. (1985). Teachers as role models: Are there gender differences in micro-computer-based mathematics and science instruction? *Sex Roles, 13* (3/4), 149–164.
Straker, A. (1989). *Children Using Computers.* Oxford: Blackwell.
Stutz, E. (1996). Is electronic entertainment hindering children's play and social development? In T. Gill (ed.), *Electronic children: How children are responding to the information revolution?* London: National Children's Bureau.
Subrahmanyam, K. & Greenfield, P. (1994). Effect of video game practice on spatial skills in girls and boys. *Journal of Applied Developmental Psychology, 15,* 13–32.
Sutton, R. E. (1991). Equity and computers in the schools: A decade of research. *Review of Educational Research, 61,* 475–503.
Todman, J. & Dick, G. (1993). Primary children and teacher's attitudes to computers. *Computers in Education, 20* (2), 199–203.
Turkle, S. (1984a). Women and computer programming. *Technology Review,* November/December, 49–50.
Turkle, S. (1984b). *The Second Self: Computers and the Human Spirit.* London: Granada.
Turkle, S. & Papert, S. (1990). Epistemological pluralism: Styles and voices within the computer culture. *Signs: Journal of Women in Culture and Society, 16,* 128–57.
Underwood, G., McCaffrey, M. & Underwood, J. (1990). Gender differences in a cooperative computer-based language task. *Educational Research, 32,* 16–21.
Underwood, J. & Underwood, G. (1999). Task effects on co-operative and collaborative learning with computers. In K. Littleton & P. Light (eds.), *Learning with computers: Analysing productive interaction* (pp. 10–23). London: Routledge.
Universities Central Council on Admissions. (1989). www.ucas.com.
Universities & Colleges Admissions Service. (1995–1999). www.ucas.com.
Watson, M. (1997). Improving groupwork at computers. In R. Wegerif & P. Scrimshaw (eds.), *Computers and talk in the primary classroom* (pp. 211–225). Clevedon: Multilingual Matters.
Webb, N. (1984). Microcomputer learning in small groups: Cognitive requirements and group processes. *Journal of Educational Psychology, 76,* 1076–1088.

Wilder, G., Mackie, D. & Cooper, J. (1985). Gender and computers: Two surveys of computer-related attitudes. *Sex Roles, 13* (3/4), 215–228.

Williams, S. & Ogletree, S. M. (1992). Pre-school children's computer interest and competence: Effects of sex and gender role. *Early Childhood Research Quarterly, 7*, 135–143.

Williams, S., Ogletree, S., Woodburn, W. & Raffeld, P. (1993). Gender roles and computer attitudes and dyadic computer interaction performance in college students. *Sex Roles, 29* (7/8), 515–525.

Willis, S. & Kenway, J. (1986). On overcoming sexism in schooling: To marginalise or mainsteam. *Australian Journal of Education, 30* (2), 132–149.

Wills, M. (2000). Keynote Speech by Undersecretary of State for Learning and Technology. Conference on Good Practice in the Use of ICT in Schools, RSA, 6 March 2000.

Wood, T. (1998). Gender and the 'new age' of computers: Identity, attitudes and use of the internet in education. *Centre for Information Technology in Education Report Number 241*. Milton Keynes: The Open University.

Yates, S. & Littleton, K. (1999). Understanding computer game cultures: A situated approach. *Information, Communication and Society, 2* (4), 566–583.

Yelland, N. (1998). Making sense of gender issues in mathematics and technology. In N. Yelland (ed.), *Gender in early childhood* (pp. 249–273). London: Routledge.

Endnotes

[1] Figures obtained from Universities Central Council on Admissions, UCCA (1989), and Universities & Colleges Admissions Service, UCAS (1995–99).

[2] The Playground Project is funded by the European Union ESPRIT/Experimental Schools Program (Project #29329).

Chapter 2

Imagining Less-Gendered Game Worlds

Katie McMillan Culp & Margaret Honey

Introduction

Like many of our colleagues, we believe that access to and fluency with technology is playing an increasingly important role in determining children's and adolescent's pathways toward success in the adult world (Glennan, 1998; Means, 1994; President's Committee of Advisors on Science and Technology, 1997; Sabelli & Dede, 1998; Task Force on Education Network Technology, 1993). This social reality has raised equity concerns in educational circles, as deep engagement with technology (e.g., designing and programming new technologies) has been demonstrated to be related both to proficiency in specific skills (Greenfield, 1984; Pea & Kurland, 1984), and to symbolic investment in particular features of technological capacity and the technological culture (Greenbaum & Kyng, 1991; Turkle & Papert, 1990; Wajcman, 1991). We have learned through our own and other's work that the nature of individuals' symbolic investment in technology can be shown to be strongly related to gender (Hawkins, Honey, Brunner, & Moeller, 1990; Honey, 1998, 1994; Turkle, 1984, 1995). While much research has focused on understanding and responding to differences in boys' and girls' opportunities to develop technology-related skills (Greenfield, 1994; Sanders & Stone, 1986;

Stone, 1986; Schofield, 1995), our work at EDC's Center for Children and Technology has focused on the role that gender plays in shaping the desires, needs, and motivations that drive individuals' engagement with technology (Brunner, Bennett & Honey, 1998; Hawkins et al., 1990). We have explored differences in the ways in which men and women, and boys and girls, construct relationships to the technologies they engage with, how they interpret and appropriate them, and how they locate technology in relation to cultures and society. Some of our investigations have examined the career paths and motivations that propel men and women to pursue technology-intensive professions (Hawkins et al., 1990; Honey, 1994). In others, we have explored the ways in which technologically sophisticated adults interpret the tools of their trades (Hawkins, 1991). We have also researched the kinds of design strategies (both applied and imaginative) that boys and girls bring to the task of creating technological devices (Bennett, 1996; Bennett, Brunner & Honey, 1996; Honey, Moeller, Brunner, Bennett, Clements & Hawkins, 1991).

What has become clear to us over time is that the issue of gender is highly over-determined, particularly with respect to technology. We use the word over-determined to characterize the multiple, interlocking forces at work, cultural, psychological, economic, and political, that help to shape our understanding and experience of gender. Gender is both shaped by these complex forces and lived and experienced by each of us as individuals and in communities. But because personal experiences are influenced by multiple and interwoven forces, grasping onto any one of them as a way to help make sense of how and why technology is gendered is always an inadequate effort. Even as we try to see clearly, for example, the sociological reality that girls are less likely than boys to take high-level math and science classes in college, our vision is clouded by the political realities of adult life that might make those choices, on an individual level, be perfectly justified, and so we accept the persistence of those course-taking patterns. On a more symbolic level, we wish that boys and girls would "naturally" choose less predictable toys but find it difficult to forbid a daughter's best friend from giving her the new Barbie™ cell phone as a birthday present (and maybe even finding it appealing ourselves).

We refer to this complicated, self-perpetuating dance as the *gender paradox*, and we find that it makes it extremely difficult for us to think our way out of more or less conventional understandings of "maleness" and "femaleness." These forces, sociological, economic, psychological, all serve to perpetuate, even as they sometimes expose, the traditional, mutually exclusive, binary relations of masculinity and femininity. The final twist in the paradox is our own participation in both questioning and reaffirming these forces, which shape our imaginations even as we try to imagine beyond them. In relation to our current topic of electronic gaming, these tensions are clear:

1. Sociologically: Girls continue to have high levels of attrition from engineering and computer science fields in college. As a result, scientific, engineering, and technological fields that make major contributions to this industry continue to be dominated by men.
2. Economically: Products that build on past successes and familiar characters and franchises are almost always seen as the safest bets for future success in the gaming industry, as in all toy and entertainment fields. Branding products with familiar licenses (e.g., Power Rangers™, Barbie™) is the surest way to claim shelf space in large retail chains. Consequently, alternative visions that might actually have broad appeal have little opportunity to prove themselves, and the track record for interactive games that are not highly and narrowly gendered remains weak.
3. Psychologically: As consumers, all of us have been strongly encouraged to collude in the kinds of narratives and story lines that the vast majority of interactive products offer, particularly in relationship to the gaming industry. The consequence of this is that when asked about preferences, it is very difficult for children to imagine non-stereotypical preferences.

Changing these complex forces is no simple task. From a research point of view, however, we need to conduct investigations that challenge our habitual participation in (and frustration with) the gender paradox. As researchers and designers we struggle with a number of questions: Should game design ignore gender? Should it focus on the preferences that we think boys and girls have? What would it mean to build environments that do not privilege gendered fantasies?

The tenacity of the gender paradox in the gaming world is well documented in a summary of a roundtable on gender and game design that was held at the Computer Game Designers' Conference in 1998 (Farmer, 1998). This roundtable, called "Babes in Boyland: Exploding Myths about Women in the Game Industry," was intended to be a discussion of the difficulties women experience as professionals working in the gaming industry. However, as Farmer's summary shows, the moderator found it impossible to entice this all-female group into discussing this issue. Instead, the group fixated on what they saw as a crucial problem with an "either-or" solution: should they be designing games that were gender free, or should they be designing "pink boxes" for girls and "blue boxes" for boys? The intensity of the session, combined with the absolute absence of any discussion of alternatives to these two paths, is striking. This incident is an important reminder of the persistence of the gender paradox, which does not become any more "soluble," necessarily, as one gains expertise, maturity, or rare access to the most intensive playing fields of the "other" gender.

It is clear that much more research is needed in order to understand the ways in which we could, in a gaming context, design effectively while responding to this notion of less-genderedness. We know that this research will need to move beyond the paradigm of standard market research, which may replicate in its methods the same pitfalls that we have just discussed in relation to specific "boy games" and "girl games." We know that, if we ask, girls will tell us they like Barbie™ dolls, and boys will tell us they like Power Rangers™. What we do not know enough about is, if they were given the opportunity to experiment and invent in technological contexts, what kinds of environments might kids choose to build, and how would they locate personally meaningful narratives in those environments?

In this chapter we hope to suggest a pathway out of these intractable, paired options of either somehow escaping gender altogether or sticking with pink and blue boxes for everyone. The escape involves, of course, rejecting the false choice of gender/no gender with an exploration of what it can mean for a game environment to be "less gendered." To us, this phrase, used in reference to game design, suggests creating game environments for an audience of players who all partake, in one way or another, in a culturally constructed range of gender roles. Gender is, most likely, an important part of who any game player is. Similarly, gendered content is going to be present in any game design. So designing for "no gender" eliminates a dimension of experience players are, inevitably, bringing to the game and is impossible to do anyway. Rather, we are interested in the idea of designing to "allow for" or "invite" gender on the player's terms rather than dictating or narrating it to the player.

Allowing for gender as one dimension of subjectivity among many is very different from designing highly codified and rule-bound images of gender. This option of "allowing for," of inviting the player to bring gender to bear on the game without dictating how that will occur, is the pathway we wish to explore. Such a game would offer up an environment that is not over-determined in the way that *Mortal Kombat* or *McKenzie & Company* are. It would allow players to construct their own meanings, to engage with the narrative issues within the game on terms that interest them, and to explore and discover the game world in ways that are inviting rather than rigid.

The pathway out of this false gender choice that we are describing is one suggested by other authors in this volume. In our chapter, we discuss two research studies and consider the ways in which their differences and similarities might suggest ways to begin imagining less-gendered game environments (Honey, 1988; McMillan, 1999).

Two Studies of Two Different Environments

In these two studies, separated by eleven years, each of us undertook an investigation of gender differences in the strategies that male and female adolescents used to appropriate and make sense of computer game environments. Our studies differed significantly in several important ways. One play environment (*Wizardry*) was highly gender over-determined, whereas the other (*Myst*) was symbolically rich but much more gender-indeterminate. These studies were also separated by many years of advances in technological development and by the increasing ubiquity of technologically rich environments in adolescents' lives. However, the spirit behind the two studies was a shared one. Both were concerned with issues of psychological investment. We wanted to examine how boys and girls established relationships in and with these game worlds. How would they fantasize about and interpret the environment and give meaning to their play? We also wanted to know what players' strategies, their interpretive and intentional choices and actions, would reveal about their play, and we wanted to understand more about the relationship between fantasy and strategic decision-making.

Both studies focused on adolescents (12–14 year olds) and used the backdrop of psychoanalytically oriented theories to analyze and interpret data. However, it is the design differences in these two games (gender over-determined and [relatively] gender-indeterminate) that were the key to helping us to think systematically about the interaction between content and players' construction of interpretive relationships with game worlds. We believe that our findings can tell us a great deal about how the symbolic content of computer and video games influences young people's play and that they began to suggest what computer and video game environments might look like if they were built to be neither rigid nor sterile along gender lines.

Wizardry: Play in the Phallic Universe

Honey's (1988) dissertation research undertook a detailed examination of how six pairs of young people (three female and three male pairs) played the computer game *Wizardry*. In the early 1980's, *Wizardry* was one of the most popular fantasy-role playing games. Released in 1981, by 1988 more than 700,000 copies of the game had been sold (personal communication, Sir Tech Software, February 9, 1988). The game was modeled on the fantasy-role-playing game Dungeons and Dragons, in which players created and named their own team of adventurers. Players decided whether their characters would be humans, elves, dwarves, gnomes, or hobbits by distributing points to various character attributes (strength, IQ, piety, vitality, agility, luck). Fighters, for example, had to have a minimum of 11 points assigned to strength, whereas mages and priests required that sufficient points be distributed to I.Q. and piety. Players assembled teams of up to six characters to form their adventurer's party. The challenge of the game was to use your characters to work through various levels of a cavernous maze, with an ultimate goal of solving the puzzle of the "Mad Overlord," a task that could take weeks or even months. Along the way, players encountered numerous and varied groups of monsters that had to be destroyed. The key to successful play lay in keeping members of the adventuring team alive, accumulating gold and other magic items, and acquiring experience points so that characters could become more skilled and sophisticated creations, capable of adventuring into increasingly complex levels of the maze.

Wizardry privileged strategies that involve risk-taking and aggression. The content of the game suggested a world that was strangely powerful, fantastic and mysterious. What made *Wizardry* an especially interesting environment to study was that while the conquest and mastery fantasies were explicit, the graphic images used in the game were very sketchy, the maze resembled a poorly lit, three-dimensional tunnel, and the monsters were represented by simple black and white graphics. Text messages appeared to tell players what they had encountered and described the action as it unfolds ("Sol is hit, two damaged"). The game was intriguing from a research point of view because it invited players to imagine for themselves what was taking place. Honey (1988) referred to the game as a "phallic universe," in which those traits associated with phallic masculinity in the psychoanalytic literature (aggression, mastery, conquest) were systematically privileged over all other traits generally, and over symbolically feminine traits specifically (relationality, nurturance, connectedness) (Benjamin, 1988; Chasseguet-Smirgel, 1970, 1985).

The study was structured so that the young people played the game in same-sex pairs. Pairs were used so that players would discuss and debate decisions and strategies. Players talked spontaneously about the characters they were creating, their reasons for fighting or fleeing groups of monsters, their decision to use certain spells, and their concerns or pride in their characters' performances. Each pair played the game a total of six times over a three-week period.

Honey's (1988) analysis was based on the psychoanalytic theories of difference in males and females relationships to aggression and mastery and focused on players' discursive associations to the game (how they talked about the play) as well as the specific strategies they used (Chasseguet-Smirgel, 1970, 1985). Honey (1988) identified four modes of engagement with the game universe: direct mastery, indirect mastery, evasion, and refusal.

With the exception of one boy, the boys' play was characterized by a single pattern, a desire to conquer the game universe, coupled with significant concern about failure and injury to their characters' well-being. On the one hand, the boys derived tremendous pleasure from their characters' conquests, and they slid easily and effortlessly into the fantasy of the game world. On the other hand, these boys paid close and careful attention to their characters' well-being, and injured characters were often hurried out of the maze for rest and repair. They identified strongly with their characters and experienced the characters' triumphs and failures as their own. In sum, they embraced the fantasy elements of the game without ambivalence, and as a group they were much more strategically successful than the girls involved in the study. One boy was something of an anomaly. He tended to worry obsessively about his characters, and his concern often overshadowed his ability to derive pleasure from their conquests.

The girls, in contrast, established more varied relationships with the game. Two of the girls engaged in what Honey (1988) termed "indirect mastery" of the game universe. These girls played more successfully than the other four girls and embraced the elements of the game that involved the acquisition of power and strength. However, they also developed relationships with the game and their characters that served to distance them from explicitly aggressive elements of the play. For one girl this was most clearly evidenced in the names she gave her characters, "Nosy," "Lucky," and "Lady." This was a stark contrast to the names chosen by the boys, "Grimsword," "Mercior," and "Vendure." For another girl, her entire relationship to the game was mediated through her one favorite character, "Taggio," whom she named after the boy in her class she was fond of. Simultaneously, these girls exhibited none of the anxiety associated with injury to their characters that was exhibited by the boys, and they never viewed their characters' injuries or deaths as personal failures. While it seemed sad to them to lose a character, the girls did not experience the same level of personal investment in character performance as did the boys. For them, the game was just a game.

The remaining four girls avoided the phallic content of the game universe in two different ways. Two of the girls evaded the signs of power and aggression, playing the game in a passive and unorganized way and avoiding engagement with all of the aggressive and phallic content of the game. Their game had a kind of depressive and defeatist quality to it, and they frequently expressed boredom and dissatisfaction.

Two other girls "refused" the phallic universe by subverting it. Their play turned the game into a parody, as they systematically took on but inverted both the aggressive and the powerful elements of the game. They did this by creating characters who were designed to be playful and silly creatures, rather than ones that would triumph over the game world. One character, in particular, served as the focal point of their subversive strategy. "Chilly-Willy," who they created to be a fighter, was named after a little penguin in a Saturday morning cartoon show. And as the girls said, "Chilly doesn't like to fight; the one thing he does best in the world is sing."

Honey's (1988) research made clear that strategic success was interwoven with the player's ability to embrace and engage the fantasy content of the game world. Despite the fact that none of the young people were avid Dungeons and Dragons players, and they did not differ from one another in their exposure to and use of computer games in general, strategically the boys did much better than the girls. Their characters lived longer, evolved into more sophisticated adventurers, and traveled to increasingly complex levels of the maze. The girls' success was much more limited. However, unlike the boys they did not take failure personally, as stated above; for them it was just a game.

What Honey's dissertation also made clear was that when the symbolic content of the game universe is highly gender over-determined, as it was in the case of *Wizardry*, young people are forced to shape their game play in response to the symbolic categories made available to them. As these young people made clear, there was *more than one way* to engage with the phallic content of a game like *Wizardry*, but one *had to engage with it*, and that requirement was so immediate that it dominated any other possible experiences of the game environment.

Honey concluded that the strategies the girls used in *Wizardry* bore a remarkably candid resemblance to the kinds of strategies that girls and women use in gender over-determined real-life situations. The girls who created the characters with the "cute" names were no doubt making a point about bringing what they understood to be dimensions of femininity into the play environment. Some women in the military or other highly masculinized professions, in a similar way, often make a point of wearing make-up on the job, as if to signal that they recognize their own difference within the highly masculine world in which they are participating.

The player who named her character after the boy in her class whom she was fond of chose, through this character, to enter the game world as a mock-boy. Her choice to name her character after this boy is familiar to many of us who longed to play traditionally masculine sports with our older brothers or neighborhood friends. It is an example of the tendency, in early adolescence, prior to the overt sexualization and romanticization of male-female relationships, to focus on the opposite sex less as an object of desire than as an object of admiration. The strategy is less about possessing this boy, and more about finding a way to be "like the boys," to find a way to join in on this game, becoming like the boys, via adopting the persona of a boy she admires.

The girls who were disengaged from the play should remind us of those who often can be heard saying "math is boring" or "I hate science." Viewed psychologically, these kinds of statements reflect the fact that math and science continue to be taught in such a way that girls find little personal relevance in what they are asked to learn (Bennett, 1996). Girls' continued attrition from advanced courses in these fields is grounded in similar experiences to those of the girls who, in their play with *Wizardry*, found no entry point that would make that gender over-determined environment meaningful to them.

Finally, the subversive strategy used by the girls who created "Chilly Willy" is not that different from that of girls who choose to create a parody of what is meant to be a serious learning situation. We can all perhaps remember middle school science labs where there always seemed to be a pair of girls who wanted to turn the experiment into comedy hour. What these various strategies suggest is that there are traditional ways of relating to gender over-determined game worlds, or subject matter, or professions, that we use to locate and preserve ourselves when confronted with situations that feel like they exclude us. What the findings of this study also reveal is that fantasies that resonate with boys can create a play context in which boys can succeed, while for girls, the same fantasies serve to make their success illusory.

Less-Gendered Environments

McMillan's (1999) dissertation research arose in part as a response to what is usually termed "effects" literature related to video game play and its impact on various socio-emotional and cognitive factors in young people. This body of research typically used as stimuli games that presented content and context that were over-determined in ways similar to *Wizardry* but did not acknowledge the role that these qualities of the game might be influencing findings related to gender differences. Instead, in this literature the "video/computer game" was usually treated as a whole and static object, the technology, the content, the rules of the game, and the narrative and environmental context were seen as being inextricable from one another (see Funk, 1992, for a review of this literature). McMillan's (1999) study was designed to tease apart some of these elements of video/computer games and gameplay, with a particular focus on the relationships that players built to a game environment, the visual content, the cues for gameplay, and the narrative cues, that were, unlike those in most video and computer game research, distinctly underdetermined in gender terms.

The question driving this study was, what kinds of relationships would male and female players build with this gaming environment, when the environment was under, rather than over-determined in terms of gender? Would gender continue to emerge as a dominant factor that differentiated and defined styles of play?

McMillan (1999) involved slighter older adolescents than Honey's (1988) study, and these subjects were invited to explore a much less symbolically constrained game environment than *Wizardry*. This study examined the strategies that forty-eight 13- and 14-year olds used to explore *Myst* Island, from the computer game *Myst* (Miller & Miller, 1993). *Myst* was one of the most popular computer games ever made and differs dramatically from *Wizardry* in both form and content. While *Wizardry* was created in the early days of graphic-interface computer games, *Myst* was, when it was released in 1993, a breakthrough in the aesthetically sophisticated use of computer graphics.

Myst Island was carefully crafted to provide a setting that is both highly evocative and highly indeterminate (Barba & DeMaria, 1995; Bodensiek, 1996; Glos & Goldin, 1998). Historical references are mixed: elements such as architectural styles, handwriting styles, and types of tools and machines present on the island are sometimes prosaic, sometimes futuristic and sometimes archaic. Many objects of unspecified function are present, such as a giant gear that will not turn, a series of switches, and a chair with a viewing screen attached. In addition, there are no characters on the island for a player to interact with. Thus the setting provided an opportunity for subjects to explore a place that is complex and engaging, without being compelled to relate to the goals, strictures, or skills involved in playing a specific game (see Barba & DeMaria, 1995, or Bodensiek, 1996, for further discussion of *Myst*).

The data for this study came from an one-on-one, 40-minute semi-structured interviews conducted with adolescents from a working-class city in New Jersey. Their explorations were analyzed with reference to a construct, established by Balint (1955, 1959), that described a subject's relative dependence on objects or on open spaces. Balint referred to these two characterological types as "ocnophilic" (clinging to objects) and "philobatic" (loving open spaces)[1]. At the beginning of the study, a small body of evidence (Hopf, 1994) suggested that these constructs were themselves highly gendered, with males being much more inclined to embrace and explore open space and females being much more likely to anchor themselves in relationships with specific objects.

Transcripts of the interviews were analyzed using a coding system that was designed to capture subjects' use of clinging and soaring strategies as they explored the island. These codes were then used to divide subjects into distinct categories using a statistical clustering process, and the characteristics of the resulting groups were examined. The coding system was structured to focus on three specific aspects of clinging and soaring that Balint emphasized: how subjects related to the objects in the environment, the fears and anxieties they experienced, and their means of coping with their own affective responses to the environment.

A pilot test of the coding system made clear that it was not capturing qualitative differences in subjects' ability to engage with the environment and to endow it with their own fantasies, expectations, and desires. This difference seemed to be independent of differences in the clinging or soaring style of relating that the subjects displayed. As a result, a dimension called "generativity" was added to the coding system to capture this capacity for play, which was not represented in Balint's system. The term "play" is being used here in Winnicott's sense of a capacity to extend the experience of transitional objects, symbolic objects through which the child negotiates an emerging understanding of the separateness of objects from the self, to spaces or environments more broadly. Winnicott (1971) uses the term "the transitional realm" to denote an environment "in which the child can play and create as if the outside world were as malleable as his own fantasy" (p. 41).

Results of the study. The coded interviews clustered into four distinct groups that exhibited different ways of relating to the *Myst* environment. There was no pattern to the distribution of male and female subjects among these four groups. The primary distinction in the analysis was between what McMillan (1999) called "anxious" and "generative" subjects. These two groups were each also secondarily divided along the lines of the "soaring" and "clinging" distinctions described by Balint, and again, gender differences did not emerge.

One of the surprising issues raised in this study was this issue of playfulness or "generativity," which arose quite unexpectedly. "Generativity" was a systematically described quality of each subjects' interaction with *Myst* Island, and this systematic examination produced no evidence of gender differences in subjects' capacity to enter into a playful, generative relationship with the environment. The following examples, in which both subjects are reacting after exploring the library on the island (which they refer to as a house) suggest the difference between a reaction that was coded as "high generativity" and one coded as "low generativity":

> It's... mmm... the house, the house is very empty but it seems like somebody still lives in there. But nobody lives in there so maybe it's a... maybe there was a... a myth or something, and someone, going around, bought the house, and before somebody died in the house, and people come to like, take pictures, I guess of

this famous house. It must, it might have been a rich person because everything's real big. But um, I don't know. The house is real empty, you could, you could tell people come to look at the house. But, I don't know.

[I want to know what this place is.] Like, where is this island, or whatever this is that I'm on? And what are the books? What does everything here do? Who used to own it? It's just empty....There's too much, too much to know, but nothing that I do know.

In the first example, the subject begins to imagine a history for the house; he creates actors, and the beginnings of a narrative, and begins to account for his own feelings of mysteriousness or ominousness within the story he creates: the house may have a "myth" associated with it, a tragic story of someone dying that has become well known. In the second example, the subject insists that the house is "empty," although this is clearly not literally true (the house contains books, a painting, and a map). Her use of the word "empty" seems to be describing her sense of frustration with the lack of clarity the place provides, that it is empty of information, or empty of clear meaning. Her desire to "know," and her expectation that there is, in fact, something *to* know clearly contrasts with the ability of the first subject to say "I don't know" but to continue imagining and describing.

With a bit of unpacking, the findings of this study may offer some important lessons about exactly how and why "less-genderedness" is a quality that can be designed for and that can invite not just the sterile genericism of supposedly "ungendered" gameworlds but a much more symbolically rich, personally evocative, and stimulating experience of play.

Making sense of generativity in this gameworld. The differences in the modes of exploration exhibited by the subjects in this study can be understood as differences in the particular desires, motivations and needs they brought to bear on this environment as they went through the experience of trying to find meaning in the island's character, tone, and content. However, as we've seen, the expression of these desires is mediated by the ability of the subject to feel able to play, to be generative in the creation of personal meanings.

A useful way to make sense of this prominent variation is to understand it as a difference in subjects' ability to make use of the gaming environment as a *transitional space* (Winnicott, 1971). Transitional space is a term used in psychoanalytic theory to describe an "area of experiencing" in which what is reality and what is fantasy are accepted as being unclear, a time and place of experience in which what we are inventing for ourselves and what is presented as "given" by the environment are not distinctly different from one another (Ogden,1992; Winnicott, 1971). This notion is useful because it relates the experience of creativity to particular experiences of space and time, as being something that occurs in concert with a particular environment rather than as something that happens in the isolated realms of an abstracted "mind."

A game like *Myst* lends itself to this type of experience because it is culturally and ontologically ambiguous. The ambiguity of its status (Does it have a history? Where, exactly, is it located? What, exactly, are the constraints and possibilities for its reinvention and reinterpretation?) invites people exploring the island to express the unconscious and highly personal, and hence, gendered in nuanced and complex ways, process of building a relationship with an environment. When the subjects in this study said things like: "I want to jump down off this mountain. Can I do that?" "That door opened when I clicked on the picture. Did I make that happen?" and "I think those pictures are a code. I think that book has a secret message about how to get out of here," they were making explicit their exploration of the freedom they have to invent this environment for themselves.

Playfulness emerged when subjects embraced this opportunity to imagine this island into being, when they allowed the boundaries between what was available to them in the environment, and what was available to them in their own imagination, to work together to create something new. This difference is evident in the contrast between these two descriptions offered by two subjects in the study, both of whom were reflecting, at the end of their exploration, on their experience:

> I like it. Cause it's like interesting, you're going into a place and you don't know what's going to happen, but you still want to go, 'cause it looks interesting...it make you think like, "What's going on?" and "Oh, I want to see that stuff," especially for somebody curious like me.

> It's just like, this is like, what is this, a missile? [The subject is looking at what appears to be a rocket] It's just a whole bunch of stuff and there's nobody here to even tell if somebody made it. It's just there. You can't tell anything about it, it's just there, but no one else is here.

This capacity for playfulness, then, is the key distinction between the "playful" soarers and clingers and the anxious soarers and clingers in this study. Different relational strategies were, in fact, used by the two types that were originally the focus of the study, the soarers (anxious or playful) seeking to make sense of the whole while the clingers were more fragmented in their explorations. But the most dramatic distinction among the subjects was the "playful versus anxious" distinction. Subjects in the "playful soaring" and "playful clinging" groups were willing to become creators of the objects that they found, by naming them, coming up with explanations of their functions, and so on. These subjects could all be described as being able to play in the transitional space of the island, and their ability to invent and imagine was not related to gender.

Conclusions of the study. This study suggests that in a virtual environment that is not over-determined in terms of gender but instead offers subjects an evocative space that allows them to do the interpretive work of making meaning of the environment, issues other than gender become apparent as important determinants in the play of subjects. Specifically, the findings of this study suggest that the modes of exploration of the subjects could be systematically distinguished on the basis of two characteristics: their soaring or clinging quality and the ability of the subjects to tolerate and build on ambiguity, as opposed to resisting and defending against it. However, because of the preliminary nature of these findings, further confirmation is needed, which will require further refinement of the coding instruments as well as conducting further studies using other virtual environments with narrative and visual features that vary from those presented in *Myst*.

These findings suggested, on a very preliminary basis, that the dimensions of game play examined in this study were not shaped or constrained by gender. Instead, because *Myst* was evocative, ambiguous, and open to interpretation drawing on multiple facets of symbolic life, other dimensions of subjective experience could be brought to bear on the gaming experience.

From Phallic *Wizardry* to Ambiguous *Myst*

We recognize that the differences in the findings of these two studies reflect many interrelated changes, changes over time, changes in subjects, changes in methods, and differences in the theoretical lenses used. These differences preclude drawing any one exhaustive conclusion, but they support the suggestion that both technological advances and the gradual appropriation of the conventions and preoccupations of electronic gaming by females can contribute to the creation of less-gendered game worlds.

In the final section of this chapter, we discuss some of the issues that arose in the *Myst* study that might be of particular interest to those attempting to imagine, or even create, these gameworlds that reach beyond phallic worlds like *Wizardry*.

What arises when gender isn't the number one issue?

Psychodynamically informed research on children's and adults' fantasies about and relationships to technology has found consistent and distinct differences between males' and females' thinking about and use of technological objects. Not only is this clear in Honey's research but Hawkins' et al. (1990) and Broughton's (1989) work also found strong gender-based distinctions in how subjects build relationships to technological objects and to technology-rich cultures. Similarly, Brunner and Bennett (this volume) describe in very concrete terms how specific design elements can shape the quality of the experiences that males and females have when they engage with various technologically mediated activities. Research from cognitive and learning sciences perspectives (Greenfield, 1994; Kafai, 1998) has also consistently documented systematic difference in adolescents' motivations for playing video games, their frequency of play, and the effects of play on various socio-emotional and cognitive factors (Funk, 1992; Greenfield, 1984). It is curious, then, that the *Myst* study does not produce similar gender-related findings.

We attribute this absence to the fact that *Myst* is a virtual environment that is not over-determined with reference to gender. Honey's (1988) study explicitly made use of a highly over-determined "phallic universe," a game world that insisted that players engage, in one way or another, with an exaggeratedly masculinized narrative of control, conquest, and mastery. By using such an environment as the context for her research, Honey implicitly required her players to demonstrate their methods of discursive and strategic negotiations with this over-determined symbolic domain.

In a similar way, the *Myst* study intentionally made use of an indeterminate, eclectic, and evocative but symbolically gender-indeterminate environment in order to invite subjects *not* to focus on negotiating with a body of tightly inter-woven and highly gendered symbolic content but to demonstrate characteristics of their favored mode of building a relationship with this environment. That is, rather than imposing highly over-determined fantasy context on players, the *Myst* study offered players a relatively unstructured space that they could appropriate and structure for themselves, using the particular modes of play and exploration that were spontaneously available to them.

The distinction between negotiation with a symbolically overdetermined domain and appropriation of a symbolically underdetermined environment is at the heart of the differences in findings between these two studies and many other studies (e.g., Funk, 1992; Greenfield, 1994; Heeter, 1994; Kafai, 1998; Sanders and Stone, 1986) of gender and its role in shaping subjects' relationship to technology. If gender is understood to be a product of language and culture, a part of self that is constructed in the context of the subject's being in relation to others, gendered individuals and a gendered culture, then gender differences should (and do) become apparent in how male and female players negotiate with and appropriate an explicitly gendered symbolic domain. As several psychoanalytically oriented theorists would argue, there is no reason for the capacity for and particular structures of play to be gendered in and of themselves, because they draw on experiences of boundedness, containment, and physical juxtaposition that predate a subject's induction into culture and, consequently, gender (Chodorow, 1989, Winnicott, 1971). The *Myst* study suggests that in the context of an underdetermined yet evocative play environment, adolescents will engage with and express dimensions of their psychological makeup that are not subsumed by gender differences. What this suggests for game designers is that we need to build games that use varied and flexible metaphors, rather than ones that represent narrow and stereotypical interpretations of male and female interests.

However, the *Wizardry* and *Myst* studies also suggest a substantial caveat to this way of thinking about game design. An important issue that was clear in both studies was the role that relative levels of creativity and rigidity played in shaping subjects' experiences. In the *Myst* study, the "anxious soaring" players and the "anxious clinging" players shared an inability or unwillingness to decide for themselves what things might mean or what might be happening in this highly indeterminate and mysterious place. By contrast, other players happily created stories explaining who might live here, where they might be, and what might happen next. The content of these stories varied widely, of course. A similar unwillingness to engage showed up in two different ways in the *Wizardry* study: first in the overwhelming anxiety one boy felt in the face of the threat of narcissistic injury, and second in the intentional passivity of two of the girls, who refused to engage with the highly constrained, phallic content of the game space. While the roots of the refusal vary in important ways across these examples, it is important to note that not all young people, regardless of gender and regardless of the nature of the environment in question, are going to be equally willing to engage in creative play with any given gaming environment. Designing game environments that aim to be inclusive of everyone, in which inclusion means catering to special interests, is, therefore, not likely to be something we should attempt to do. It is our belief that this way of thinking has given rise to the "pinkwear" phenomenon exemplified in games like *McKenzie and Company* and *Barbie™ Fashion Show*. Rather than inviting flexibility in interpretation, this strategy tends to reinforce culturally ascribed notions of gender. We need to think of gaming metaphors that lend themselves to multiple interpretations, different readings and different associations. This is a vision of game design in which meanings are not condensed but rather opened up. Rather than offering up the constraints and codes and conventions of either the phallic or feminine universe, a game like *Myst* invites us to explore a world which is sure to mean something, but exactly what it means is up to us. A round room with stars on the ceiling? A giant gear? A clock tower standing in water? A combination safe? These evocative but somehow slippery objects are provocative enough to invite us in but elusive enough to leave the storytelling up to us. This is the combination of richness and ambiguity that, we believe, is central to creating gaming experiences that are not for boys *or* for girls but are for all of us to engage with deeply.

The experiences of the players as they "ambled about" on *Myst* Island provide evidence that virtual environments can be conceived of as places in which players can explore and elaborate the interplay of subjective experience and objective reality, perhaps not so differently than they do in the "real world," only with vastly expanded opportunities for variation and creativity. This opportunity for diversity should not be taken lightly; one characteristic shared by many of the players in the *Myst* study, most of whom had little experience of any social or physical environment outside of their New Jersey town, was simply pleasure at the prospect of exploring a place that was distinctly different from anything they had ever seen before. As virtual worlds become an increasing part of our real life experiences, metaphors that invite rich and varied engagement and expose us to situations that invite interpretation should be something we keep in mind.

References

Balint, M. (1955). Friendly expanses, horrid empty spaces. *International Journal of Psycho-Analysis, 36* (4–5), 225–241.

Balint, M. (1959). *Thrills and regressions.* New York: International Universities Press.

Barba, R. & DeMaria, R. (1995). *Myst: The official strategy guide: Prima's secrets of the games* (Vol. 1) (Rev. ed.). New York: Prima Publishing.

Benjamin, J. (1988). *The bonds of love: Psychoanalysis, feminism and the problem of domination.* New York: Pantheon Books.

Bennett, D. (1996, May). *Voices of young women in engineering.* Technical Report CCTR4, Center for Children and Technology, Education Development Center, New York. Original paper presented at the 10th International Conference on Technology in Education, Boston, Massachusetts, Massachusetts Institute of Technology, 1993.

Bennett, D., Brunner C. & Honey, M. (1996, June). Gender and technology: Designing for diversity. Paper written for the regional equity forum on math, science and technology education co-sponsored by the EDC's WEEA Equity Resource Center, Northeastern University Comprehensive Resource Center for Minorities, TERC, MassPep.

Bodensiek, P. (1996). *Complete Myst: Hints and solutions.* New York: Macmillan Computer Publisher.

Broughton, J. M. (1989). Machine dreams: Computers in the fantasies of young adults. In R.W. Ricker (ed.), *Individual, society and communication: Tribute to Gregory Bateson.* New York: Cambridge University Press.

Brunner, C., Bennett, D. & Honey, M. (1998). Girl games and technological desire. In Cassell, J. & Jenkins, H. (eds.), *From Barbie to Mortal Kombat: Gender and computer games.* Cambridge, MA: MIT Press.

Chasseguet-Smirgel, J. (1970). *Female sexuality; new psychoanalytic views.* Ann Arbor, MI: University of Michigan Press.

Chasseguet-Smirgel, J. (1985). *The ego ideal: A psychoanalytic essay on the malady of the ideal.* (Barrows, P., Trans.) London: Free Association Books.

Chodorow, N. (1989). *Feminism and psychoanalytic theory.* New Haven: Yale University Press.

Farmer, M. A. (1998). *Babes in boyland: Exploding myths about women in the game industry.* CGDC'98 Roundtable report, May, 1998. http:// www.gamasutra.com/ connection/threads/cgdc_reports1998/women_gaming.htm

Funk, J. B. (1992). Video games: Benign or malignant? *Journal of Developmental & Behavioral Pediatrics, 13* (1), 53–54.

Glennan, T. K. (1998). *Elements of a national security strategy to foster effective use of technology in elementary and secondary education.* Document T–145. Santa Monica, CA: Rand Corporation.

Glos, J. & Goldin, S. (1998). An interview with Marsha Kinder (Intertexts Multimedia). In Cassell, J. & Jenkins, H. (eds.), *From Barbie to Mortal Kombat. Gender and computer games.* Cambridge, MA: The MIT Press.

Greenbaum, J. & Kyng, M. (eds.), (1991). *Design at work: Cooperative design of computer systems.* Hillsdale, N. J.: Lawrence Erlbaum Associates.

Greenfield, P. M. (1984). *Mind and media: The effects of television, video games, and computers.* Cambridge, MA: Harvard University Press.

Greenfield, P. M. (1994). Video games as cultural artifacts. *Journal of Applied Developmental Psychology, 15* (1), 3–12.

Hawkins, J. (1991). *The Aesthetics of Understanding.* Paper presented at Women, Work and Computerization. July 1991, Helsinki, Finland.

Hawkins, J., Brunner, C., Clements, P., Honey, M. & Moeller, B. (1990). *Women and technology: A new basis for understanding.* Final report to the Spencer Foundation. New York: Bank Street College of Education, Center for Children and Technology.

Hawkins, J., Honey, M., Brunner, C. & Moeller, B. (1990). *Women and technology: A new basis for understanding:* Final report to the Spencer Foundation. New York: Center for Children and Technology/Education Development Center.

Heeter, C. (1994). Gender differences and VR: A non-user survey of what women want. *Virtual Reality World,* March.

Honey, M. (1988). At play in the phallic universe. Unpublished doctoral dissertation. New York: Teachers College, Columbia University.

Honey, M. (1994). The maternal voice in the technological universe. In D. Bassin, M. Honey, & M. Kaplan (eds.), *Representations of motherhood.* New Haven: Yale University Press.

Honey, M., Moeller, B., Brunner, C. Bennett, D. T., Clements, P. & Hawkins, J. (1991). *Girls and design: Exploring the question of technological imagination.* (Tech Rep. No. 17). New York: Bank Street College of Education, Center for Technology in Education.

Hopf, H. H. (1992). Geschlechtsunterschiede in Traumen: Inhaltsanalytische Erfassung von oknophilen und philobatischen Traumbildern in den Traumen von Kindern und Jugendlichen. *Praxis der Kinderpsychologie et Kinderpsychiatrie, 41,* 176–184.

Kafai, Y. B. (1998). Video game designs by girls and boys: Variability and consistency of gender differences. In Cassell, J. & Jenkins, H., (eds.), *From Barbie to Mortal Kombat: Gender and computer games.* Cambridge, MA: The MIT Press.

McMillan, Katherine (1999). Gender and subjective experience in a virtual environment. Unpublished doctoral dissertation, Teachers College, Columbia University.

Means, B. (1994) (ed.). *Technology and education reform.* San Francisco: Jossey-Bass.

Miller, R. & Miller, R. (1993). *Myst: The surrealistic adventure that will become your world.* Novato, CA: Broderbund Software and Cyan, Inc.

Ogden, T. (1992). The dialectically constituted/decentred subject of psychoanalysis, II. The contributions of Klein and Winnicott. *International Journal of Psycho-Analysis, 73,* 613–626.

Pea, R. & Kurland, D. (1984). On the cognitive effects of learning programming. *New Ideas in Psychology, 2* (2), 137–168.

President's Committee of Advisors on Science and Technology, Panel on Educational Technology (1997). *Report to the president on the use of technology to strengthen K–12 education in the United States.* Washington, DC: USGPO.

Sabelli, N. & Dede, C. (1998). *Integrating educational research and practice: Reconceptualizing the goals and process of research to improve educational practice.*

Sanders, J. & Stone, A. (1986). *The neuter computer: Computers for girls and boys.* New York: Neal-Schuman Publishers.

Schofield, J. W. (1995). *Computers and classroom culture.* New York: Cambridge University Press.

SirTech Software (1988). *Personal communication*, February 9, 1988.
Task Force on Education Network Technology (1993). *Achieving educational excellence by increasing access to knowledge.* Discussion document: Report to the National Education Goals Panel: Washington, DC.
Turkle, S. & Papert, S. (1990). Epistemological pluralism: Styles and voices within the computer culture. *Signs: Journal of Women in Culture and Society, 16* (1), 128–157.
Turkle, S. (1984). *The second self: Computers and the human spirit.* New York: Simon & Schuster.
Turkle, S. (1995). *Life on the screen: Identity on the Internet.* New York: Simon & Schuster.
Wajcman, J. (1991). *Feminism confronts technology.* State College, PA: Pennsylvania State University Press.
Winnicott, D. W. (1971). *Playing and reality.* London: Tavistock Press.

Endnote

[1] Since these terms are very unwieldly these types will be referred to for the rest of this chapter as "soaring" (philobatic) and "clinging" (ocnophilic).

Chapter 3

Who's Afraid of a Mouse?—Grrrls, Information Technology and Educational Pleasures

Elizabeth Bullen & Jane Kenway

Introduction

It is often argued that as a generation, the young people of today are characterized by their command of information and communication technologies (ICT). They have been variously labelled "the computer generation" (Papert, 1993, p. x), "the Nintendo generation," "techno-kids" (Green, Reid & Bigum, 1998, p. 19, 21), and "cyberkids" (Sefton-Green, 1998, p. 2). As these labels suggest, much about contemporary child and youth cultures relates to ICT and more specifically computers, computer games and the Internet. Further, Spender argues that "Young people are already exhibiting the qualities and characteristics that go with the new technologies and which are setting the cultural patterns of the knowledge economy" (quoted in Bagnall, 2000). Whether one subscribes to Spender's tendency towards technological determinism and utopianism or not, it is certainly the case that digital technology has become an integral part of many young people's leisure and education in the so-called First World. But do such generalizations hold equally for all young people or do digital divides exist?

Such discussions about the generations tend not to consider whether ICT will map onto current social inequalities or create new types of inequality. Access is a base-line issue and includes issues related to cost, availability and competence with new information technologies. Matters of poverty, social and geographic isolation, disability, gender and generation as they overlap and intersect are particularly pertinent here. Given that technological literacy is commonly regarded as a "new basic" of education, equal access and competence must be a fundamental premise of any consideration of ways to ensure basic skill levels are achieved. Additionally, access issues include the question, "access to what?" What will the nature and quality of the interactions and content be and how will social relationships and individual and group identities be constructed within them? From a feminist point of view, these are standard curriculum questions which become all the more pressing as we witness the intransigence of many unfortunate aspects of the relationship among girls, young women and computer technology.

While aspects of elementary school girls' access to and interest in computer technology is not unproblematic, by the teenage years a digital gender divide is often clearly apparent. Girls' enrolments in information and computer technology courses fall dramatically once they enter the final years of their schooling and are able to make their own subject selections. In the Information Age, such choices may have long-term consequences. As Collins, Kenway, and McLeod (2000, p. 7) warn, "Girls" low participation in subjects that result in information technology literacy leads them to risk becoming members of the information poor and exclusion from the information society. It also excludes them from a range of emerging and important employment opportunities'. Women made up a mere 19% of enrolments in post-secondary Information Technology and Telecommunications (IT&T) courses in Australia over the past five years and their participation in the industry workforce stands at 20% (Newmarch, Taylor-Steele & Cumpston, 2000). While the figures for some Mediterranean and Asian countries show far more equal participation rates for men and women (Newmarch et al., 2000), women's representation in the field in the United States is similarly poor (American Association of University Women, 2000a).

Clearly there is a problem. But the key question is, how is it best understood and dealt with? In addressing this question we turn to cultural studies of young people and to cyberfeminism. The latter possibly needs some explanation.

Cyberfeminism is a contested term (Hall, 1996; Braidotti, accessed 1999; Wilding, accessed 1999). In general though it can be understood as a feminist politics in, about and around women's relationships to digitized, networked and increasingly converging information and communication technologies (ICT) and their surrounding contexts and cultures. It comes in many modalities (Kenway & Langmead, forthcoming).

Elsewhere (Kenway & Langmead, forthcoming) we have separated cyberfeminists into two broad groups, the conventionalist and the avant-garde. As we explain, the former explore issues and propose modes of gender politics which occupy very familiar feminist terrains such as access, participation, voice, gender dynamics, symbolic violence, power /knowledge and control. The latter distance themselves from such issues and pursue somewhat less feminist concerns. Of particular interest amongst the cyberfeminist avant-garde is the technopolitics of pleasure and play. While in parts of this paper we will draw on research that fits into the category of cyberfeminist conventionalism, for the main part we will seek to build upon the work of the cyberfeminist avant-garde through reference to the power of pleasure as a curriculum resource. In doing so, we will draw on Barthes' (1975) theorization of pleasure and, in particular, the concepts of plaisir and jouissance.

We will argue that conventional feminist responses to this problem are limited because they do not attend to the ways in which technology and consumption connect with gender, generation, pleasure and identity. They thus fail to consider what such matters might tell us about the ways in which girls and young women might be engaged through education. Accordingly, we begin by looking more closely at the current generation of young people.

The Y Generation

It is well documented that digital technologies play a major role in the ways in which today's children and youth are characterized and in how they construct their own identities. This is the case for those born between 1980 and 1995, popularly called the Y Generation. As the offspring of the late Baby Boomers, they are also known as the Echo Boomers. Unlike their parents, however, who:

> ...grew up in the confines of cookie-cutter suburbia, these kids are developing their interests in a world of exploding technological opportunity, learning through computers, video and a bursting array of cable options. This sophisticated,

mouse-wielding, joystick-operating group grew up with advanced eye-hand coordination and a low threshold for boredom. Within five years, they are expected to produce term papers with full-motion video. All the conventions that shaped a more traditional past are being left behind as these early adopters rush into ever-changing technology. (O'Leary, 1998, p. 49)

O'Leary (1998, p. 49) argues further that "There are no rules for this group.... With all the media stimulus, things like the Internet, there's no one authority for them." They themselves defy easy generalizations.

The Y Generation is regarded as being "highly consumption oriented and sophisticated in terms of their tastes, aspirations and shopping skills" (Schneiderman, 2000). Marketers seeking to target this generation are already recognizing the imperative of reaching them through the new media forms. Nucifora (2000) predicts that:

Because they spend so much of their time attached to their computers, online marketing and the Web will be dominant strategies for developing a marketing relationship with the Ys. This is also a generation with heretofore unheard of access to consumer information. Couple that with expanded choice and what results is greater individuality and self-expression in how they select and interact with their brands and provide feedback. To that point, communicating through e-mail is essential to this group. (Accessed, 2000)

These young people have great influence over household spending, particularly in regard to technological products (Schneiderman, 2000). As the number of children per household decrease, they are becoming the beneficiaries of the even-greater spending of often guilt-ridden and stressed working parents (Mackay 1997). Overall, as we have demonstrated elsewhere (Kenway & Bullen, forthcoming), among the young media-consumer culture has increasingly become an important although not unproblematic resource for identity building and an important source of pleasure and agency.

However, there are some paradoxes at the heart of the Y Generation. While its members exemplify technological and consumer pleasure and agency and frequently reject the long-term, instrumental outlook of their parents, they are possibly more dependent on parents, education and welfare than earlier generations. It has been argued that children are becoming "adult-like" at an earlier age (Postman, 1994; Meyrowitz, 1985; see also Buckingham, 2000 for a discussion of the debate surrounding the "disappearance of childhood") but also that the period of their economic and social "dependency" is being extended (Kociumbas, 1997). Older generations understand employment as the key to independence and identity building. However, because steady employment is not as readily gained as it was for previous generations, identity is potentially gained in other ways for the Y generation. Mackay's (1997) research on those born in the 1970s shows that similar paradoxes characterize that generation too and that they assert their identity through style and image, much of it derived from media-consumer culture. The trend towards identity building through style, image and the screen is intensified in the Y Generation.

In this context and paradoxically again, youthful identity is both "individualized" and "standardized" (Beck, 1992). This contradiction can, in part, be linked to the information and telecommunications technology revolution and to the technologically mediated convergence of entertainment and advertising. On the one hand, Internet technology has intensified the homogenizing force of globalization. For instance, racial and ethnic divisions have become more muted as along with corporate globalization, ICT have offered First World children and youth access to the same cultural influences. To the extent that the Internet transcends time and space, it connects members of Y Generation with their First World peers globally. On the other hand, the Net has simultaneously promoted diversification or what has become known as the new youthful tribalism. Whereas "adolescents could pretty much be divided into jocks, rockers and preps" in the 70s and 80s, today "there are at least a dozen "tribes" defined by their fashion, music and magazines" (*Maclean's*, accessed 2000). Each has its own style and aesthetic. Importantly, this all suggests that our efforts to engage the female members of the Y generation must attend to this diversification and to issues of pleasure and agency.

Contrary to O'Leary's (1998) pronouncement, however, not all of "the conventions that shaped a more traditional past are being left behind." Intransigent fundamentalist constructions of gender appear to be contributing in some ways to girls' and young women's rather unproductive relationships to computer and information technology in terms of curriculum and job preferences. The Y Generation is only just beginning to enter the post-school job market, although being employed part-time or casually while at school is a major trend for them. Nonetheless, as we have indicated, current data show that girls remain markedly under-represented in Information Technology courses in the final years of secondary school, in post-secondary vocational courses, and in the job sector. In fact, their participation rate is actually decreasing (American Association of University Women, 2000a). Given that girls' knowledge and use of computers "is almost as high as boys' in [the elementary and middle] school years" (Newmarch, et al., 2000, accessed 2000), what are the influences that limit young women's engagement with computer and information technologies in the middle teenage years?

In the search to find the reasons why this is the case for the majority of girls, it is interesting to note that Butler's (2000) survey of the literature on girls and technology since the 1980s reveals a number of recurring themes. In the following, we look briefly at some of these, concentrating on home, popular and school cultures as they affect girls' interest, access and participation in information and computer technology. These factors are in the main structural and the effects evidently cumulative. We are also particularly interested in the factors that determine the choices that 15- and 16-year-old girls make in respect to IT and how the problem of their low participation might be resolved. In this regard, we once again look to popular culture, understanding it to be a resource for identity and community building and a source of pleasure for Y Generation girls. The possibility of bringing pleasure into the IT curriculum may be the key to retaining their interest. However, given that popular culture also limits and constrains the identities and pleasures available to girls, we look to cyberfeminist avante-garde Net-practices for our exemplar.

Girls and Computers

Computer games became an important children's medium during the 1990s and, indeed, since the 1980s, access to them has been extended from mainly teenage boys to younger children and girls. This can be viewed as simply a consequence of the need to expand markets. Accordingly, the subject matter of these games diversified from initially boy-targeted, violent and often misogynist and homophobic action fare which Alloway and Gilbert (1998, p. 97) argue:

> ...align[s] masculinity with power, with aggression, with victory and winning, with superiority and strength—and, of course, violent action. They offer positions for young male game players that promise success as masculine subjects.

However, the subject positions that girls have been offered in girl-oriented games are frequently just as timeworn. In 1999, one media analyst described the interactive industry's courtship of girl gamers as "sluggish", and observed that "Still pretty in pink, girl-specific interactive games aren't branching out much beyond the feminine stereotypes of the kinds of activities girls like—namely, creativity, communication and, of course, fashion" (Barker, 1999).

The strongly gendered nature of computer games has other consequences. It has been argued that interactive entertainment is reconfiguring the relationship between gender and space. As literature on girls' and youth culture has shown, the home is the traditional site for young females' leisure activities. Now, as a function of computers, computer games and the Internet, young males are spending more time indoors. This is leading to struggles between girls and boys over access to ICT in the home and creating a gendered geography of cyberspace access in the home and, consequently, in cyberspace itself. The fact that girls play computer games less frequently than their brothers may be due to the fact that "for some girls, their access to computers and video games is controlled by their brothers" (McNamee, 1998, p. 197). McNamee argues that boys and "young men are controlling and policing their sisters' access to computer and video games in the expression of their masculine identity" and, as a consequence, "girls' use of domestic space as resistance to boys' domination of the streets...is now being eroded" (1998, p. 204). Boys also tend to monopolize computers at school with Newmarch et al. (2000) noting that "computer rooms often become *boys' clubs.*"

Newmarch et al. (2000) also identify another disquieting dimension of the question of access. Their data show that "parents are more likely to buy computers for boys than girls because they are more likely to believe that male children will have a future career in IT" and that "Around 32% of boys own their own computers compared with 23% of girls" (Newmarch et al., 2000). They are also far more likely to have access to a modem. Consequently, boys are more likely to acquire their computer skills at home, and this then gives them the edge in the classroom. Being more confident, they are then more likely to experiment and more likely to be the focus of the teachers' attention. Conversely, teachers are also likely to encourage boys to problem solve and trouble shoot, but to take over and complete tasks for girls. There are also some data which suggest that girls from all-girls' schools may be more likely to pursue studies in IT. Newmarch et al. (2000) note that "at UTS [the University of Technology, Sydney] which has one of the highest Australian participation rates of women in undergraduate courses, over 90% of female undergraduates went to an all-girls school."

Nevertheless, with women making up such a small proportion of enrolments in IT courses in Australia as well as in the industry workforce, the reasons for the imbalance cannot be reduced to a simple matter of the dominance of boys in the home and the school. Newmarch et al. (2000)

suggest that girls themselves also have preconceptions about IT and IT professionals which are self-limiting. It is generally thought to be a career that is "lonely and dull with little human interaction." The typical IT professional is understood to be technically adept but socially inadequate and usually male but not exclusively. Despite some exceptions (for instance, the technically adept but socially isolated Sandra Bullock in *The Net)*, IT is most often a background to the main action in popular cultural representations likely to appeal to female audiences. Given this, it is not altogether surprising that preconceptions about image are sometimes compounded by the fact that girls do not appear to know what IT professionals actually do. One wonders whether their teachers know either. Overall, it appears that girls' perception of information technology and computer science curriculum and work are that they are dull, tedious and just plain boring.

Conventionalist cyberfeminist approaches to women and technology focus on the themes we have outlined above: access to and control of ICT, gender dynamics, and inclusion of significantly disempowered women such as the young, the poor, and ethnic and racial minorities, those whom Negroponte (1995) calls the "digitally homeless." They advocate a range of strategies to enable access and to promote women's participation in cyberspace. Reflecting the cyberfeminist conventionalist position, the GirlTECH and Women's College Coalition have made a number of recommendations for parents seeking to encourage their daughters in technology. These begin with "truly believing" that girls have an aptitude for math, science and technology and that they are suited to careers in these field and go on to list ways of being proactive in promoting girls' interest and participation in technology both in the home and at school. Recommendations for the home range from preventing boys from monopolizing the family computer, through spending time on the computer with daughters, to giving girls gift certificates to a computer store and encouraging the purchase of "fun but beneficial products" (Rapp, 1998). Strategies aimed at the school include encouraging a technical mentoring program for girls and advocating homework that includes complex problem solving. While these suggestions appear to have potential, they do not necessarily address girls' and young women's immediate and diverse interests, desires or fantasies.

The Power of Pleasure

As previously stated, by age 15 or 16 many girls seem to have lost interest in computers other than for their own personal use (Internet surfing, homework, email). It is often inferred from this that there is no flow-on effect from personal use to participation in senior school and higher education computer training or in the job sector. The AAUW's commission report, *Tech-Savvy: Educating Girls in the New Computer Age* (2000), makes this point explicitly, arguing that girls' current ways of participating in computer culture do not promote true technological literacy or "fluency." Their use of the Internet, email or publishing software does not count when evaluated in the context of traditional views of technology, even though they are valued and enjoyed so much by them.

This is not to say that the AAUW report takes a deficit view of girls and we agree with co-chair of the commission, Sherry Turkle, who has noted:

> The commission makes it clear that girls are critical of the computer culture, not computer phobic.... Instead of trying to make girls fit into the existing computer culture, the computer culture must become more inviting to girls. (American Association of University Women, 2000b)

However, we would go further to suggest that rather than dismissing the relevance of girls' existing personal interests and propensities in regard to cybertechnology, we should be looking to them for insight. They may offer ways of interesting young women in technology, of consolidating and extending their skills base, of creating confidence, and of deconstructing the current social misfit image of IT and IT professionals in ways that the traditional IT curriculum does not. As the president and CEO of Girl Games, Laura Groppe, explains:

> Technology is not an end in itself, but a vehicle for what one really likes to do.... Girls do not want to learn to like a computer, but rather the outcome of what it and other technology can offer. Only then can they see the merit of it, and seek to become the coders, creators, and producers of technology. You kind of go through the back door. (Rapp, 1998)

Indeed, we suggest that if we are to succeed in attracting the current generation of girls to IT, then we must to go beyond the cyberfeminist conventionalist thinking which situates technology as instrumental or enabling and, like the cyberfeminist avant-garde, position it as pleasurable.

What do we mean by pleasure here? Barthes (1975) has defined two types, jouissance and plaisir, and we think the distinction important. Grace and Tobin (1997, p. 177) explain the difference between them thus:

> Plaisir represents conscious enjoyment and is capable of being expressed in language. It is more conservative, accommodating, and conformist than jouissance. Where plaisir is a particular pleasure, jouissance is more diffuse; it is pleasure without separation—bliss, ecstasy, pure affect. Jouissance is an intense, heightened form of pleasure, involving a momentary loss of subjectivity. It knows no bounds. Fiske (1989) sees the roots of plaisir in the dominant ideology. Plaisir produces the pleasures of relating to the social order; jouissance produces the pleasures of evading it.

Ultimately, jouissance is transgressive.

In many cases, the pleasure teenage girls currently derive from computer and information technologies falls into the category of plaisir. ICT is clearly a means of relating (both literally and semiotically) to the technological social order which, if anything, characterizes the Y Generation. But such pleasure is also constrained by its roots in the dominant (masculinist) ideology. Those girls who at 15 or 16 years of age lose interest in ICT are also those who are negotiating their (gendered) identity as young women. Image and style are important. So are the positions they assume in relation to peers of the same and, in particular, the opposite sex. In this context, the level of their engagement with technology is self-conscious, hardly the stuff of jouissance. The expression of rapt attention on face of the young child engrossed in Nintendo might as easily belong to a little girl as a little boy. Theirs is a pleasure without separation. The boy who explores, experiments and improvises with technology is not constrained by the fear of breaking the machine or the rules. His is a pleasure that disregards boundaries. Are there pleasures of this kind available to young women in contemporary technoculture? A brief look at some of the cyberfeminist avant-garde and girl-oriented websites suggests that there are girls who do experience the trangressive pleasure of jouissance in and through technology.

The proliferation of cyberfeminist avant-garde and girl-oriented websites not only indicates that some young women and girls are interested in technology but also in the pleasurable transgression of gender constructions around women and technology. These sites are not simply girls' or women's magazines published on the net or the equivalent of Barbie software for big girls. They are hybrids which have hijacked elements of Y Generation media-consumer culture to blend politics with pleasure. In doing so, they offer girls and young women opportunities to enjoy the very objects they want to subvert. They frequently celebrate the new technologies and associated technological know-how. The new wave of young feminists, in particular, those seeking "Grrrl power" in, and through new technology, offer insights into the ways in which girls and young women might be engaged.

"Grrrl power" websites are youth oriented and aim for wide popular appeal. They are not about the "girl power" which one United Kingdom group, the Spice Girls, famously promoted to a predominantly pre-teen audience in the 1990s. With single, double and triple R variations on the spelling, theirs is the power of "girls spelt with a growl and not an I" (Driscoll, 1999, p. 179). The origins of grrrl power are in the US punk music scene of the early 1990s and girl bands like Bikini Kill. Their typical audience is older, college- or university-aged young women. Unlike the Spice Girl version of "girl power" which "seem[s] amenable to the sometimes limited range of spaces popularly allowed to girls," the so-called:

> "Alternative" forms of girl culture, like the riot grrls or the cybergirls... often question the boundaries or definitions of such "girl space."(Driscoll, 1999, p. 176).

It could be argued that the one is the conformist space of plaisir and the other, the hybrid, trangressive space of jouissance, respectively. It is by virtue of its hybridization of popular culture and politics, technology and style, that grrrl power suggests itself as a means of attracting to technology those 15- and 16-year-old girls whose notions of pleasure and identity are in a flux of conformity and rebellion, power and powerlessness and who aspire to emulate their more sophisticated older "sisters."

Unlike conventional classroom instruction which many girls find boring or irrelevant, such sites offer technological advice, and funky "role models," in ways which are feisty, subversive, politicized, alternative, celebratory, impassioned, fun, chic and sexy. The Cybergrrl website, for instance, runs regular features on women in technology: web producers, developers, consultants and mistresses; systems administrators, analysts and computer programmers. These sites offer tech tips on subjects ranging from DLS vs. Cable Internet (September 11, 2000) to "Is your mother a technophobe?" (May 3, 1999). They have cool and credibility. They offer girls and young women opportunities for information sharing, collaboration, creativity and self-expression. They provide a forum within which they can "distribute" their voices and views in ways that they enjoy because it offers them the opportunity to blend the playful and earnest.

Whereas conventional Information Technology pedagogies appear to encourage girls' passivity, the message of these girlsites is, "Do it yourselves (DIY)" and "Do what you like" rather than waiting for someone to do it for you.

Unlike much of the "Barbie-fied" technologies to which young girls of the Y Generation are introduced, they take into account the polymorphous character of Third Wave feminism and the heterogeneity of the Y Generation. This diversity is indicated by sites like chickclick.com with its network of links to "girl sites that don't fake it". These sites include the Riotgrrrl, Riotgrrl and Cybergrrl websites and webrings; Wired Woman ("explores how technology affects women's lives"); Smarty-Pants ("mixes style with substance"); Bohos (a comic about four teenagers and "what it means to be cool in a world gone mad"); as well as Lawgirl, Teengrrl, gURL, Breakup Girl, Hissyfit, GrrlGamer and DjDazy. These are all elements of the grrrl power story. As Kenway and Langmead (forthcoming) explain, "Grrrl power is an offspring of consumer/techno culture which venerates speed and change, the new, the novel, virtuality, simulation" and is part of a broader subcultural movement which combines politics with style through its appropriation and subversion of the forms and genres of popular mass media and culture.

Garrison (2000) takes Riot Grrrl as typical of the youth or Third Wave feminist movement. She describes it as "an alternative subculture built around the opposition to presuppositions that young (usually white) US girls and women are too preoccupied with themselves and boys to be interested in being political, creative, and loud" (2000, pp. 142–143). "The tensions between this expectation and the political desires of members," she argues, "offers [sic] a powerful opportunity to learn different ways of resisting in a consumer-oriented culture" (2000, p. 143). Indeed, as Garrison goes on to add:

> For more and more subcultures (youth or otherwise), the ability to intertwine politics and style is a risky and necessary tactic in a cultural-historical period marked by 'the logic of late capitalism' in which the commodification of resistance is a hegemonic strategy. The hybrid political texts and distribution networks produced by feminists like Riot Grrrls are...both 'popular' and subcultural, they provide spaces for youth-controlled conversations, and they can operate as an interface between different Third Wave cohorts (2000, p. 143).

Such emphasis on style and content in the school curriculum is crucial if young women are to go against expectations, to invest in the production and politicization of elements of their own learning culture, to aspire to technological competence, and to take pleasure in these things. Of course it is also crucial if educators are to encourage girls and young women to question their own and others' sociocultural assumptions about gender and technology.

There is no doubt that information technology is currently developing as "masculine gender *territory*" (Collins et al., 2000, p. 41) in schools. However, the success of avant-garde cyberfeminism in exploiting the new "democratized technologies" to produce "hybrid political texts" in cyberspace (Garrison, 2000, p. 144) offers an alternative conceptual space from which to think about the education of girls in technology. A comparable hybridization of literacy and technology, of the popular and political, of entertainment and education, of "hard" and "soft" subjects, and individual and collaborative projects may be one way of dismantling the binary opposition which currently underpins the gender imbalance in technology. But it should go beyond the mere integration of technology into the broader school curriculum.

If future IT curricula are to attract and retain girls, they should invoke what Garrison (2000) has termed a new "technologic." She links the character and advancement of Third Wave feminism with a "technologic" which combines "diverse technologies to construct powerful cultural expressions of oppositional consciousness [,] involves a particular way of articulating one's awareness of the ways information travels [and] merge[s] identity, politics and technology" (2000, pp. 150–1). This "technologic," Garrison argues, "is a means for networking across cultural-technological spaces" (2000, p. 162).

Integrating a new "technologic" into the current information technology curriculum is imperative. A curriculum thus informed would take into account the fact that IT is not merely about technical discipline or skill but about relationships and social interaction, the sharing of knowledge and creativity, things that are regarded as being important and pleasurable to girls. In this regard, then, we argue that pleasure be acknowledged as an additional and vital element of a new "technologic" for curriculum development. Such a "technologic" would attend to information technology as a means not an end and, importantly, to the pleasures, desires and aspirations of girls as members of the Y Generation.

References

Alloway, N. & Gilbert, P. (1998). Video game culture: playing with masculinity, violence and pleasure. In S. Howard (ed.), *Wired-up: Young people and the electronic media* (pp. 95–114). London: UCL Press.

American Association of University Women. (2000a). Executive Summary. *Tech-Savvy: Educating girls in the new computer age* [Online]. Available: http:// www.aauw.org/ 2000/techsexecsum.html [2000, 24 October].

American Association of University Women. (2000b). Research. *Tech-savvy: Educating girls in the new computer age* [Online]. Available: http:// www.aauw.org/ 2000/techsavvybd.html [2000, 24 October].

Bagnall, D. (2000, 15 August). Born to be wired. *The Bulletin*, 24–29.

Barker, K. (1999, August). Girls games are in the pink. *Kidscreen* [Online]. Available: http://www.kidscreen.com/articles/ks26270.asp [2000, 6 June].

Barthes, R. (1975). *The pleasure of the text*. Trans. R. Miller. New York: Hill and Wang.

Beck, U. (1993) *Risk society*. London: Sage Publication.

Beck, U. Giddens, A. & Lash, S. (1994). Preface In: U. Beck, A. Giddens, & S. Lash, *Reflexive modernization: Politics, tradition and aesthetics in the modern social order.* (pp.vi–viii). Cambridge: Polity Press.

Braidotti, R. Cyberfeminism with a difference. [Online]. Available HTTP: http://www.let. ruu.nl/womens_studies/rosi/cyberfem.htm (July 1999).

Buckingham, D. (2000). *After the death of childhood: Growing up in the age of electronic media.* Cambridge: Polity Press.

Butler, D. (2000). Gender, girls, and computer technology: What's the status now? *The Clearing House, 73*(4), 225–229.

Collins, C., Kenway, J. & McLeod, J. (2000). *Factors influencing the educational performance of males and females in school and their initial destinations after leaving school.* Canberra, ACT: Commonwealth Department of Education and Training.

Driscoll, C. (1999). Girl culture, revenge and global capitalism: cybergirls, riot grrls, Spice Girls, *Australian Feminist Studies. 14* (29), 173–193.

Fiske, J. (1989). *Understanding popular culture*. London: Unwin Hyman.

Garrison, E. K. (2000). US feminism—grrrl style! Youth (sub)cultures and the technologics of the third wave. *Feminist Studies. 26* (1), 141–170.

Grace, D. J. & Tobin, J. (1997). Carnival in the classroom: Elementary students making videos. In J. Tobin (ed.), *Making a Place for Pleasure in Early Childhood Education.* New Haven: Yale University Press.

Green, B., Reid, J. A. & Bigum, C. (1998). Teaching the Nintendo generation?: Children, computer culture and popular technologies. In S. Howard (ed.), *Wired-up: Young people and the electronic media* (pp. 19–41). London: UCL Press.

Hall, K. (1996). Cyberfeminism. In S.C. Herring (ed.), *Computer mediated communication: Linguistic, social and cross-cultural perspectives*, Amsterdam & Philadelphia: J. Benjamins.

Howard, S. (ed.), (1998). *Wired-up: Young people and the electronic media.* London: UCL Press.

Kenway, J. & Bullen, E. (forthcoming). *Consuming children: Entertainment, advertising, education.* Buckingham: Open University Presss.

Kenway, J. & Langmead, D. (forthcoming). Cyber-feminism and citizenship? Challenging the political imaginary. In M. Arnot & J. Dillabough (eds.), *Challenging democracy: Feminist perspectives on the education of citizens*. London: Routledge.

Kociumbas, J. (1997). *Australian childhood: A history*. St Leonards: Allen & Unwin.

Mackay, H. (1997). *Generations: Baby Boomers, their parents and their children*. Sydney: Pan Macmillan.

Maclean's. (1999, 22 March). How teens got the power: Gen Y has the cash, the cool—and a burgeoning consumer culture. *Maclean's* [Online]. Available: *http://web4.infotrac.galegroup.com, Article A54833728* [2000, 27 June].

McNamee, S. (1998). Youth, gender and video games: Power and control in the home. In T. Skelton & G. Valentine (eds.), *Cool places: Geographies of youth culture*. London: Routledge.

Meyrowitz, J. (1985). *No sense of place: The impact of electronic media on social behavior*. New York: Oxford University Press.

Negroponte, N. (1995). *Being Digital*. New York: Knopf.

Newmarch, E., Taylor-Steele, S. & Cumpston, A. (2000, March). Women in IT—what are the barriers? Paper presented at the Network of Women in Further Education Conference, Net Gains: Women, Information Technology and Emerging Issues, [Online]. Available: http://www/detya.gov.au/iae/analysis/womeninit.htm [2000, 23 October].

Nucifora, A. (2000). Advertising age: Generation Y bears watching in marketing mix. *Houston Business Journal*, 30 (44) [Online]. Available: http:// web4.infotrac. galegroup.com/itw/infomark/566/946/ [2000, 27 June].

O'Leary, N. (1998, 18 May). The boom boom tube. *Adweek*, 45–52 [Online]. Available: http://www.adweek.com [2000, 27 June].

Papert, S. (1993). *The children's machine: Rethinking school in the age of the computer*. New York: Basic Books.

Postman, N. (1994). *The disappearance of childhood*. New York and Toronto: Vintage Books (first published 1982).

Rapp, T. (1998, 22 April). A high-tech career of her own. *TechWeb* [Online]. Available: http://www.crpc.rice.edu/CRPC/news/archive/techweb 422 98.html [2000, 23 October].

Schneiderman, I. (2000, 3 February). Echo boomers: staggering spending power. *WWD* [Online]. Available: http://web4.infotrac.galegroup.com, Article A59221600 [2000, 27 June].

Sefton-Green, J. (1998). Introduction: being young in the digital age. In J. Sefton-Green (ed.), *Digital diversions: Youth culture in the age of multimedia*. London and Bristol: UCL Press.

Wilding, F. Where is feminism in cyberspace? [Online]. Available: http:// www. studioxx.org/xwords/cyberfemme.html [1999, July].

Chapter 4

The Feminization of Technology

Cornelia Brunner & Dorothy Bennett

Introduction:
What We Mean by "Feminization"

In our research about the educational uses of technology (e.g., Bennett, 1993, 1996; Bennett, Brunner & Honey, 1996; Brunner, 1991; Brunner, Bennett & Honey, 1998; Brunner, Hawkins & Honey, 1988; Hawkins, 1991; Hawkins et al., 1990; Honey, 1994; Honey et al., 1991; Honey et al., 1994), we have come to recognize two very-distinct attitudes toward technology, two ways of looking at it, thinking about it, and making use of it. One seems recognizably "feminine" because it supports and reflects the values associated most strongly with women. It contrasts with a more traditionally "masculine" perspective about technology, more often represented in the mass media, which supports values more commonly associated with men.

This feminine perspective regards technology almost as a fellow creature, needing care and feeding to stay in balance with the environment, both social and physical, that surrounds it. A feminine perspective wants technology to be small and versatile, to permit conversation and connection, the sharing of ideas and feelings and experiences. It focuses on technology as one medium among many for expression and creation as well as a way to integrate our home and work lives.

The masculine perspective asks that technology grant the user transcendence over time, space and the limitations of the physical body. It sees technology as affording power, command, and control. In this view, the primary function of technology is instrumental, not expressive. This perspective prizes speed and efficiency. The feminine perspective prefers flexibility and effectiveness. In a masculine voice, there is talk about consuming technology, about needing it to exploit resources and potentialities. With a feminine voice, talk is about using it to explore worlds, to communicate and to share ideas.

Our previous work (e.g., Brunner, Bennett & Honey, 1998) has revealed that the "ideal" masculine technology of the future might be characterized as one that can provide its wearer with all the wisdom of great men throughout history, at the blink of an eye, to solve an ordinary problem, or to create cities and mountains either in the cyberworld or in the real one. The "ideal" feminine technology might be characterized as a tiny, portable device that can transform itself into many useful tools, depending on need or environment. Many boys imagine vehicles that can take them anywhere at any time, without depriving them of junk food and TV. Many girls imagine helpful companion creatures, or small boxes that heal all the ills of the world.

We began studying the gendered nature of technological desire in the late eighties and early nineties, before the explosion of the World Wide Web (e.g., Bennett, 1993, 1996; Brunner, Hawkins & Honey, 1988; Brunner, 1991; Hawkins, Brunner, Clements, Honey & Moeller, 1990; Honey, Moeller, Brunner et al., 1991; Honey, 1994). The people we interviewed for these studies ranged from highly trained technology users to adults and children who had never used computers. The gendered difference in what they expected of technology seemed to prevail regardless of their level of technical sophistication. But most of our work was done when the world was not yet wired. It is now timely to revisit those insights, to see if they still ring true in an age where digital technology has become a ubiquitous medium for communication rather than a set of isolated computational devices.

We have begun to explore ways in which women and girls make use of new media and the ways in which women's values shape the use and design of new technologies. For this chapter, we offer five examples: a look at how girls and boys imagine the Internet, an examination of how girls talk to their women mentors online, a glimpse at girls playing in a virtual world for kids, a glance at design features in women-made information interfaces, and finally, a snapshot of young women's perspectives on virtual reality.

Gendered Conceptions of the Internet

In some ways this new medium, the Internet, looks like the answer to both genders' prayers for technology. On one hand, it is the biggest and most accessible library imaginable. Using it feels amazingly close to wild masculine fantasies, such as dialing up Gandhi to get some advice on an important decision. As a frontier, the Internet provides new worlds to conquer with speed and bandwidth! However, the Internet is also a more feminine "talk" medium, a space to connect with others, to collaborate, to chat and to shop.

Rather than focus on the Internet as a device for information, we are just beginning to understand a more feminized view of the Internet in which sharing and collaboration are primary motivators for connecting with others. How do girls really view the Internet? There is evidence that girls think about and use the net differently than boys (Brunner, Bennett & Honey, 1998; Cassell, 1998). In the context of a larger Web-based research and development project, we investigated how children ages 8 to 12 think of the Internet and how they see themselves in relation to it (Bennett, Brunner, Hupert, Meade & Honey, 1999). To get a sense of these issues, we asked a range of children, from novices to regular users, to describe the Internet to someone who did not know about it and to create a poster or cartoon of it to go along with their description. We wanted to see whether the gendered conceptions of technology we saw in our earlier research persist in the current wired world.

The Internet seems to be a meaningful concept to nearly all children we talked to. Both boys and girls had a plethora of ideas about what the Internet was for and how you might navigate it. This was true for novice users as well as experienced Internet users. They described surfing the net, instant messaging, Web pages, and searching for specific information. There appear to be differences in how girls and boys conceptualize the purpose of the Internet.

Boys tended to emphasize the technical features of navigating and accessing the Internet rather than the broader functions one could perform and needs one could fulfill. They described how you connect, type in addresses, or access servers to use on your TV. When boys did speak of functions of the Internet, they tended to focus on how it is a tool for accessing information; as one boy explained, "It puts the encyclopedia to rest."

While girls often included terminology about how you might access the World Wide Web or the Internet, they more often described the multiple functions of the Internet (e.g., "it helps you look up things, shop, have fun, talk, and email people"). Rather than focus on its informational features exclusively, they tended to describe the Internet as a tool for connection and communication; as one girl said, "It connects people to games and other people."

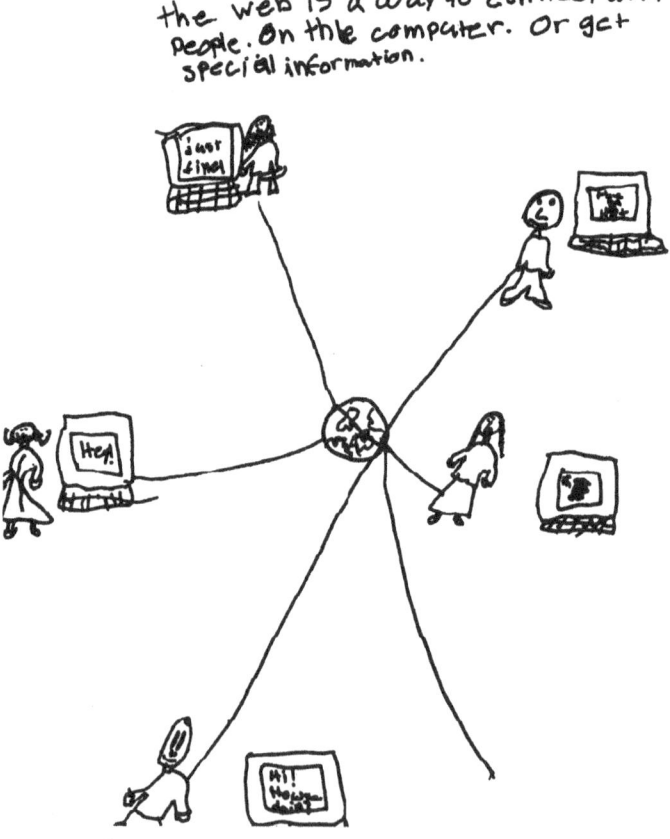

Figure 4.1: One girl's image of the Internet

These gendered conceptions of the net were most evident in the drawings that children created. A recurrent metaphor that girls included in

The Feminization of Technology

their drawings was the earth or world with connections going around it. When they drew computers, they often included images of people on the screens or standing by the machines. For the girls, the Internet was in many ways depicted as a party line where you get to see who is on and what they might be saying (see Figure 4.1).

Boys, on the other hand, tended to be drawn into the Internet as a technological object to be explored and manipulated. They drew literal versions of Web pages interspersed with Web "lingo" such as: download, email, and search. They also incorporated spider webs into the computer screens or illustrated the networks between machines rather than between people. In these cases, features of the technology itself, for example, the computer screen and the information tools one might use, were prominent (Figure 4.2).

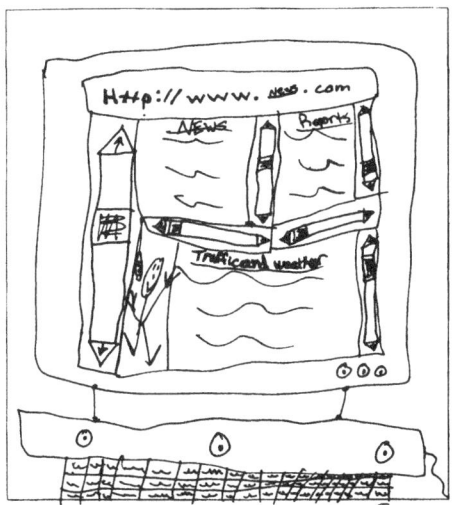

Figure 4.2: One boy's image of the Internet

As we listened to children describing the Internet, we were struck by how often girls emphasized the *communication* aspects of the Internet rather than the informational aspects that boys frequently highlighted. Ultimately, these different visions of the Internet have implications for how we interest girls in technology. At present, the Internet has primarily been seen as a space for information gathering, and more tactical search engines continue to be developed. Far fewer innovations exist that build on the expressive and communicative potential of the Internet. As we move ahead, we need to look more closely at what fosters productive conversation online and how women are beginning to make the Internet their own.

Feminization of One-to-One and Group Discussions: The Art of Online Facilitation

When people communicate face to face, conversation is generally a turn-taking game, while one talks, the listener picks up on when it is her or his time to speak. In everyday face-to-face conversation, you can assure someone that you are listening with a nod of the head, a reassuring look into the other person's eyes, or a quick utterance of approval. On line, these cues are absent or awkward at best. Many designers of online educational programs are beginning to realize that new skills are needed to ensure that productive online conversation can take place. Since in general women tend to use the Internet for ongoing conversation more than men do (Bennett, Hupert et al., 1998), it makes sense to study their uses of telecommunications to inform the design of future tools that may transform the Internet into a truly expressive and communicative medium.

One could argue that reading between the lines and monitoring the pulse of conversation is what women and girls are socialized at a very early age to do. Women are often finely attuned to the subtext in conversations, thinking not only about what is being said but what is not being said and how the words might be received by others. According to linguists, women tend to engage in "interaction work" (e.g., active listening and building on the utterances of others) while men tend to want to hold the floor and interrupt more (Fishman, 1983; Tannen, 1990). From years of conversational experience, many women become particularly good at taking turns and extending the conversations of others. These skills are critical in a medium that is pared down and has limited forms for two-way dialogue.

For the past five years, we have been experimenting with communication technologies to create new environments that support young women. One such project is the Telementoring program, which used telecommunications to link high school women to practicing female professionals in science and technology-related fields for ongoing advice and support. Through online conversations and discussions, we envisioned that professional women could address many of the girls' apprehensions, tensions, and questions about pursuing science and technical studies and, in turn, help sustain their interest in these fields.

Through this work, we have learned a great deal about specific facilitation skills and conversational strategies needed to support prolonged, purposeful conversation over the Internet (Bennett, Hupert, Tsikalas, Meade & Honey, 1998; Bennett, Tsikalas, Hupert, Meade & Honey, 1998). The program evolved a range of formats for students and mentors to engage in online conversation (one-on-one exchanges as well as topical group discussions and informal peer group exchanges). Each format and approach offers insight into the strengths and weaknesses of the medium itself and the unique set of strategies women and girls used to connect to each other.

One-on-One Discussions

The mentoring exchanges took place via private email between the mentor, from her workplace or home, and the student, who had access through school connections and occasionally through a home computer. To introduce themselves to their students, mentors emailed short autobiographies to their students and then followed up with "Day in a Life" messages, descriptive accounts of mentors' lives inside and outside of the workplace. From then on, mentors and students negotiated the frequency and content of their electronic conversations.

In speaking with students about their Telementoring relationships, it was clear that students and mentors took multiple pathways in order to connect at a deep level. The inclusion of personal information in a mentor's autobiography often helped generate more substantive conversation. Similarly, through exploring common interests (e.g., music, major hobbies, television programs), student-mentor conversations often wandered into deeper fundamental issues around career perceptions and aspirations. Humor and lightheartedness in mentor communications often gave students permission to be "silly" as well as serious. And finally, direct questioning about the details of one's daily life sometimes led to larger questions and issues, such as how to handle leaving home to go away to college.

These approaches to online communication seemed to echo the feminine voice we heard in our early studies of gender and technology (Bennett, 1993, 1996; Bennett, Brunner & Honey, 1996; Hawkins, et al., 1990; Hawkins, 1991; Honey, 1994). In the context of this project, women and girls were particularly keen on somehow "humanizing" the medium and were generally more concerned about how their messages would be received emotionally rather than how efficiently they disseminated information. Mentors and students made an effort to couch information in a personal and conversational tone. Mentors who could paint a picture of who they were, by describing in words, the setting they worked in and their feelings at the moment were particularly successful in establishing strong communications with students. Emoticons (e.g., smiley faces made with punctuation), little drawings at the bottom of messages, anecdotes of daily life, and humor seemed especially important to the students' increased sense of their mentors as people. Similarly, mentors who would pick up on a student's mention of small details in her emails appeared to communicate to students that their mentors really listened or cared about them. These techniques are illustrated in the following section.

Examples of mentors creating personal presence and attending to detail

- Rotten week...why do things always seem to happen together like that? Haven't figured that one out yet. I'm sorry to hear about....
- Anyway, my fingers are saying hasta la vista or, since you're a member of the French club, a bientot et bonne nuit!!
- I thought you had been taken hostage by the Oppians [Opp is the neighboring town and key opponent of the student's school.] ;>) since I hadn't heard from you in so long. sorry about the basketball loss, but there's always next year... (I know you won't be there then, but still...).

These professional women and high school girls became quite skilful at determining the boundaries of conversation, that is, which topics were appropriate for discussion and which were better left untouched. To help them decide what was appropriate and inappropriate, students described posing test questions to their mentors. For instance, one student said, "I tested to see if she would respond to something personal, like church. But she didn't, so I didn't bring it up anymore."

Over the course of the project, we observed a set of facilitation skills that were critical for starting and sustaining conversation. These skills included:

- Developing personal presence

- Paying attention to personal details
- Offering direct affirmations to students
- Avoiding long lapses between communications
- Acknowledging the boundaries of conversation, what could and couldn't be discussed

As telementoring has grown quite popular in education, teachers and program developers are recognizing that these "soft" skills are essential to build worthwhile online experiences for children, especially for girls. Yet programs often learn this the hard way, after they experience long silences online. Women in our program seemed particularly adept at these skills, but obviously not all women are. To ensure that outside experts are up to the task of engaging in meaningful exchanges with students online, we found it was important to provide adults with opportunities to practice responding to questions and issues that girls might raise in collaboration with their peers. To do this, we created online training sessions for 15 to 20 mentors that took place via mailing lists and were facilitated by project staff. This kind of community building and support enabled mentors to see multiple ways of responding to the same message and to experience some of the skills firsthand as modeled by facilitators. This added training feature ultimately proved to be essential to the success of the program. It reiterated for us that the nature of online discourse is much more nuanced than getting information out quickly and effectively.

Group discussions

Group conversations offer further insight into the complex skills involved in facilitating discussions. Many individuals, even those with some technical knowledge, often have no mental image of how a conversation might take place online among groups of diverse people. This is especially true for large-group discussions that take place via electronic mailing lists where people never meet face to face. Without this understanding, participants are often unsure of what to post, how to frame postings, and how to respond to postings from others. In an online discussion this can lead to long online silences, a lack of participation, and a breakdown in communication.

In the Telementoring program we designed a range of activities and techniques that encouraged girls and mentors to engage in topical online group discussions. Central to large-group discussions was the use of online scenarios where participants could respond to a hypothetical situation that was designed to resonate with their own lives. Scenarios were deliberately created so that they were multifaceted and complex and able to capture some of the competing concerns that students often face in making life decisions. For example, in the following scenario the theme is choosing an appropriate college.

Scenario: college and you

Maria was accepted to a university out of state that has many courses she would like to take. Yet she is considering going to the local community college since it is affordable and she thinks she could transfer to a four-year college down the road. Deep down, the real deal is that Maria is conflicted about what to do since she would like to go away for college, but at the same time she is not sure she is ready to leave her family and her hometown.

Her friend Karyl is a junior-year student and is interested in an environmental engineering program at a top college. The only problem is that she is not positive she wants to pursue engineering exclusively (she likes the performing arts) and there do not seem to be many interesting performing arts courses that she could take at this college.

You are eavesdropping on Maria and Karyl's phone conversation.

What do they talk about? What choices do they have?

The scenario was designed to invite students and mentors to share their ideas about choosing colleges. The most striking aspect of ensuing discussions was the broad range of issues touched on in response to a discussion on college choices. Topics ranged from conflicts with parents, careers, and relationships, to peer pressure, and attitudes toward mathematics. This discussion environment, stimulated by a complex scenario and guided by skilled mentors, supported the integration of multiple ideas and concerns and led to the kind of multilayered conversation that girls appeared to enjoy most.

What follows is a sample of both a student's and a mentor's response to the college scenario discussion.

Student response

Hey, everybody,

This is gonna be quick because I'm really tired. I'm not really sure where I'm going. Maybe Lehman College, maybe Long Island University, maybe the University of the Arts in Philly. The only thing I'm sure of is that I'll be getting my degree in music. I might also get my degree in music therapy. I wanted to do engineering, but I hate math. I'm kind of confused to say the least.

I have college problems and high school problems and boyfriend problems, and can anyone tell me if they stop soon? I feel like a slacker sometimes. Well it's time for bed so,

Later! J

Mentor response

Hi J, Glib answer:

—boyfriend problems stop when you ditch boyfriend

—high school problems stop when you graduate from high school

—college problems stop when you get out of college

So yes, in about 4 years, these problems will probably be over unless you forget to ditch boyfriend!

Actually, you don't sound like a slacker; you sound like you have a dream, having music in your career, whether as a musician or a therapist (or other ways which you might discover in your future). Having a dream is a good place to start, because you can think about your choices in the context of that dream. Good things happen to those who actively pursue their dreams, I think they turn out to be happier people for it.

So ask yourself how the programs available at Lehman, Long Island University, and University of Arts in Philly fit in with your music interests. Tell us about it, we'd like to know! If there's other college issues on your mind, you can dump those here too. Maybe some other participants have similar college questions or suggestions. Get some sleep! (Mentor)

A critical factor in the success of these discussions was the presence of skilled adult facilitators who could affirm, validate, and highlight salient issues raised in the forum. Successful facilitators were able to deal with the multiplicity of issues that girls raised about their life choices as was the case of the above-mentioned mentor. Here, the mentor not only acknowledged the key issue of applying to college and finding her dreams but, with humor, also acknowledged the student's anxiety about her boyfriend and prompted for others to join in and offer advice. It seems in this case, a host of facilitation skills were critical in making such multilayered conversation possible. These skills involved:

- Responding to affective as well as pragmatic issues
- Validating and highlighting issues raised by participants
- Offering options for further investigation
- Using a conversational tone
- Inviting other viewpoints/contributions

Designs for the future

While there were many successful conversations and relationships in the Telementoring project, there were also examples of miscommunication (Bennett, Brunner & Honey, 1996). In light of these, the project team identified design principles that could establish an online community by affirming that each person's words are heard.

The lack of nonverbal communication in the online environment can make conversation difficult. We considered how the design of new communication interfaces that valued the nuances of communication as well as the dissemination of information might alleviate such problems. For example, conferencing software that included personal icons that allowed girls to establish a sense of personal presence online could enrich the communication possibilities. Means for expressing tone and emotion beyond smiley faces would also add a dimension to communication that might make it more attractive to girls.

Given the multilayered conversations we saw girls engage in with the mentors and groups in this study, we also see a need to develop tools that do not organize group conversation linearly as so many current online discussion tools do. Many discussion environments privilege a topical or temporal organization of messages, which may not suit participants who are trying to follow the flow and engage in conversation on a personal level. For example, many pieces of conferencing software present individual messages as a long list of postings from individuals nested under the original message. More useful might be a visual interface that enables a discussion facilitator to see who is in the discussion and who has been silent, at a virtual table if you will. Maps that depict the pattern of conversation from one to another could provide a sense of the ebb and flow of conversation rather than the quantity of messages and support a richer sort of communication.

New communication and collaboration tools are being developed by many software companies. The insights gained from women and girls in current online programs are critical in shaping the next generation of conversational tools so that they are more feminine in nature and take into consideration the many dimensions of conversation. This would not only encourage more women and girls to participate but would also have the potential to facilitate richer exchanges among women and men.

In *KAHootZ*: Feminizing an Online Design World

Based on the insights gained from the telementoring project and related work, we have been developing a curriculum that invites girls, and boys, into the digital universe[1]. The curriculum provides opportunities for girls and boys to express their technological imaginations by designing technologies of the future. The technological substrate is *KAHootZ*, designed by the Australian Children's Television Foundation[2]. *KAHootZ* is an Internet-based, multimedia construction environment that allows children to create computer games or cartoons, known as Xpressions, which children can show to and discuss with one another. In essence, *KAHootZ* combines the power to make complex constructions and show them off to a world of peers with the potential for connection, conversation, and sharing.

The tools in *KAHootZ* include a large collection of clip art, including many categories of graphic stamps, backgrounds, and patterns; easy animation tools; and sound effects that allow users to add simple sounds or to compose complex music. There is personal email and a powerful chat room interface, in which the children are represented by icons of their own making, distributed around the border of the window. At the centre of the screen is an Xpression that a user has published for others to view and discuss. What the children write in the chat room appears in speech balloons emanating from their icons. In *KAHootZ*, a conversational centrepiece always exists, and it is clear who is talking.

Using the capabilities of *KAHootZ*, an "Imagination Place channel," is created where girls in particular—though not exclusively—are invited to join in a set of relatively structured design activities with other users to create fantastic inventions that solve problems they identify. To do so, we developed a set of additional graphics for the *KAHootZ* tools including the kinds of backgrounds that evoke stories that girls are interested in creating and a set of whimsical, charming and evocative parts that can be used to construct complex, fantastic machines. We have also designed structured learning activities to foster girls' technological imagination. The activities invite girls to think about design in the real world, to imagine themselves as future inventors, and to go through a process, using the *KAHootZ* animation tools, that helps them think systematically (though not necessarily realistically) about inventing technological objects.

In many ways, *KAHootZ* appeared to be the perfect gender-neutral vehicle for our curriculum, since it would offer girls opportunities to not only create inventions but also talk about them and share them with peers. When *KAHootZ* was launched, Australian creators stressed the adult-free nature of this world, a place where kids could just "hang out" with each other and talk and make "cool stuff." There were no adults, no structured activities, nothing but what the kids themselves invented. The inclusion of our new channel, "Imagination Place!" represents a shift away from the totally "free" space they had imagined to a somewhat more traditional environment with specific places to go and things to do. To use a frontier metaphor, congruent with pioneering Australians, we are feminizing their world, civilizing this particular cyberfrontier, as women have so often done, after it has been carved out of the wilderness with the aid of brilliant and powerful masculine tools.

In the course of the project, we noticed that there were a number of important features missing in the *KAHootZ* world that were critical for encouraging girls to create constructions. For one thing, the *KAHootZ* world was not as girl-friendly as it seemed at first because there were no meeting places. There was no central place or landscape in this world, just people and things. It is an inviting online world for kids who want to make something "cool" and share it with others; making something and sending it out into the world is easy. Finding someone in that world to talk to, to collaborate with, to make something with, or to play with, however, is much harder. The friendly interface makes chatting easy, but finding somebody to chat with is hard because there are no permanent chat rooms to join. There are only private parties here. It is early in the life of this world, but from what we can tell so far, boys seem to make things and look at each other's creations without much desire to discuss them. Girls, on the other hand, seem to want to chat. They send out invitations rather than constructions.

In addition to recognizing the need for a "place" for girls to meet in this new online world, we noticed several aspects of the environment that needed to be "feminized" so they were more appealing to girls.

Neatness. *KAHootZ* contains wonderful graphic tools that make changing size, shape, color, layers and other graphic properties easy. But there is no way to align graphic objects neatly or to lock a carefully designed arrangement of objects so it does not get disturbed when new things are added. We have found that there are a number of ways that neatness

The Feminization of Technology

comes into play during the design and invention process for girls.

Table 4.1: What boys and girls care about

What girls care about	What boys care about
Decoration: neatly aligning flowers or ten stars on an invention or Xpression they have created.	Model numbers and horsepower and other performance characteristics of inventions they are creating.
Ability to interact with things or "Xpressions" other people have made without the fear of "messing them up."	Ability to take things apart and put them back together without caring much about how neatly parts are rearranged.
Alignment of parts of machines they create, wheels should be aligned properly on a space vehicle.	Showing that the space vehicle has wheels is satisfying enough.

One of our modifications, then, was to add new tools that allowed girls to have more control over details of their inventions, particularly in relation to carefully aligning decoration or machine parts.

Symmetry. We found through our work that girls are more likely to want to construct creatures or humanoids, even when they are designing technologies, while boys seem to be more content constructing vehicles. To create such symmetrical creatures, users need a horizontal flip tool. However, The *KAHootZ* drawing tools allow you to rotate any object easily and freely up to 360 degrees but not to flip them horizontally. This means that after creating, using freehand drawing tools, one non-symmetrical object, such as an ear, the user cannot simply duplicate it to make an ear for the other side of the creature's head. While this omission had no bearing on the types of designs or games boys would typically create, it was a serious limitation for girls who wanted make creatures or complex symmetrical patterns. Until we started the process of "feminizing" *KAHootZ*, the lack of a horizontal flip feature had not been noticed.

Sounds. The sound capabilities of the *KAHootZ* tools are impressive. One can compose complex musical scores and select from a vast library of clear sound effects and musical phrases which are easily attached to objects and play either automatically or when clicked. *KAHootZ* contains sound elements that are not available in any other animation program that we have encountered. These include alien sounds, animal sounds, bath and kitchen sounds, cartoon sound effects, many different musical instruments, communication sounds, vehicle sounds, people sounds and environmental sounds. There are ten different laugh sounds. There are also six different fart sounds and seven different vomit sounds. Girls often complete their designs without such a highly differentiated choice of fart and vomit sounds, while boys will make entire constructions inspired by those very sounds. For "Imagination Place!" where we invite girls to invent fantastic machines to solve real social problems, the world needs a new set of sounds, which might best be called "process sounds." These are the sounds parts make when they are working together with other parts, sounds that characterize what things do when they're not shooting or traveling through space or exploding. Creating a set of such "process sounds," small sounds that indicate that things are working, will further feminize this world.

Movement. We became aware of an important feature that needed to be included in the *KAHootZ* tool set when we had girls attempt to map out their own inventions using the available animation capabilities. For example, to illustrate how her Dirt-to-Food Machine worked, one girl included a "bread loaf" graphic stamp coming out of her machine as an end product. The problem with many of the stamps, however, is that they move incessantly once a construction is played. That student's bread kept slicing and unslicing even though she did not assign that action to her bread loaf.

Even more problematic was that the *KAHootZ* animation tools do not allow an object to be moved along a user-defined path. Instead, most of the animation tools only allow objects to be moved across the screen in a prescribed set of patterns (for example, in a ricochet or an up-and-down motion). This movement is useful for making the kinds of computer games boys tend to create—where the player often has to catch or shoot a fast-moving object by directly clicking on it. We discovered, however, that without a great deal of clever manipulation amounting to a "trick," it is impossible to move an object from one place to another, to move from point A to point B and then stop. The kinds of narrative or practical constructions girls are often interested in making require just that kind of simple, functional movement.

These are small concerns in an otherwise excellent tool set. A school version of *KAHootZ* is currently in the works. Interestingly, it seems that many of the features girls need to make "Xpressions" that interest them are not very different from the kinds of tools that teachers want for their students. Teachers have noted that it would be useful for students to create narratives which express their knowledge and demonstrate their understanding of process through animation. We feel that schools will "domesticate" this cyberworld because good teaching is not about showing off how clever you are but about providing opportunities for children to express and share the knowledge they are constructing. To make room for effective teaching and learning, the *KAHootZ* world will need to be adapted to become more appealing to girls and thus more "feminized." In the interim, we are designing a space called "Imagination Place!" in the *KAHootZ* world, as a place for girls to meet, to think about worlds that they can design and to imagine themselves as the powerful inventors of new, wonderful technologies that have the potential to solve many problems of the real world. The real "feminization" of this particular corner of the cyberuniverse will occur when girls feel comfortable enough to share their designs with each other by talking about them, collaborating and using their inventions as a common ground for building a community of young inventors on the Internet.

Information Interfaces

What would it mean to design a Website that begins from the narrative/emotional perspective more common in women, rather than the more strictly informational approach that fits a more masculine perspective? What might such a new esthetic look like, one which met users' information needs on an emotional level? In this section we describe a health information Website, created by young women for young women, whose goals are to explore the space of possible designs and to identify design principles that could support this new, more feminine, esthetic.

A group of young Australian women recently developed a Website in which young women shared stories and information with each other, a mix of information and expression. The Website is called *Somazone*[3] and its purpose is to provide young people, especially young Australian women, with a place to talk about the issues that concern them. These include health, sex, and relationships. At the current time we don't have information about access and use of the site, but we are interested in it as an example of the ways in which an information interface might incorporate some of the "feminine" sensibility defined by our previous research.

This site was developed against a backdrop of our continually increasing use of the Web to find information which can have an immediate and profound effect on our lives. In the current view of the medium, information is power. Search engines can help direct our attention, whether by asking for keywords or through organizing known, established sites into a system of categories. Either way, the information is out there, and our goal is to find it by sifting through all the irrelevant and misleading information until we reach the nuggets of real stuff we want. There is something challenging and even exciting about this search process. Boys, in particular, seem to enjoy getting thousands of hits on a Web search. Some girls, on the other hand, would rather not be presented with an enormous number of responses to their query and then have to figure out how to whittle them down. While search engines are becoming more sophisticated, interpret queries more intelligently and do a better job of ranking "hits" according to some criterion, the basic premise is still that the information comes first and that we have to figure out how to get it. In this context, speed and efficiency are the benchmarks by which we evaluate the merit of an information interface. In a "masculine view," a good search engine allows clever users to penetrate the information thicket elegantly and swiftly, to locate everything potentially relevant to a specific topic in record time.

A more "feminine" perspective on information interfaces reverses this that premise. In this view, the user's informational *needs* come first, and information is important only in so far as it addresses those needs. Some information interfaces that take this perspective have been developed by the entertainment industry and are now being adopted in other domains, including medicine. In this approach, information-seekers are asked to identify a set of concerns, supply some information about themselves, from demographics to diagnoses, so that a profile of the user can be established and relevant information can then be customized This is likely to be a more appropriate way to provide access to people with information needs for whom neither speed nor inclusiveness are the primary criteria. It saves them from having to sift through sometimes misleading, and in medical matters, sometimes terrifying, material to get to what they want. In other domains, however, there is no obvious analogue of demographics and diagnosis. What might be a different path to the information?

The *Somazone* site provides a glimpse of another possibility, one that may be more consistent with young women's world views and esthetic

The Feminization of Technology

perspectives. In a way, this interface borrows from atmospheric games such as *Myst* but combines these features with a considerable amount of (growing) information.

The *Somazone* "homepage" is dark and cavelike but has the appearance of being warm because of the use of soft colors. Pulsing, delicate, round icons represent body parts and offer five options. When the cursor touches one of the circles, a label appears, and an additional piece of information gently flows in and out of the shadows for as long as the cursor rests on the icon. The impression it creates is one of quiet, gentle waving.

The "offerings" are little points of light in the darkness. The pixel-like dots of the wide, textured border eventually come to look like the side of a face. The icons next to it are evocative: the circle with two faces is a soft blue and represents "personal stories." An open hand, friendly and waving stands for "questions & answers," the gently beating heart for "interactives," the soft, purple toes are for "support networks," and the silver brain for the credits. Each icon moves a little, subtly changing size or position when the cursor touches it. The entire screen is highly responsive.

These techniques are used in many Websites. The remarkable thing here is the simplicity, creating a look that is clean and uncluttered while being dark and mysterious but gently, without intending to scare. The interface immediately communicates to the user that this is about people and their bodies.

The first content section, "personals" is as dark as the homepage. The small shape in the center is green. On closer inspection, it turns out to be a pair of crossed feet. The small type above it reads "1:10, 2:10, ..." and identifies the circle as a kind of clock face, creating a visual pun about feet and hands: clock feet. The body theme is continued from the home page icons. The invitation above the story clock face invites the user to "tell us your story." As the cursor rolls over each spike around the circle, the image inside the circle changes to another subtle biological image. What these images represent is not immediately obvious though all have a photo-realistic look, alluding to the mysteries of the real body touched upon in this virtual world.

The words that appear next to each spike indicate a kind of story: "Anorexia has been in my life for 6 long years now," or "I was very young and needed some support; my family had problems." The stories themselves are told in short, horizontally aligned chunks. Each is accompanied by a graphic, something like a face or a body part, a more complete image than the small icons but equally mysterious. The images take on meaning as you look at and in some cases, a graphic accompanying each paragraph adds to the meaning more directly. In one story about identity, for instance, the soft white rectangle next to the first part of the story gradually becomes a face as the young woman telling her story about leaving home at 16 describes coming to terms with her identity. In another story about anorexia, a face slowly disappears as the story progresses, and the protagonist grows thinner.

The "q & a" section of the site shows translucent blue hands against a white background. Written on each finger is one category of questions the site is designed to answer: general health, independence, harassment, body image, sexuality, relationships, drugs, and mental health. Touching a finger produces a screen with questions and answers. The questions seem genuine, as if real adolescents had asked them. For example, for body image the question is: "My best friend has recently lost a lot of weight. I think that she is vomiting up her food but I am not sure. How can I tell and what should I do?" or "I have really big breasts and they make me feel uncomfortable. What can I do to make them look smaller?" The answers seem to be sensible and give the impression that the information was gathered from the cited sources, mostly social service agencies, and was translated into appropriate language by young women who can sympathize with the questioner and understand that sometimes there is another question underlying the one stated.

The aesthetics are interesting; coming upon the white background in this section after the dark, mysterious homepage and "personals" section is not a visual shock, but it does have the function of making the visitor feel as if a light has just been turned on, as if things are clear here. The x-ray-like graphic of the hands still hints at interiority, at looking deep inside, but things are well lit and in the open.

The "support" section of the site continues the visual theme of translucent blue body parts against a white background, this time with toes rather than fingers. The section offers three areas of support: a map of Australia from which to select regional services for the kinds of issues dealt with in this site, including gay and lesbian youth services, a page of links to other on-line youth health sites, and a page explaining how to go about getting various kinds of help: immediate help, specific help, going to the doctor, getting a Medicare card, and community health centers. "Going to a doctor" is a good example of the quality of the help:

The Feminization of Technology

> You should feel comfortable with your doctor and be able to tell them [sic] what you are thinking and how you are feeling. If you are unsure about how you feel about your doctor, ask yourself—does my doctor:
>
> • Spend time getting to know me?
>
> • Really understand where I am coming from?
>
> • Listen to what I have to say?
>
> • Explain things in a way that I understand them?
>
> • Answer my questions?
>
> By law, any consultation with your doctor or any health professional is confidential, UNLESS you are under 16 and they believe you are not able to make an informed decision. Or they feel that you are in emotional or physical danger.

This focus on advocacy more than information is a different approach from the more "naked" informational sites that don't explicitly address their audience in such an intimate way. This consideration of the reader's needs above and beyond information one may know how to ask for is part of what we are calling "feminine."

Finally, there is the "about" section. The photographs of the young people who made this site are clear. Clicking on any photograph produces a larger version of it on the right side of the screen, with a quote by the person about her involvement in the project and a direct email link.

This site exemplifies, or suggests, several of the attributes of an information interface that we think of as "feminine." In the "personal" section, for example, we imagine that the stories were intended as a kind of diagnostic, as a way for young women to identify their problems and needs. While reading through them, a user might signal "I have a similar issue" or "I have a question about this." This would be a way to identify one's own informational needs based on a complex narrative in which such issues are placed in a rich context. Some part of a story may sound "right" to a visitor to *Somazone*, and this could be a place to start an inquiry, a way to select information and to guide the user through a more complex search. There might be a more specific set of questions attached to any point in a story, a naming of related issues, that would more narrowly indicate what information would be useful. The aesthetics of the screens in *Somazone* seem to work well with this notion. The darkness and the body images allow young visitors to feel understood even before they have "said" anything about themselves. An information interface of this sort signals that clear, efficient, diagnostically accurate knowledge of one's information needs is not necessary here, that it is sufficient to empathize, to identify with someone, to say "me, too."

The "q & a" section of *Somazone* is a more direct version of a "feminine" information interface. Here authentic questions by visitors are answered by experts and translated into non-technical language by young people who understand both the question and the answer in a social context. Those kinds of information interfaces are often expensive because they are labor intensive, requiring a human behind the scenes to direct the flow of information, a cyberlibrarian, as it were.

The hoped-for result of these features is that either through the stories or a direct question, users can identify what they want to know about in the *Somazone* site. The program could then produce a page specially created for a visitor, with links to other Websites and other resources. Going back to change or add an issue in one of the stories would produce further links and possibly eliminate some less relevant ones. If this were done well, users would feel understood, and the responses could help them. The information itself, instead of being primary, would be part of a service performed in the background. It would be part of a process of identifying one's concerns and recognizing that they are shared by many others. That, in itself, is often the most important information service. What strikes us as "feminine" in this slant on information interfaces, then, is the emphasis on sharing rather than having, on identifying and empathizing rather than on efficiency or quantity of the information "goods." In this sense, this Website, made by young women for young women, is a beginning example of the feminization of this medium. This Website is distinctive and attractive to girls because it invites them into information using metaphors and strategies that are frequently missing from many informational Websites, particularly in an area as important as health. We think the features employed by these young women for young women holds great promise in redefining how we access and make use of information.

Looking Toward the Future:
Girls' Visions of Visualization Tools and Virtual Reality

There are always new technologies to explore and new questions about their use by women. Two of the most recent of these are visualization software and virtual reality, which offer new ways to communicate information, visualize processes, and creatively express ideas. The power often associated with virtual reality is the ability to see and feel things that would otherwise be impossible to explore. With data gloves, joysticks, or wands in hand, users can navigate through a range of three-dimensional worlds and interact with virtual objects. These virtual worlds may consist of realistic buildings, landscapes, underwater shipwrecks, the interior of the human anatomy, or abstract worlds such as molecular fields, mathematical systems, or artistic constructions. In some cases, sound and tactile feedback are provided, offering ways to design and test ideas that would otherwise be dangerous or near impossible, from automobile design and crash-testing, to the re-enactment of crime scenes, to microscopic operations on the human body. In education, we often hear a great deal of talk about how virtual reality can help children transcend the barriers of time, space, and environment to see and experience worlds they could never see before. But what might be important to experience in these worlds from an educational standpoint? What kind of feminist perspective might be brought to bear on the use of these new resources in education?

In our work with schools, for example, we have started to investigate what a "feminized" view of such tools might be. Girls spoke to us about the visualization tools they were using in their science and technology classes, and many felt that they provided an interesting means for investigating ideas. However, girls also expressed some caveats. Several described how visualization tools sometimes made concepts even more difficult to understand. They complained that tools such as Spyglass did not allow them to "break down" the data or to get a sense of how graphical representations are constructed. This last point was particularly true for girls working on a study of earthquakes. These students explained that drawing their graphs by hand allowed them to know what each data point meant, whereas a computational visualization tool that plotted data quickly and three-dimensionally did not.

When we asked them for additional ideas about what kinds of visualization tools they would like to use in their classes, girls immediately mentioned virtual reality applications they had seen in the movies that provided a sense of being there even when you're not. For them, virtual reality would help make the *invisible, visible*, not by observing and manipulating information but by becoming part of it. They wanted to be active participants who could feel the transformations of data taking place. They wanted to see protons and electrons. They wanted to know how atoms come together and collide, and they wanted to be able to experience the collisions themselves in some way. They also described how they wanted to see a quark and to understand it through a simulated hands-on experience.

The girls also described how they wanted to explore mechanical and electrical processes that they were studying as part of their pre-engineering courses. They wanted to see a visualization of the inside of a motor in order to know how the energy is transferred from one part to another and suggested that it could use sparks to show the energy transformations taking place within the motor, helping them to understand the inner workings. They also wanted to understand and experience how gas runs a car and how energy is converted into motion. Yet another student described how she wanted to get inside a TV and feel how the signal is received and how the TV knows it is there.

Young women thus longed for a more intuitive, organic understanding of mechanisms, systems, and the invisible theories (e.g., energy transformations) that they are expected to understand in the context of their science, physics, and engineering classes. They did not want to take what they learned about these systems on faith. The kinds of visualizations and tools that students described could be key to opening up these topics to them in a way that they haven't been before. Their descriptions echo the musings of the famous geneticist, Barbara McClintock who described her approach to studying the genetics of maize by "getting a feeling for the organism." Rather than use tools that enable them to merely transcend natural barriers, girls, in essence are asking that tools enable them to become one with phenomena so they can understand them better from the inside out.

Through their exploration and use of the latest digital technologies, women and girls are redefining the purposes and designs of our most fantastic and futuristic technological tools. Their voices hint that there is a feminization of technology underway that could lead to exciting new directions for technology and education as a whole.

References

Bennett, D. (1996, May). Voices of young women in engineering. Technical Report CCTR4, Center for Children and Technology, Education Development Center, New York. Originally paper presentation for MIT Symposium.

Bennett, D. (1993). *Voices of young women in engineering.* Paper presented at the 10th International Conference on Technology in Education, Boston, Massachusetts, Massachusetts Institute of Technology.

Bennett, D., Brunner C. & Honey, M. (1996, June). *Gender and technology: Designing for diversity*. Paper written for the regional equity forum on math, science and technology education co-sponsored by the EDC's WEEA Equity Resource Center, Northeastern University Comprehensive Resource Center for Minorities, TERC, MassPep.

Bennett, D. T., Brunner, C., Hupert, N., Meade, T. & Honey, M. (1999). Imagination Place! Interim report to the National Science Foundation. New York: EDC's Center for Children and Technology.

Bennett, D. T., Hupert, N., Tsikalas, K., Meade, T. & Honey, M. (1998, September). *Critical issues in the design of telementoring environments*. CCT Reports. New York: EDC's Center for Children and Technology.

Bennett, D. T., Tsikalas, K., Hupert, N., Meade, T. & Honey, M. (1998, September). *The benefits of online mentoring for high school girls: Year three evaluation of the telementoring young women in science, engineering, and computing project*. CCT Reports. New York: EDC's Center for Children and Technology.

Brunner, C. (1991). Gender and distance learning. In L. Roberts & V. Horner (eds.), *The Annals of political and social science*. (pp. 133–145). Beverly Hills, CA: Sage Press.

Brunner, C., Bennett, D. T. & Honey, M. (1998). Girls' games and technological desire. In J. Cassell & H. Jenkins, (eds.), *From Barbie to Mortal Kombat. Gender and computer games,* (pp. 72–87). Cambridge, Mass.: MIT Press.

Brunner, C., Hawkins, J. & Honey, M. (1988). Making meaning: technological expertise and the use of metaphor. Paper presented at the American Educational Research Association, New Orleans, LA.

Cassell, J. (1998). Storytelling as a nexus for change in the relationship between gender and technology: A feminist approach to software design. In J. Cassell and H. Jenkins, eds., *From Barbie to Mortal Kombat: Gender and computer games,* (pp. 298–322). Cambridge: MIT Press.

Fishman, P.M. (1983). Interaction: The work women do. In B. Thorne, C. Kramarae, and N. Henley, (eds.), *Language, gender, and society*, (pp. 89–101). Cambridge: Newbury House Publishers/Harper and Row, Inc.

Hawkins, J. (1991). The aesthetics of understanding. Paper presented at Women, Work and Computerization. Helsinki, Finland.

Hawkins, J., Brunner, C., Clements, P., Honey, M. & Moeller, B. (1990). *Women and technology: A new basis for understanding*. Final report to the Spencer Foundation. New York: Bank Street College of Education, Center for Children and Technology.

Honey, M. (1994). The maternal voice in the technological universe. In Bassin, D., Honey, M., Kaplan, M. (eds.), *Representations of motherhood*. New Haven: Yale University Press.

Honey, M., Brunner, C., Bennett, D., Meade, T. & Tsen, V. (1994). *Designing for equity: A new approach for girls and engineering*. Final Report to the National Science Foundation.

Honey, M., Moeller, B., Brunner, C., Bennett, D.T., Clements, P. & Hawkins, J. (1991). Girls and design: Exploring the question of technological imagination. (Tech Rep. No. 17). New York: Bank Street College of Education, Center for Technology in Education.

KAHooTZ. http//www.kahootz.com.au.
Somazone. http://www.somazone.com.au

Tannen, D. (1990). *You just don't understand: Women and men in conversation.* New York: Ballantine Books.

Endnotes

[1] Under a grant from the National Science Foundation, NSF-HRD 9714749
[2] *KAHooTZ* can be located at http://www.kahootz.com.au
[3] *Somazone* can be located at http://www.somazone.com.au

Chapter 5

Women Artists and Their Relations to Technologies

Zoë Sofia

The research on which this chapter is based was conducted by myself (a humanities academic) and Virginia Barratt (a performance and visual artist) when we interviewed a number of women arts practitioners at different stages of their careers, including well-known and mature artists, as well as some just learning to use computers for visual art at a summer workshop run by the Australian Network for Art and Technology (ANAT). We wanted to study women artists in order to find out what was involved in the creative and playful use of digital technologies by women who were making and expressing new ideas and cultural productions with, through and about these technologies. The questions we asked covered a range of topics, including the interviewees' technical backgrounds, which technologies they used and how and where they used them in their art practice, issues of access to equipment, what ideas they had about the aesthetics of machines and the future of technology for women and art, questions of technophilia and technophobia, and details of how they related physically and emotionally to equipment. This chapter dwells mainly on these last two questions and is particularly focussed on what interviewees reported about how they used and related to equipment, and how their relations to technologies changed over time and in different contexts. In other papers I have discussed some of the artworks made by various of these artists[1], but here my emphasis is on the technology relation itself, not the art[2].

Women artists are an interesting and arguably an important population to research in relation to questions about gender and technology. As a group they are diverse within themselves indeed their career success depends in part on their being able to differentiate themselves for originality and uniqueness, and they have some distinct features compared to other groups studied by gender and technology research. Unlike workers, for whom the use of technologies is often not optional, and in contrast to schoolchildren who may be forced to undertake computer lessons in the context of a curriculum, a social setting and broader sociotechnical agenda which they are relatively powerless to define, artists elect to involve themselves with computers or other digital media precisely for the purpose of creative and expressive activity. Unlike students who generally have to demonstrate their individual mastery of all stages of a process, artists have the liberty of being able to incorporate the work of other technicians and experts into a project of which they have conceived. Some of the women we interviewed had occasionally found themselves learning about computers or other electronic technologies in all-male classes with socially incompetent and sexist instructors and classmates (some examples of which are given below). But as adult learners who are likely to have had further training in some field and who already are competent practitioners of other (pre-digital) forms of art or technique, these women could access a variety of resources, strategies and people to assist them in becoming competent. Artists are very willing and "high yield" subjects for researchers to interview on topics of relations to technologies not only because they are typically quite keen to talk about themselves and their work, but more importantly they are experienced at being reflective about their own technical practice and may well be conceptually engaged with broad questions about the meanings of technology and specific technologies which are pursued in their work. In contrast, the feelings that students, or workers, may have about technologies may sometimes be observed by researchers, especially in social psychology (e.g., Turkle, 1984, 1988, 1996; Turkle & Papert, 1990) but are usually relegated to the margins or background in relation to the more pragmatic aspects of using technologies for externally defined purposes. For artists, though, whose self-definition is conceptualized in terms of being creative people rather than technicians or productive workers, feelings about technologies are recognized as a legitimate and important aspect of technological experience and comprise part of what may be worked through and expressed in the final artwork. Thus, from studying women artists working in technological media, we may gain further insight into some of the issues and potential obstacles that face women users in other kinds of learning contexts.

Pragmatic Use of Tools

A common finding in studies of gender and technology is that whereas boys and men spend more time simply playing with the equipment and "loving the machine for itself" (as Turkle [1984] titled a chapter on computer hackers), women tend to be more interested in using it for specific tasks in meaningful contexts. The visual artist and designer Sarah Waterson, who at the time of interview was also teaching computing at high school (she now is a university academic in Design), made the following observation about gender differences, echoing findings of a number of more systematic researches into this question:

> Boys have a response more in terms of having to be masters of it, and to be masters of it in terms of being to name all the bits and know how it works, and be able to program it. Whereas the girls can program it just as well, but unless it satisfies her means or ends she won't bother doing it, whereas the boys will do it to exhibit something that's admirable for them, for their peers.... That's the only thing I notice about it. It's more task-specific for the girls, whereas for the boys it would be more like kudos or prestige.

Her school found it worthwhile to schedule a girls-only computer day in the lab, so as to give girls the chance to learn on the machines and develop confidence on their own terms.

In writings published prior to conducting the research on women artists (Sofia, 1999, 1993), I critiqued Turkle's (1988) interpretation regarding the tendency of women and girls to reject the computer as a kind of "second self" in favor of a more pragmatic approach to equipment as "just a tool" as the result of a feminine and romantic emotional reaction against the idea of intimacy with the machine. Instead, I have argued that the expectation that users ought to enthusiastically embrace the technology as a miraculous brain-child or another version of themselves was related to those masculinist irrational ideas about technologies which have become normalized in high-tech culture. For example, the idea of tools as brain-children and compensations for male womb-envy that can become objects of narcissistic identification or the idea that computers provide an attractive microworld for exercising fantasies of control and domination of space. The flip side of those fantasies, of giving up oneself to oceanic absorption by the virtual world, is one of the irrationalities with which women may have, at best, an ambivalent relationship (see also Sofia, 1998). I have suggested that women who insist that computers are "just tools" were perhaps reacting not so much against the "hyper-rationality" of the machine as against the masculinist *ir*rationalities associated with it. Conducting the interviews with women artists was a way to find out whether these theories were supportable by their reported experiences.

Like other groups of women users of technology, most of our artist interviewees when asked, claimed that to them, the computer is "just a tool" they did not see themselves as getting terribly emotionally involved in equipment and basically were interested in using it for what it could do in particular project contexts rather than loving it for what it was in itself or for how it might enhance their status. Joyce Hinterding, a mid-career artist who had explored various kinds of technologies and art involving electricity, described her approach in these terms: "I use what I need to use, not for the sake of it. I learn for specific contexts and purposes." The pragmatic approach to the technology as something that satisfies "her means and ends" was also articulated by Linda Dement in her written response to our question "Once you know what a new piece of equipment or software can do, are you easily bored with it? Or will you stick with it if it does what you need it to?"

> I am still finding out things about programs I have been using for years. Upgrades come so thick and fast there is no time to be settled about it anyway. I think the thing for me though is that I work. If I am working then that is absorbing me and the fascination is not with the toy so much as with solving the problems in order to continue to work. Technology is a big part of that but if I didn't have problems to solve or a project underway or something to do I wouldn't even bother turning the machine on. I would be bored with the technology if I didn't have things I particularly wanted to do with it.

For her, the chief criteria for choosing new hardware and software were:

> What it costs. What it can do, will it enable me to make what I want to make? Is it flexible, can I use it in ways that it might not have been intended to go? Can I control the aspects I want to control? ...I tend to avoid software that has too much preset automatic stuff.

This kind of dispassionate and pragmatic attitude to technology tends to be regarded as somehow less mature or appropriate in a cultural or educational climate that promotes masculinist models of technophilia and enthusiastic embrace of the new as norms for all users. However as we learn from psychologist Winnicott (1989b), the fact that a subject relates to an object (whether thing or human) offers no assurance of a genuine self-other relation, because the subject may narcissistically identify with the object in the form of a phantasmic or ideal projection of itself as, perhaps, in male ego-identification with computers or computer space. But in the use of an object, perhaps as a tool or a means to complete a project, the subject may achieve a genuine appreciation of the object's alterity, the fact that it is not-self, and is not amenable to omnipotent control. A key moment in progress towards use of the object is its survival of subject's efforts to destroy it, for this survival proves the object's independent existence. From this perspective, those with the dispassionate "just a tool" attitude are more mature than the technophiles who narcisisstically identify with equipment and programs.

Pragmatic attitudes to technology were also evident in answers people gave to our questions about what criteria they used for choosing equipment and programs, whether they sought out high-end equipment, and how long they persisted with using certain programs. An interest in high-end equipment is generally tempered by concerns with affordability and access, not to mention suspicion of the rapidity of changes: "State of the art equipment implies to me something which isn't very practical and is ridiculously expensive; it also implies hype," said Rosie Cross. As Isobel Delmotte pointed out when discussing her use of a second-hand Silicon Graphics workstation (donated by the company), artists are not under the same time pressures as commercially based workers and so do not have the same need for the latest, which usually means the fastest, hardware and software. Moira Corby, who confessed she was "fully devoted to high-end Silicon Graphics workstations and what they can do for me as an artist" also expressed an alternate attitude in her comments on gender differences in attitudes to new equipment and ways of learning about it:

> I've learned by myself, I've got the catalogue, and learned, through trial and error, trial and error. ... They're fantastic tools, you can just get lost in them forever, there's so much to learn. With the boy's thing it's always, "Oh! Here's the latest new software. Let's do what we can do with it, then throw it out and get the newest software." There's this big competition thing happening, whereas that doesn't happen amongst the women I know. We like to spend a bit more time on one thing, and really explore it. You come up with things that so-called experts on the machines don't even know you could do. That's happened to me several times.

Despite her devotion to high-end equipment, Corby was clearly not interested in dumping familiar software just because something newer had come along. On the other hand, this interest in thorough learning can sometimes go too far, as SuePhil acknowledged: "I wouldn't be honest if

I didn't admit that the investment in the learning curve can often keep me stuck to a technology or process long beyond its use-by-date."

Like Moira Corby, Linda Dement confessed to harboring her own "techno-lust" but she also rejected the idea that the newest is the best just because it is new:

> I do experience techno consumer lust and I love playing with new toys, but, when it comes to working and producing, I find that it is most important to be as familiar as possible with the tools being used and finding the most appropriate form for the work (this may be the latest & greatest software or it may be a pen & paper). ...I think that tools are important in the formation of artworks and to switch repeatedly to whatever is new won't always be the best path to take. I am also finding at the moment that the constant hype around whatever is new is really sickening and tedious. I just want them to shut up so we can get on with the work, but they seem to need to invoke fear of being left behind in the consuming public, so we will buy more stuff and really, more stuff might enable you to make it faster or bigger or something but it won't make your work any better, not ever.

Sometimes women had tried more advanced systems but went back to earlier ones because they better matched the aesthetics and technical demands of their projects. To quote Dement again:

> There was a new version of a program I had & I played with it then I put it away and finished the work I was doing with the old version. I didn't have time to learn the new version then finish the work before the deadline. I also didn't think that that new version would suit the way I was going with the piece.

Elena Popa likewise reported that when working on her artistic animation piece Sintu she at one point changed from the 2D program she was using to a 3D program but then reverted back to the 2D version because "it had a better reaction than the 3D work." She thought that its aesthetic qualities were more suited to what she was trying to convey. So rather than seeing equipment as something to idealize or wanting to get the newest and latest and most "high-end" simply because it is that, these artists are taking more of an "appropriate technology" line, trying to optimally match the capacities of the equipment to the task in hand.

Various Woman-Technology-World Relations

Although many of the artists interviewed described computers or other high-tech equipment as mere tools, their actual relationships to technologies were quite varied in practice. We asked women a variety of questions about their relationships to technologies, including one which asked them to interpret these relationships in terms of the framework of philosopher of technology Ihde's phenomenological analysis of varieties of human-technology-world relations (Ihde, 1990, esp.pp. 72–123) and others that explored the similar points in more everyday language. Basically, Ihde outlines five main kinds of relations:

- Embodiment, tool as extension of body or as prosthesis; ideal of transparent relation to world via this extension; focus of senses not on the tool but on the sensory data it transmits or the motive force it translates. e.g., hand-held hammer.
- Hermeneutic, tool as text or code to be deciphered; for example, a map or an array of dials and gauges reporting on the state of a system; sensory focus is on the "text," the language, code or data transmitted in the technology; focus on the map more than the territory.
- Alterity, three main senses of this (1) sensory and psychological focus on the properties, qualities and behavior of the technology as a thing in itself with little attention to the broader world or context; (2) tool as an entity, quasi-person or rival, a "second self"(Turkle, 1984) as experienced in computer or video games; (3) tool as stubborn, intractable thing, especially experienced when user cannot control the tool or when it breaks down (see also Heidegger, 1962, pp. 102–107, on the non-transparency of relations to tools that have broken down).
- Background, tool as shelter, cocoon, environment; the technology itself becomes a kind of world or microworld, and the relation is one of inhabiting that world e.g., clothing, house, shopping mall, space ship.
- Horizontal, boundary/category breakdowns between human, technology, world, for example, various kinds of cyborgs which break down human-technology distinction; or experience of being at one with computer and adrift in the cyberspace microworld (see Sofia, 1995, for a discussion of horizontality and cyberculture).

We found that the interviewees were engaged in a full range of relationships with technologies, including total absorption into the computer microworld (background and horizontal relations) and moments of passionate engagement with the machine as an "other" to love or hate or wonder at its capacities (alterity). Much depended on what the machines were being used for and where.

For Elena Popa, an animation artist, the computer became "an extension of you, like when you are driving your car"; for her, embodiment relations were most important. Consonant with her attention to the computer as an extension of the body, this artist went on to voice concerns with the health problems associated with the use of computers in high-pressure work in the commercial world. Moira Corby commented that "The interface of mouse and screen is probably not as tactile as it could be, but then I'm very familiar with the use of that kind of technology." Sarah Waterson expressed her sense of wanting the computer to be more or less invisible while she was working on it: "it does come down to it's a tool and you want it to be hidden as being that tool," and "maybe it might come down to it being a part of your thought processes like you want it to happen and it does, invisibly...." She was using an IBM at work and a Mac at home and found the IBM noisier, clunkier, and thus more obtrusive during work. Other women contrasted the tactility, physicality and multi-sensory qualities of working in mediums such as sculpture or screen-printing with the more mono-sensory work with computers. Linda Connoli, whose work as a screen printer was quite physically demanding since she used "really big screens and you have to throw yourself on top of them, and you pull the ink down," found it was "really hard to adjust to this visual/conceptual thing" with computers, where the main interface was a screen to simply look at.

Filmmaker and sculptor Mahalya Middlemist explored this kind of difference by contrasting the different sensory experiences and perceptual focus entailed when working on a three-dimensional sculptural object compared to using a computer or optical printer to manipulate a virtual or visual entity:

> [Working on computers is]...different from making a 3-dimensional object because [there] you're running around physically in a space, and you're constantly picking up a tool, like dealing with a hammer, and then you're going back to the thing that you're making and dealing with that. [With optical printer and computer]...you're always focussed on the object, and you can get into a really fluid, way of thinking...and you're constantly thinking about it, and every movement that you're making to manipulate it is directly at it. If you're making a plaster mould or whatever, you're dealing with the plaster, that's not the object whereas with optical printing or using the computer, the space is sort of constrained, and every tool or process you bring to bear is directly on the object. My whole body is focussed towards my eyes.

She points out how a real-world production process involves physical and sensory attention to the materials in space, and intermittent attention to the object being produced, whereas in working with the computer or optical printer, space is more or less collapsed into the virtual space of the machine, and the primary sensory attention is fixed on the virtual or visual objects more or less the whole time. This is a good description of the perceptual array in what Ihde would call "hermeneutic technics," in which other sensory modes are subordinated to vision (and, in some cases, hearing) in order to decipher and manipulate coded representations of objects via a textual interface. The comments also highlight a degree of crossover between hermeneutic and embodiment relations: when working on a computer are you looking at the box, reading the box, or looking at something through the box? These things can be going on simultaneously or can phase in and out. As Ihde puts it, there is a "double sense in which a technology may be used. It may be used simultaneously both as something through which one experiences and as something to which one relates" (Ihde,1990, p. 93). Depending on what one is doing at a particular moment, the perceptual focus may be on the represented object, and the computer becomes "transparent" (that is, like embodiment relations where the technology itself is not the focus of attention) or it may shift to the screen and representation itself (hermeneutic relation).

Although as I have suggested women and girls may downplay the sense of a computer as a "second self" for ideological reasons, that is, not wanting to identify themselves with a male-defined technofetishism bordering on worship of the machine and the futury attached to it, it was nevertheless apparent that alterity relations were part of the computer experience for many users. Artist Amelia Bardon made the following comments which revealed a sense of the computer's alterity:

> If you say you are trying to do something it won't always work out the way you want it to. It depends whether you are exploring or whether you are working with a field you know, but it might come up with something you are not expecting, and it might be great, and you might work with that again, it does have a fair amount of give and take. I really like that. I certainly wouldn't say that it dictates to me, but I like that fact that sometimes it does things, even if it makes a mistake, sometimes computers do things that they just shouldn't do....
>
> I enjoy the meditative side of working with a machine, sitting there, knowing that there are layers and processes and things you can work with that it can present to you and you can present to it.

Heather Fernon made a similar comment about the way programs can interrelate with the user:

> You ask it to do something, and it gives you back more than you had hoped for...great, I didn't know you could do that also. ...[It] gives you something unexpected back...some people want to thump it occasionally.

These quotes suggest a kind of alterity relation in which the computer is not so much a rival or friend but a kind of partner ("it can present to you and you can present to it") which sometimes exhibits its own forms of autonomy, such as coming up with unanticipated results or maneuvers which can inspire admiration ("great, I didn't know you could do that also"). These serendipitous moments can be experienced as pleasurable and helpful to the creative process. Though as Fernon's quote suggests, on occasion the computer's autonomous agency is experienced as that other form of alterity in which the user's "quasi-love" relations to it flip over into "quasi-hate" (Ihde, 1990, pp.105–106), and it becomes a stubborn, non-compliant thing that goads the user into giving it some "percussive maintenance."

While the above comments are mainly about the computer or programs as functioning agents, we also remind ourselves that at the most basic level, alterity relations are also caught up in the physical properties of the equipment itself. We explored feelings about this in the questions "Are the material or physical attributes of the equipment important to you?" and "Do you like to personalize your equipment, and if so, how?" Not everyone had comments on these questions, suggesting they weren't important for everybody. Corby, who found the screen/mouse interface insufficiently tactile, took the trouble to personalize her computer by giving it a feminine name with a special screen-saver and decorating it with little shrines and stickers. Likewise magazine editor Rosie Cross used "lots of stickers...and some shiny things, gold dust, fake gems" to decorate her machine. Several artists commented on the boring greys and beiges of computer equipment, and one student reported on a friend of hers who didn't like the plastic and made her computer into a tree, decorating it with bark.

Linda Dement's analysis of her computer's material attributes is interesting for its detail and how she separated out pleasing and displeasing elements of it:

> I find the way my computer looks is annoyingly ugly. Bad design, dumb shapes, bad color...I almost didn't buy the model I got as it looks so bad. I really like my external drive as it is so tiny. The colors & shapes are not great, but size, the way things are getting tiny, I love. There is something wonderful about these small machines being able to perform incredibly well or contain huge amounts of information yet they are so minute. It is a nice *Dr. Who* Tardis aesthetic, bigger on

the inside than on the outside. The little birdlike sounds my monitor and external drive make I really like. There is something very appealing about these little techno noises. They sound expensive, efficient, well working and are pleasant to listen to. The sound of the computer itself is fine but unremarkable. I am really sick of beige and grey plastic. I like the black rubbery feel of the Newton. I like the color of the SGI Indigo.

This attention to particular aesthetic details of the computers suggests a somewhat critical mode of appropriation of the computer: it is not being admired as a whole or worshipped completely as an aesthetic object in its own terms, but aspects of it may be appreciated. Significantly, the aspect most appreciated by Dement is the "Tardis aesthetic" of miniaturization, which is directly related to its functionality.

There are two main ways of looking at the computer in terms of background relations. One is the way the computer itself may be experienced as an environment or "microworld" that is inhabited by the user; the other is to look at the computer (or other high high-tech equipment) in relation to *its* background, that is, the context(s) or lifeworld in which it is experienced; our interviews covered both these dimensions.

In my earlier writings (e.g., Sofia, 1993, 1999) I argued that it seemed to be mainly men who enjoyed, on the one hand, the oceanic experience of losing themselves inside the computer and, on the other, the power to control a computer microworld when they had little power in the outside world. But women artists also experienced some versions of these powers and pleasures. The sense of the computer as a personal space was highlighted by Dement, an advanced computer user who felt her computer "is personal in the way that my bedroom is personal. Everything is set up in the way I want it." Corby, whose computer image-making draws on sculpture and architecture, found herself frustrated in sculptural practice by the limitations of materials and her lack of architectural training; she wanted to occupy and control the whole space:

> I started using computers because in the space that I am using I've got a completely unlimited space, a virtual space that I populate myself...I do all the lights, all the camera action, all the models in the space, I have complete power over *everything* that I'm making in that space....It's almost like I am a whole film crew or I am God/Goddess. That sort of power, it's great.... So I've got this unlimited space, I can create any form I want in it.

A few of our interview subjects also referred to the sense of absorption by/into the computer. For example, Liz Edwards, one of the ANAT students, recounted her experience of the computer as an absorbing microworld:

> I'm not conscious of myself when I'm working. I really don't feel like I'm there at all. I don't feel like I'm really existing. I feel like I'm right in there inside there, so I can just work for hours and hours...the time just seems to go by so fast....

This account posed the computer as a space in which to work and is what in Ihde's terms might be an "horizontal" case of "background" relations, for the boundaries between the user and the technological environment have become blurred. Edwards felt like she was not really in the world and was not conscious of herself but at the same time felt she was existing inside the computer. By contrast, Middlemist, who was at that time still learning to use computers, did acknowledge that "losing oneself" inside the machine is a possibility contingent on familiarity:

> I enjoy losing myself in making something and not being aware of time passing. I don't always lose myself in work, it depends very much on the environment, the equipment I'm using and how familiar with it I am.

Aware of the feminist critiques of "nerds" who lost themselves inside computers and neglected real-life relationships and sensitized by painful experience to the health problems arising from too many work hours per day spent at the keyboard, Rosie Cross, founding editor of the innovative grrrl-zine *Geekgirl*, outlined her changing relationship to the computer world and to the use of the computer as a tool:

> I don't find the machine supplants my social relations as it used to, I don't spend 12 hrs a day on it anymore, generally I spend about 3 getting my work done and trying to avoid flames and obnoxious bods. I use it to contact friends and sometimes ward off foes. I use it sometimes as a cathartic exercise to blow off steam and to subjugate myself to feelings of frustration about my level of knowledge and computer competency. I also use it as a reminder to acknowledge just how much I do know, how far I have come and what fantastic opportunities await me in the future. I laugh, cry and above all depend on my machine! depend on my machine!

As I have elsewhere noted (Sofia, 1998, p.34) it is interesting that even amongst self-confessed "cyberfeminists," "geek girls" and "wired women," the computer world tends to be seen as complementary to the real world of social interaction rather than a substitute for it. As Elizabeth Reba Weise has stated about computer-mediated communication in her introduction to *Wired Women*:

> Being online is an adjunct, a backyard fence, a coffee shop, a favorite hangout, a weekly support group. It's not my life, but it's a nice medium to have in one's life. It is not a social revolution, but at times...it can be a revelation. (Cherny & Weise, 1996, xv)

Like other women training for non-traditional vocations, many of our interviewees reported difficulties in learning or accessing equipment in the male-dominated and woman-unfriendly contexts of classrooms and laboratories. Two participants at the ANAT Summer School told the following stories illustrative of the kind of sexism that is sometimes encountered in training situations:

> One fellow who ran the computer lab, he was self-taught, was proud of a program to make a reflection upwards of something that wasn't there. There was a picture of a woman standing in front of a motor cycle and it's a reflection of looking up her crotch, and that's what you see the moment you go into the computer lab...[It was] one of the most disgusting displays of technology I've ever seen. He was very proud of this computer that could think for itself, obviously he couldn't!

> There was a lecturer in computing design at art school. A [female] student went in early in the morning and found the guy in the studio sitting in his underpants waiting to greet her. The studio was air conditioned; he was just waiting for her to arrive.

In contrast to learning in these kinds of contexts, being able to work on computers in a friendly learning environment with other artists was much appreciated by students at the ANAT School. Having to access labs at night when there are few people around can prove a barrier to some women's participation in computer learning and creating, but for those who overcome the transport issues and fears and social difficulties there are some rewards as outlined by Linda Dement:

> Before I bought my own computer and was working at school, there were almost always other people around. I hate having someone look over my shoulder as I work. I also disliked working under the systems & controls set up by others. The room back then too was awful, no windows, no heating, no air conditioning, chemical smells coming off the carpet, fluoro light...I did like doing late nights and weekends there when no one else was around and I could have the run of this vast institutional space and all these computers to play with. Also I liked it that I had to get organized and go in at particular times and that was the time when I did the art work, it kind of separated it out from my living time or employed time. Now [that she has a computer at home] it gets a little blurred. ...Sometimes I was really lost as there was no one to ask questions of, but I also really loved working stuff out for myself, it made me feel so clever.

Linda went on to discuss the enjoyment of working at home:

> Working at home has just been fantastic. I can work all night with bad late movies on TV or with the stereo going, dance around the room, drink coffee, whatever. I can work whenever the mood strikes me, and I always do something every day. It is perfect for me. I wondered before I bought the computer whether my fantasy that having one at home would mean I would work more and better was

true or just a delusion. It really has turned out to be true and I am happily surprised.

The kinds of feelings, experiences and relations women had about/with computers varied according to the context(s) of learning and work. The following quote from Sarah Waterson indicated how different kinds of relationships and degrees of intimacy may be experienced with working on computers at work compared to at home:

> My relationship to the computer is a pretty intimate one. I do use it as a tool, and I do have an intimate relationship with it in terms of doing personal writing on it. It's a different relationship with just mine at home [compared] to using it at work.... Mine at home is actually more me, whereas the ones at work I use for work and I wouldn't do a thing personal on it. ... It's almost as though you need your computer in your space to be your personal bit, even though you can transport the disks. ... [My] relationship to it [has more to do with] what I do on the computer, not it itself. It never becomes just a machine, it's more what I would do on a particular machine, not it itself.

For Corby, who was earlier quoted on the pleasure of controlling the space inside the computer, the context in which the computer was located was not as relevant as the project within computer space:

> I use different machines. I do have the same relationship with each place, it doesn't matter where I am, it matters [more] where I am in my project, or in my environment.

We might speculate that the relationship to the computer as an environment is especially important for these artists because they are seeking to do creative work. According to Winnicott (1989a), adult creativity involves a re-invocation of the "potential space" experienced in early infancy, where the mother was nearby but not directly present, and the child could safely play around with "transitional objects" on the borders of fantasy and reality without having to decide whether these objects were discoveries or inventions. People seem to vary in the extent to which they need their "potential space" to be entirely their own. Waterson said she had a "more intimate" relation to her home computer than the one at work and referred to the idea of potential space in claiming that "you need your computer in your space to be your personal bit," that is, a free and intimate space for play and creative experiencing. For Corby, this space seemed to be equally present at work and at home and was invoked in her relation to the project itself. For Dement, the isolation and quietness of the late night computer lab helped delineate it as a space for producing artwork, while the newer experience of working at home produced another variety of creative and intimate space, in which creative work at the computer could be interspersed with other playful or relaxing activities, such as dancing or watching television. Several other artists referred to the convenience of working at home, and it may well be that the increased accessibility and affordability of domestic computers has been a major factor in encouraging more women to develop as digital art-makers, which they can do at least in part within the more "feminized" space of the home, instead of the more technicist, unhomely and male-dominated spaces of the on-campus or corporate-based computer laboratory (though these spaces may still be needed for aspects of work requiring "high-end" equipment)[3]. Overall though, it might be noted that for artists, who almost by (Winnicottian) definition are playing and creating at the borders of illusion and reality, there is perhaps a greater tolerance of ambiguity and less need to definitively resolve those ontological and epistemological worries over the reality and intelligence of computers which emerge for students, "hackers," technically oriented users and full-time "netizens" as researched, for example, by Turkle (1996): artists are always already, and for the most part happily, engaged with virtuality, and the turning of it into artworks.

Multiple and Dynamic Relationships with Equipment

I have so far presented quotes from various artists' interviews to illustrate each of the different kinds of human-technology-world relationships discussed by Ihde. But it is important to stress that these relationships do not simply occur in isolation from each other. Unlike simple hand-tools such as the proverbial hammer, which offers only limited relational possibilities, high-tech equipment affords a range of relational modes which may be experienced sequentially or simultaneously by users. As Turkle summarizes it, "the computer encourages a natural diversity of responses. Different people make the computer their own in their own ways" (1996, p. 267). Thus Colleen Cruise, for example, said she had a "number of different relationships to it [the computer], depending on the function. Mostly as a tool. A communications device. I'm interested in the space, not the materiality." Here the artist seemed to primarily characterize the computer as a tool, implying a kind of embodiment relationship. But as I have wanted to show, this characterization is probably more ideological than phenomenological and does not precisely capture the range of actual relationships experienced. When Cruise said it was a communications device, the emphasis was on the hermeneutic dimension, and when she claimed to be interested in the space, not the materiality, she highlighted the way the computer functions as a cyber*space*, operating in background relations.

It is also interesting to track how people's relationships with computers change as they become more familiar and competent with them. In the following quote, some of which appears above, image-maker Heather Fernon describes a change in her relationship to the computer:

> View it firstly as a tool, then later it becomes a dialogue as you can see how the machine modifies an image under your instruction, until "the computer's done the job for you," you can communicate with it. You ask it to do something, and it gives you back more than you had hoped for...great, I didn't know you could do that also.

For Heather, the computer starts off as a "mere" tool, something she uses to accomplish a task, but after work with it, communication becomes possible, implying here both a hermeneutic relationship (the machine as a communicative text or surface) as well as the dialogical relationship of alterity, where the computer becomes an agent that can surprise the user.

The ability to lose oneself in a technological environment is related to one's familiarity with it, as Mahalya Middlemist explained:

> I enjoy losing myself in making something and not being aware of time passing. I don't always lose myself in work, it depends very much on the environment, the equipment I'm using and how familiar with it I am....If you walk into a studio that you don't know how to use, you are really aware of the banks of machines and the chairs. And if you walk into a studio that you do know how to use, you just slide into the chair and you just turn everything on and you're actually dealing with what's inside the machine, you're not dealing with the surfaces of the machines....In a [familiar] big video studio you'll just be backskating around on the wheels of the chair which is really similar to just clicking on things with your mouse...you're not aware of what sort of floor covering there is, or where things are positioned, how far away you've got to slide. Your body knows that you've got to slide backwards a bit and stretch your arm out to turn that on, or it's the same sort of idea.

Here Middlemist likens the computer space to a video lab, an analogy which poses the computer in *background* relations, as a space to be inhabited. She then describes the kinds of *embodied* knowledges and work practices possible with familiar equipment and set-up ("you just slide into the chair"; "your body knows that you've got to slide backwards a bit"), which allow the technologies to function more or less transparently while one focuses on the task, without having to think too hard about the body movements and equipment manipulations needed to achieve the desired results. But in an unfamiliar lab, and by analogy, an unfamiliar computing environment, you don't have that automatic physical knowledge, and you have to deal "with the surfaces of the machines" instead of "what's inside" them. In dealing with these surfaces, one has to actually pay close attention to all the unfamiliar switches, dials, menus, etc, and this kind of attention to the equipment and the physical environment implies at once *hermeneutic* relations to the equipment, their surfaces are texts to be deciphered as well as *alterity* relations: they are material objects with properties of which one is aware, even when they have no bearing on the task at hand ("what sort of floor covering there is").

Clearly there was a broad diversity in the ways women artists related to computers and other high-tech equipment, and everyone had her own narrative of becoming familiar with technology[4]. If we were to project a generalized narrative from this, one tentative model could involve moving through different kinds of relationships. To begin with, a form of alterity relations predominates: the computer is an unfamiliar and alien thing that stubbornly imposes its own logic onto tasks and does things the user does not understand. Then the user has to become familiar with its logic and codes, which are very much in the realm of hermeneutic relationships, predominant in computers whose programming is largely language based (different kinds of codes and programming languages) and where the main interface is a complex visual display: the screen with its various pull-down menus, icons, dialogue boxes. Simultaneously the user has to learn to embody herself in the machine via the manual interface of keyboard and mouse. Once familiarity with both physical and virtual interfaces is achieved, often through a painstaking process of trial and error (for example, with assistance from various sources, including manuals, help screens, other users), it becomes possible to adopt more relaxed ways of relating to the machine or the electronic environment, in which the parameters of the hardware and software become taken for granted. Equipment can then be experienced as a more or less transparent means for performing the task at hand, or computer space experienced as an environment to be inhabited, explored and manipulated for one's own purposes. Here, in Ihde's terminology, the relation becomes more like one of embodiment, of feeling it as an extension of oneself, and/or it becomes a space, a background environment in which to work. But at any time, the other kinds of relationships can re-emerge: for example, when the machine breaks down or fails to do what you want it to, it reappears as an alien entity; when new programs or new parts of programs are learned, the hermeneutic operations of decoding and recoding become more definitive of the experience. And, as we saw in the example of Fernon, what starts off as a pragmatic effort to use and control the machine for certain purposes can with more intense use settle into a dialogue between user and machine, in a more friendly version of alterity relationships.

Conclusion

This chapter has considered various layers and dynamics involved in how women artists in digital media relate to the technological equipment they use. The research materials amassed by Virginia Barratt and myself cover other salient factors which space constraints did not permit to discuss here, including more on questions of access, feelings of technophobia and ways to get around them, ideas about the technology and the future, and different attitudes of women coming to technology from different backgrounds. It has been found that while most artists claim to use the computer as "just a tool", and did in fact adopt a pragmatic "appropriate technology" approach to choosing equipment and software, the actual range of relations and responses to equipment is more diverse than suggested by this phrase. This gave support to my earlier contentions that the "just a tool" attitude was more about an ideological position with respect to masculinist technophilia than a phenomenologically accurate description of the woman-machine relation. Because the artists are involved in creative practice, the sense of comfort and familiarity with the machine is an important factor in facilitating work on it. The context in which computers were used, and the length of time over which women had been using them could account for some of the different kinds of relationships reported.

Acknowledgments

The author would like to acknowledge Virginia Barratt's work on our "Double Agents" project; Virginia was responsible for the interviews with Moira Corby, Amelia Bardon, SuePhil and Heather Fernon quoted here and was co-interviewer of Sarah Waterson and the ANAT summer school group. We are indebted to the artists for their time in answering our questions, and especially to Rosie Cross, Linda Dement and SuePhil for providing us written responses to the questions. This research was supported with grants from the Australia Council, ANAT and Murdoch University, which are gratefully acknowledged.

References

Cherny, L. & Weise. E. R. (eds.), (1996). *Wired women: Gender and new realities in cyberspace*. Seattle: Seal Press.

Heidegger, M. (1962). *Being and time*. (J. Macquarie & E. Robinson, trans.). New York: Harper & Row. (Original work published 1927).

Ihde, D. (1990). *Technology and the lifeworld*. Bloomington: Indiana University Press.

Lally, E. (2000). The computer at home: material culture and the relationship of ownership. Ph.D. dissertation, School of Cultural Histories and Futures, University of Western Sydney.

Sofia, Z. (1993). *Whose second self? Gender and (ir)rationality in computer culture*. Geelong: Deakin University Press.

Sofia, Z. (1995). Of spanners and cyborgs: de-homogenising feminist thinking on technology. In B. Caine & R. Pringle (eds.), *Transitions: New Australian feminisms* (pp. 147–163). Sydney: Allen & Unwin.

Sofia, Z. (1998). The mythic machine: gendered irrationalities and computer culture. In H. Bromley & M. W. Apple (eds.), *Education/ technology/ power: Educational computing as a social practice* (pp. 29–51). Albany, NY: SUNY.

Sofia, Z. (1999). Virtual corporeality: A feminist perspective. In J. Wolmark (ed.), *Cybersexualities: A reader on feminist theory, cyborgs and cyberspace* (pp. 55–68). Edinburgh: Edinburgh University Press. (Reprinted from *Australian Feminist Studies* 15 (1992), 11–24.)

Turkle, S. (1984). *The second self: Computers and the human spirit*. New York: Simon and Schuster.

Turkle, S. (1988) Computational reticence: why women fear the intimate machine. In C. Kramarae (ed.), *Technology and women's voices: Keeping in touch* (pp. 41–61). New York: Routledge & Kegan Paul.

Turkle, S. (1996). *Life on the screen: Identity in the age of the Internet*. London: Weidenfeld & Nicolson.

Turkle, S. & Papert, S. (1990). Epistemological pluralism: styles and voices within the computer culture. *Signs, 16* (1), 128–57.

Watson, G. (2000). Just do IT: Australian women in cyberspace. Ph.D. dissertation, School of Cultural Histories and Futures, University of Western Sydney.

Winnicott, D.W. (1989a). Transitional objects and transitional phenomena. In *Playing and Reality* (1–25). New York: Routledge. (Original work published 1953.)

Winnicott, D.W. (1989b). The use of an object and relating through identifications. In *Playing and Reality* (pp. 86–94). New York: Routledge. (Original work published 1969.)

Endnotes

[1] Writings by the author related to the research reported on here include (1994) "Technoscientific Poesis: Joan Brassil, Joyce Hinterding, Sarah Waterson," *Continuum* 8 (11), 364-375; (1994) "Slime in the matrix: Post-phallic formations in women's art in new media," in Jill Julius Matthews (ed.), *Jane Gallop Seminar Papers* (pp.83–106);

Canberra: Humanities Research Centre, ANU, (1995) "Creative ambivalence and 'Interactivity'" *Geekgirl* 003, 21; (1996) "Contested zones: Futurity and technological art," *Leonardo: Journal of the International Society for the Arts, Sciences, and Technology* 29 (1): 59-66; (Spring 1996) "Interactivity, intersubjectivity and the Artwork/Network," *Mesh: Journal of Experimental Media Art 10*, 32–35; "Nola Farman and the Artwork/Network," in T. Snell and J. Goddard (eds.), *Objects and spaces*, Perth: University of Western Australia Press, (in press 2002).

[2] For discussions of, and interviews with, Australian technological artists, including some who were part of Barratt's and my research, see *Continuum 8* (11) (1994) special issue edited by Nick Zurbrugg on "Electronic Arts in Australia," also *Photofile* 42 (June 1994), special issue "Natural/Unnatural," *Mesh: Journal of Experimenta Media Art* 10 (Spring 1996) supplement on women@art.technology.au (also available at *Mesh* Website, http://www/peg.apc.org/~experimental), and Cracked Metal Productions (Producer) & Jonathan Cohen (Director), (1993) *Artists in Cyberculture*, Sydney: Ronin Films.

[3] For a fascinating Australian study of the domestication of the computer which looks at how it becomes incorporated into familial and working lives, see Lally (2000).

[4] For more detailed accounts of getting familiar with technologies and overcoming technophobia, including the way different personal and political backgrounds influenced women's engagements with cyberspace, see the extensive study by Glenice Watson of Australian women activists and pioneers in cyberspace (Watson, 2000), whose subjects include a couple of the people referred to in the present study.

Part Two

New Ways of Learning with Technology in Schools and Communities

Chapter 6

Learning by Design: Environments That Support Girls' Learning with Technology

Laurie D. Edwards

Introduction

It is a few weeks before Christmas. I am looking at an advertisement in the Sunday supplement magazine of my local newspaper. The ad is divided into two panels: the top panel shouts "NEW... Barbie™ Computer Designed Just For Girls!" We see a photograph of the computer; it is white and pink; colorful daisies cover every surface, including the mouse pad, speakers, and CD-ROM case. A pink-clad Barbie™ with long blonde hair smiles out from the monitor screen. An inset adds: "Included! Barbie™ Digital Camera!"

In the second panel, we see an identical computer with identical components: keyboard, monitor, "mini-tower" CPU, speakers, and mouse pad. This computer, however, is "Designed Just for Boys!" and its "hook" is the popular collectible series of miniature cars called Hot Wheels™. The color scheme is quite different; the "boy's" computer is blue, with a yellow "flame" motif featured on all components. Instead of a digital camera, the Hot Wheels™ computer comes with a steering wheel and pedals, for playing the drag car racing simulation shown on the monitor.

The advertisement described here seems to reflect the conjunction of two historical/cultural trends. One trend is economic: the price of technology has continued to decline over the past decade, to the point where a complete computer system, rather than being an expensive capital investment for businesses, can now be mass marketed as a brand-name children's toy. At the same time, the feminism of the 1970's that strongly disapproved of gender stereotyping in children's toys seems to have become more muted in recent years. Given the documented reluctance of girls to embrace technology and technical subjects (Oakes, 1990), one might argue that targeting a computer system to young girls is not such a bad thing. A "Barbie™ computer" might at least encourage an engagement with technology by girls who might not otherwise choose to put their hands on a keyboard. However, a closer look at the software included with the Barbie™ and Hot Wheels™ computers discourages this optimistic view and reveals some disturbing underlying assumptions about the ways in which boys and girls differ in their interests and intellectual capabilities.

Half of the software packages that come with the girl's computer are Barbie™ programs. Distinctive in their pink boxes, these titles offer activities such as jewelry design and pony care. The other titles include an encyclopedia, a world atlas, a typing tutor, a program from National Geographic, and an educational package called *Body Works*. The popular exploratory fantasy game *Myst* is the only non-Barbie™ game included.

The boy's computer includes the same reference set (e.g., encyclopedia, atlas, typing tutor) featured with the Barbie™ system. However, whereas fully half of the software offered with the girl's computer consists of *Barbie*™ titles, the boy's collection includes only four *Hot Wheels*™ games. The remaining boy's software includes such educational titles as *The Logical Journey of the Zoombinis*, two additional mathematics games, two interdisciplinary learning games, and *Chessmaster 5000*. *Myst* is the only game found in both collections.

The gender stereotyping in the boy's and girl's software is troubling. It assumes that girls are not expected to enjoy or appreciate logic and mathematics, even when presented in a game format. In fact, educational software makes up less than a third of the titles accompanying the Barbie™ system but represents a majority of the programs included with the Hot Wheels™ computer. In contrast to learning mathematics or exploring logic games or chess, the girls are offered the opportunity to select and create hairstyles, play with jewelry, and design high-fashion outfits to be modeled by their virtual dolls.

The Barbie™ computer exemplifies one approach to encouraging girls' use of computers. This strategy is characterized by modifying the

Learning by Design 121

technology to make it less threatening, or more appealing, to girls. In this approach, software is tailored to what are conceptualized as girls' interests, that is, fashion, design, creativity, and interpersonal relationships as in the case of recent "role-playing" software that features adolescent intrigues and friendships. This approach may have some benefits: at the least, it has served to broaden the kinds of activities instantiated in computer software for children and young people beyond simple "shoot-em-up" games or drill and practice programs. Yet, there are clear disadvantages, most specifically in reinforcing gender stereotypes that steer girls away from science, mathematics, and other "gateway" subjects.

The stereotyping so obvious in the Barbie™ and Hot Wheels™ computers may seem to work most clearly against the interests of girls. Yet it also impacts (and limits) what are considered appropriate activities for boys. Much of the Barbie™ software focuses on creativity and design, an aspect of play and learning not represented in the Hot Wheels™ collection. The digital camera is an accessory for the Barbie™ computer but is not offered to boys who purchase the Hot Wheels™ system. Why should it be assumed that boys are uninterested in artistic or creative production, like digital photography, and, instead, would rather spend their time in competitive games?

The purpose of this chapter is to describe a gender equity project, funded by the National Science Foundation[1] (Edwards, 1996) that attempted to avoid gender polarization in the use of technology with children, to offer a technology-centered learning environment that challenged girls to utilize logic and problem solving, while at the same time providing opportunities for imagination, design, and creativity. Rather than modifying computers or software to appeal to girls, the project situated traditionally "male" activities, engineering and programming, in a setting intended to both support and expand girls' interests. The overall goal of the project was to provide an opportunity for young women to engage with technology in new, personally meaningful ways, and to come to see themselves as successful designers, builders, and programmers within the context of information and communication technologies (ICT).

Project SAME

Project SAME ("Science and Mathematics Equity") was funded through the National Science Foundation's Special Programs for Girls and Women (Matute-Bianchi, Stoddart, Edwards, Landesman & Gaiberson,

1994). The purpose of the project was to enhance girls' interest and self-confidence in science, mathematics, and technology by immersing them in challenging, hands-on design and programming activities. The project focused on the age range from upper elementary through early high school, a period during which many female students lose interest in science, technology, and mathematics (Oakes, 1990; Sadker, M. & Sadker, D., 1994). In an effort to encourage the girls' on-going engagement in these subjects, the project also involved their parents and teachers, who worked alongside the girls as learners with technology. During the two years of the project, a total of 66 girls and 12 teachers participated in two intensive summer workshops, with follow-up activities involving a total of six schools and 268 students of both sexes.

Project SAME was based on a view of science and technology as "messy," exploratory disciplines, whose practice includes both planned and fortuitous actions (Latour & Woolgar, 1986). Science, mathematics, and technology are often portrayed as subjects requiring what Turkle has called "hard mastery" (Turkle, 1984; Turkle & Papert, 1992), a top-down, structured, rule-driven process in which plans are completely specified in advance, and then carried out step by step, leaving nothing to chance. Project SAME encouraged a different kind of engagement with technology and science, corresponding more closely to what Turkle calls "soft" mastery. The project offered girls the chance to develop personal interests and relationships with technology, learning primarily through "tinkering" and open-ended exploration, rather than through highly structured "cookbook"-style lessons. This kind of "soft mastery", although it draws on logic and problem solving, also leaves room for intuition, chance, and spontaneity. Rather than learning by being told or by following specific instructions, this is a kind of "learning by tinkering" (Turkle, 1995).

In designing the project, we wanted to provide the girls with opportunities for original and authentic activity with technology. By authentic activity, I refer to a way of working in which learning the technology is not an end in itself (e.g., achieving "computer literacy" or reaching a level of mastery in a particular video game) or a means of meeting goals dictated by others (e.g., completing school assignments) but a way to reach goals conceptualized and chosen by the learner herself. Only certain technology-based environments can support this type of authentic, creative activity. For Project SAME, we chose the design, construction, and programming environment known as *LEGO/Logo* (Lego® Dacta, n.d.)[2].

LEGO/Logo

LEGO/Logo combines the internationally popular Lego® building pieces with a simple programming language to allow the learner to build and control functioning physical machines (Resnick & Ocko, 1991). *LEGO/Logo* materials include standard and custom-designed Lego® bricks as well as a specialized version of the programming language Logo used to issue commands to the custom Lego® pieces. These special pieces include, as output devices, a 9-volt motor, a small lamp, and a sound element that makes two different "siren" noises. Input devices, which take real-time data from the environment and make it available to the program or user, include touch, temperature, light, and angle sensors. By using these pieces in combination with regular Lego® bricks, a user can build a wide variety of machines

LEGO/Logo was developed at the Massachusetts Institute of Technology by Seymour Papert and Mitchel Resnick and exemplifies an educational philosophy, constructionism, that emphasizes children's learning through the construction of physical and electronic artifacts (Harel & Papert, 1991). The thesis of constructionism is that powerful learning occurs when students engage in the design and creation of new objects and productions that are personally meaningful. This notion is, of course, an extension of Piaget's dictum that knowledge derives from action, but in this case, the action results in a tangible, shareable product. According to constructionism, students are highly motivated to reach their personal goals and to share the concrete results of their efforts with others.

Existing research with *LEGO/Logo* suggests that it is effective in promoting idea-generation, hypothesis-testing, spatial imagery, and problem solving (Palumbo & Palumbo, 1993). Some studies report gender differences in how children work with *LEGO/Logo*, although results are not consistent between studies (Faulkner & Anderson, 1991; Yelland, 1994). The variations in research findings may be related to differences in how *LEGO/Logo* is presented to the children, that is, in the specific activities and social context featured in the design of the projects. This chapter will focus on the social and contextual aspects of Project SAME, since the context of an educational technology project is at least as significant for outcomes as the particular technology itself. As Hawkins noted in discussing gender differences in children's work with technology, "sex differences emerge in relation to the functions computers serve and the organization of learning settings of which they are a part" (Hawkins,

1985, p. 165).

Principles used in designing Project SAME

The central activity setting of Project SAME was a two-week long summer workshop for girls and their teachers, in which the participants worked with *LEGO/Logo* for three hours a day and also carried out hands-on mathematics activities involving art and design. The *LEGO/Logo* workshops were followed up with academic-year activities at three school sites involving both girls and boys as well as with "family science" weekends that incorporated and expanded upon the *LEGO/Logo* activities. The design of the summer workshop was based on five general principles intended to increase the girls' engagement with, and enjoyment of, technology, and to support a constructionist, soft-mastery style of learning. These principles were:

- a girls-only setting and the use of girls as peer experts,
- a focus on design and creativity,
- scaffolded instruction and learning through tinkering (Turkle, 1995),
- peer collaboration, and
- the public sharing of products.

The remainder of this chapter will review and discuss each principle, along with selected research that addresses its efficacy, as a framework for presenting outcomes and illustrative results from the project.

A girls-only setting and girls as peer experts

From the initial stages of planning for Project SAME, it was decided that the *LEGO/Logo* summer workshops would be offered in a single-sex, girls-only setting. Although there have been methodological criticisms of some studies of single-sex instruction, the majority of such studies have concluded that, "[g]irls in single-sex schools have higher self-esteem, are more interested in nontraditional subjects such as science and math, and are less likely to stereotype jobs and careers" than girls in co-educational schools (Sadker, M. & Sadker, D., 1994, p. 233). Given the disparity in attention favoring boys in mixed-sex classrooms, with boys demanding and gaining more instructor time than girls (ibid.), as well as the fact that Lego® materials are far more popular among boys than girls after the age of six (Burns, 1989), we felt that a girls-only setting would provide participants the greatest chance for working successfully (and unselfconsciously) with *LEGO/Logo*.

Interviews with participants after the summer workshop were unambiguously positive with regards to the choice of single-sex setting. No girls interviewed said they would have preferred a workshop with boys. One participant seemed aware of the tendency for teachers to spend extra time responding to boys in mixed-sex classrooms, stating, "I thought it was good without boys, 'cause usually boys slow down the class." In fact, in another study in a mixed-sex setting, we found that boys-only groups called for help more often than did girls-only or mixed-gender groups (Edwards, Coddington & Caterina, 1997). Additionally, boys also showed less persistence and autonomy in completing their projects and made derogatory comments, both to other boys and to girls, something that was not observed among the girls.

Although the study described above took place in a mixed-sex setting, it was designed to offer girls a more active role than might be the case in a typical mixed-sex classroom. During each three-day workshop, two girls were selected by lottery to become peer experts (the lottery was necessary because almost all of the girls wanted to be trained as peer experts). After receiving preliminary instruction in *LEGO/Logo*, as well as recommendations on how best to provide assistance to their fellow students, the girls helped to introduce *LEGO/Logo*, and then were "on-call" to help other students as they worked on their projects. This use of girls as peer experts was very successful: the other students treated the girls as more knowledgeable others and took advantage of the advice they offered, and the girls themselves took their responsibilities seriously and expressed pride in being able to assist their classmates. For example, one of the girls in the follow-up study described how it felt to help other students with their *LEGO/Logo* projects:

> Well, I learned a lot and it was fun, like when someone needed help, that I knew what to do, so I helped them... I enjoyed it and, um, and I'm sort of, proud. At the end, when someone makes you feel proud.... (Edwards et al., 1997, p. 43)

In summary, responses to the single-sex summer workshops indicated that the girls-only setting offered a safe and positive context for learning *LEGO/Logo*, one that was appreciated by the participants. In subsequent mixed-sex settings, the opportunity to act as peer experts gave girls a sense of accomplishment, pride, and satisfaction. These results suggest that offering a single-sex setting, and/or allowing girls to act as peer experts may be advisable elements in the design of technology projects for girls.

Focus on design and creativity

Despite efforts to broaden the appeal of technology, research has shown that when computers are introduced as a subject closely aligned with mathematics or science, girls transfer negative attitudes toward these disciplines to computers as well (Collis, 1987; Damarin, 1989). A remark made by one of the high school students describing her initial feelings about participating in Project SAME illustrated this attitude:

> At first I thought it would be kinda like school, because I was, kinda like, well, it's kinda summer vacation and I don't really want to go to school and do stuff with math books, but then when I got there, it was, like, a lot different than I thought.

A slightly younger student stated, "Before, I always thought that stuff like this was, you know, kind of stupid and boring." In Project SAME, we wanted to give participants a different kind of experience of learning with technology, one that would be positive and engaging.

Mathematics and science, as traditionally taught in schools and universities, are subjects associated with Turkle's "hard mastery" (Turkle, 1984), a hierarchical, top-down, distanced stance toward knowledge, which contrasts with a more negotiated, concrete, and relational "soft mastery." In regards to learning to program computers, Turkle's research suggested that "[w]hen people are free to explore programming without preconceptions about the "right" way to do it, more women use soft approaches and more men hard approaches" (Turkle & Papert, 1992). In a study of middle-school students learning Logo programming, Sutherland and Hoyles noted that "the girls more often chose to work on loosely-defined, exploratory goals in creating Logo programs, whereas the boys generally worked on well-defined, specific goals" (Sutherland & Hoyles, 1988). One of the goals of Project SAME was to engage girls in activities typically associated with "hard" science, that is, computer programming and mechanics but in a way that left room for "soft mastery", exploration, design and creativity.

The *LEGO/Logo* materials, as they come "out of the box," don't necessarily support an open-ended kind of creativity. The bricks, motors, and sensors are packaged with step-by-step instructions for building machines of varying complexity, along with sample Logo programs for controlling

Learning by Design

them. For example, complete instructions are provided for building a walking dinosaur, a vending machine, or a temperature-controlled greenhouse.

In order to encourage creativity and to avoid communicating the idea that there is a "right" or "wrong" way to build a *LEGO/Logo* machine, we decided not to show the participants the step-by-step building instructions during the first week of the workshop. In our view, learning *LEGO/Logo* does not consist of being able to interpret and follow instructions but instead of understanding the mechanical, programming, and systemic elements that function together in a working *LEGO/Logo* device. We believed that, with scaffolded instruction and sufficient time to explore and experiment with the materials, the girls would be capable of learning *LEGO/Logo* at this conceptual level and of applying their creativity to the design of original, functioning devices.

During the second week, the girls worked in small groups to create machines for display during the culminating Technology and Design Fair. They were given the choice of using supplied instructions, or continuing to work on projects of their own design. The majority of the girls chose to build original devices. Table 6.1 indicates the variety of original projects as well as pre-designed projects constructed from supplied instructions.

Table 6.1: Original and pre-designed *LEGO/Logo* projects

Original projects	Projects from supplied instructions
Doll/elevator factory	Elevator
"Gear factory"	Printer
"Willy Wonka" machine	Motorized wheelchair
Roller coaster	Greenhouse
Dump truck and crane	Robotic arm
Castle and drawbridge	
Jumping frog	
Car wash	
Police car	
Airplane	
Helicopter	

Many of the girls' original projects were whimsical and imaginative, in contrast to the fairly utilitarian pre-designed devices found in the supplied examples. It is interesting to note that even the example projects provided in the *LEGO/Logo* kits were usually adapted or personalized in some way by the participants. For example, the elevator, a fairly simple example project, was placed inside an elaborate cardboard "art museum" designed by the girls, complete with small figures brought from home to represent visitors to the museum. The motorized wheelchair, a more challenging machine built from supplied instructions, took one group most of the second week to construct. On the final day, one of the girls who built the wheelchair brought a Barbie™ to sit in it, integrating this toy into technology in a manner quite different from that found in the Barbie™ computer.

In addition to encouraging the participants to use *LEGO/Logo* to build "anything they liked," at the end of the first week, we offered a specific activity emphasizing art and creativity. The girls were shown a short video of kinetic art created by twentieth century artists and were invited to create their own kinetic sculptures, using an assortment of artistic materials (e.g., mylar, colored paper, stickers) which they attached to *LEGO/Logo* substructures they designed[3]. The girls enjoyed this activity, and created a diverse range of original, colorful and whimsical moving sculptures.

Scaffolded Instruction and Learning Through Tinkering

Although the workshop focused on creativity and was designed to immerse the girls in technical subjects in a way that did not replicate their school experience, we did not follow a "pure discovery" model of learning (Bruner, 1960). Given the need to learn the conventions of a programming language, as well as the functions of a new type of artifact, a "scaffolded" model of instruction was implemented. The instructional sequence was based on Vygotsky's (1978) model of learning as progression through a zone of proximal development toward independent performance. The first week of instruction began with a brief demonstration of a completed *LEGO/Logo* machine (the walking dinosaur). The goal of this first week was to assist the girls to learn progressively more of the skills and knowledge needed to create a project of similar complexity on their own (or, rather, within a small group of peers). During the second week, the participants would work on projects of their own choosing, with further instruction provided "on demand" by the adult instructors.

To scaffold the learning process, during the first week, a series of design challenges, which increased in difficulty throughout the week, were presented to the participants. At the time a challenge was presented, the instructor would also demonstrate the individual Lego® elements and the relevant Logo commands that could be used in order to solve the problem. The girls were then left to discover a solution, working in groups of two to four. The instructor and teaching assistant would circulate to help the students, assisting them when they encountered an obstacle that they could not resolve on their own.

The challenges set during the first week of instruction included:

- locating and identifying specific Lego® elements (e.g., motors, lamps, gears);
- assembling a motor and propeller to make a fan;
- using a motor, wheels, and gears or pulleys to make a moving vehicle;
- determining how long a Logo "tick" was (a "tick" is used to control the length of time that a Lego® element such as a motor or a lamp is turned on);
- writing a Logo procedure to control the vehicle;
- adding a touch sensor to the vehicle and writing a program so that it stops when it hits something;
- using a temperature and light sensor to control the fan; and,
- making a vehicle that can climb a hill.

Once all the groups had built vehicles, a race was conducted, and the speed of each vehicle was entered into a chart that also included information about the gear mechanism used in the design of the vehicle. This part of the instruction was the most structured; the goal was to assist the participants to discover how gear ratios help to determine a vehicle's speed and/or power (torque).

This scaffolded style of instruction contrasts with the typical top-down, procedure-driven science lesson. In typical science labs or computer lessons, all steps are spelled out in advance, and success depends on faithfully following instructions to a pre-determined outcome. Instead, during Project SAME, the girls were expected to find multiple, different solutions to the initial challenges and to develop their own goals as they consulted with their partners and decided on their *LEGO/Logo* projects. Rather than learning by reproducing "correct" procedures, the girls engaged in what Turkle has called "learning by tinkering" (Turkle, 1995). The participants constructed their devices in a bottom-up fashion, combining trial-and-error, existing informal mechanical knowledge, and newly learned procedures that had first been practiced on smaller "toy" problems. This style of working conforms to what Turkle and Papert, following Lévi-Strauss, call "bricolage," a process of "arranging and rearranging...negotiating and renegotiating with a set of well known materials" (Turkle & Papert, 1992, p. 12).

The following segment of dialogue between two sixth-grade girls, engaged in building their first *LEGO/Logo* vehicle, gives a flavor of this bricolage, or learning through tinkering:

S: Oh, I know a perfect wheel to work, to make the wheels work.
M: What?
S: Here, I'll tell you.... OK, what happened to those skinny wheels?
M: We have them here.
S: Well, wait, never mind.
M: Why do we have this, what do you think it's for?
S: I don't know, it's like a motor.... Let's just, well, we could use it.
M: I don't know.
S: It's kind of big.
M: I have no place to put it.... Oh yeah, I do.
S: Here, I'll show you, OK, here's the wheel.
[...]
S: So you want to do that?
M: I don't know, I want to see what I come up with.
S: Kind of, yeah, doing whatever's on my mind. If you want to.
M: Do you want to have two motors?
S: Actually, it would be better....
M: I have a really good idea...we have two propellers, right?
S: Yeah.
M: We could maybe, I don't think this will work, 'cause....
S: No, it won't work.
M: Why?
S: 'Cause two propellers can't lift them up like that. Plus I don't think they can fly.

In the dialogue above, the girls continually negotiated and renegotiated their design goals, modifying and rebuilding their vehicle, taking into account their evolving goals and the affordances of the parts available to them.

The use of scaffolded instruction and learning by tinkering, intended to distinguish the *LEGO/Logo* experience from typical school teaching, was noted appreciatively by one participant, who said:

> It wasn't like someone standing up there and like lecturing and saying, like, this is how you do this and this and this, but it was more like, OK, go ahead and try something out and see if that works.

Collaboration

The dialogue between the two sixth-grade girls cited above also illustrates another important element of the *LEGO/Logo* workshop, specifically, its emphasis on peer collaboration, and the intensely social character of the girls' work. In planning the workshop, we took into account prior research indicating that girls prefer working in groups and receiving help from peers when learning Logo (Sutherland & Hoyles, 1988), and other studies that showed enhanced performance for girls in mathematics courses when working in collaborative settings (Peterson & Fennema, 1985).

In the summer workshops, we organized the girls into two groups, an older group (13–14 years) and a younger group (11–12 years). Within each age level, the girls were invited to form self-chosen small groups containing two to four members. There were some changes in membership during the first few days, but by the end of the week, the girls had settled on partners with whom to design and construct their final projects. All of the groups exhibited continuous and effective collaborations, both in making decisions about what machines to build and how to program them, and in carrying out those decisions. There were certain age-related variations in the type of collaboration within the small groups. The younger girls more often worked side by side in more flexible, "parallel" collaborations, or established specialized roles within the group (for example, one girl worked on building the project while the other attempted to program a part of it). When girls in the younger groups encountered obstacles, sometimes one girl would "take over" the project from her partner, rather than working together to find a solution. Conversely, the girls in the older group more typically sought full consensus in both planning and problem solving and carried out construction and programming tasks in concert rather than in parallel.

Even among the younger group of girls, however, it was clear that each group member was engaged in building a joint project. This collaboration within the groups was mirrored by between-group cooperation as well. For the most part, this took the form of sharing Lego® pieces as well as seeking or offering help with construction or programming problems. One of the most impressive collaborations during the first summer workshop went well beyond sharing advice or pieces. This was a joint project, conceived, spontaneously, as a collaboration between two groups of younger girls, who happened to be working next to each other. In discussing various possibilities for their final projects, the two groups came up with the idea of building a project with two parts: first, a crane, which would be able to swivel on its base and lift and lower a load, and second, a dump truck fitted with an "electric eye" in the truck bed, so that when a load was lowered into it, it would automatically drive away. The successful completion of this complex, compound project not only required the pooling of the girls' developing *LEGO/Logo* expertise but also involved a fairly heavy management load in coordinating the decisions and actions of the five young participants.

Sharing of Productions

In traditional school settings, students are regularly asked to complete work that is generally seen only by the classroom teacher. The work assigned by the teacher is intended not only to help the student learn new material but to serve as evidence of that learning. Although some students may be intrinsically motivated to learn the material, others work primarily to gain a good grade (or avoid a poor one). Yet many students are neither intrinsically, nor extrinsically, motivated to learn in school and, in fact, may reject performing tasks that they perceive as having no meaning to their lives.

One approach to increasing students' motivation in school has been to open the classroom, by involving students in activities for which the audience is not the teacher alone. The use of projects and presentations is one method of engaging students in more personally meaningful, authentic tasks, and the motivating aspects of these activities may be enhanced when they are shared with peers, family, and community.

This approach, involving the sharing of products and productions, was taken in the design of Project SAME. Although the emphasis of the summer workshops was on learning through exploration of *LEGO/Logo*, each two-week session was structured around a culminating activity, called the Technology and Design Fair. During the Fair, which took place on the last day of each session, the girls' families, friends, and teachers, as well as members of the university and school communities, were invited to view the *LEGO/Logo* projects that the girls had developed. In addition to building and programming a project, each group was also responsible for creating a computer interface to allow a user to operate the project. This was done by creating a "Project Page" which linked the Logo procedures to visual icons such as on/off switches, sliders to modify power levels, and so forth. The project pages also had to include a brief description of the project as well as a list of the group members.

The Technology and Design Fair was an unqualified success. The girls were proud of their work and confident in demonstrating their projects, and parents were able to see for themselves what it was that had excited and engrossed their daughters so dramatically during the previous two weeks. During the first Technology and Design Fair, for example, we learned that several girls had been meeting daily at each others' homes to continue planning and researching their projects. Another parent, a father, expressed his amazement about the day his daughter came home and asked for an algebra book, stating that she had shown no previous interest in mathematics or science. This kind of informal feedback, offered during the Fair, helped to validate the design of the workshop. The Technology and Design Fair provided the girls with a very public acknowledgment (including a front-page story in the local newspaper) of their accomplishments. The public sharing of productions is a way to link a personal connection with technology to a broader social context that can encourage on-going engagement with mathematics, science, and computing.

Discussion

The strategy used to encourage girls' involvement with technology by Project SAME was intentionally different than that found in the traditional school science or mathematics classroom. Yet, at the same time, we did not wish to take a "pink Lego® bricks" approach, in which activities tailored to stereotypical girls' interests were offered. Instead, we chose to create challenging, authentic design, engineering, and programming tasks and embed them in a social setting that would make it comfortable for girls to explore new interests that have traditionally been constructed as "male" in orientation. In order to reduce competition for the instructors' time and possible self-consciousness about doing "boy's work," we decided to make the summer workshops single-sex, so that girls could engage fully with the activities. The focus of the workshops was on creating original *LEGO/Logo* projects, not on correctly following instructions to a pre-determined end. The girls worked in small collaborative groups, and had the opportunity to share their *LEGO/Logo* productions at a concluding community event.

The instructional sequence during the workshops combined small design and programming challenges with the opportunity to use the resulting new knowledge in larger, self-chosen projects. The scaffolded instruction model was designed to help the participants become capable of independent performance in implementing their own *LEGO/Logo* designs. The girls built their projects through a process accurately described as bricolage, or learning through tinkering. In a literal sense, they put together bits and pieces of the *LEGO/Logo* materials, constructing and reconstructing their devices until they met their self-determined design goals. But the participants also worked conceptually as bricoleurs, assembling an understanding of this new domain from a combination of existing informal knowledge in mathematics and science, newly-learned Logo commands, and general problem-solving and logical skills. The central premise of Project SAME was that an intensive experience with *LEGO/Logo* would not only call upon these kinds of skills and knowledge but would help to strengthen and expand them.

LEGO/Logo and "Soft Mastery"

All of these elements were intended to support a different way of working with computers, a kind of "soft mastery" that contrasts sharply with the structured, top-down, "objective" "hard mastery" more typically associated with science and technology. One of the elements of "soft mastery" described by Turkle (Turkle & Papert, 1992) is a tendency to identify with the materials, a kind of closeness or affective link with the subject under study. As a final observation, it is interesting to note that this kind of identification and anthropomorphization was found throughout the girls' work with *LEGO/Logo*. Participants regularly gave names to the objects, procedures, and variables they created, as is typical in programming. However, rather than using arbitrary labels ("X" or "Motor1"), many girls used personally meaningful names. These were sometimes nonsense words ("Fugi," "Kooka"), and sometimes names of people, for example, boys, whom they knew. This gave rise to remarks like "What are we going to do to Brian?" (with subsequent reactions of hilarity).

The girls also expressed emotion and affection toward their creations, including expressions of sadness at having to disassemble them. In the school-based follow-up study, one of the girls cradled her *LEGO/Logo* vehicle, referring to it as her "baby." This provoked a dismissive reaction by one of the boys, who said, "Your baby belongs in the SPCA." This interchange is reminiscent of an incident described by Turkle and Papert (1992) in which a boy reacts negatively to another boy's description of "being a [Logo] sprite," stating, "That's baby talk... I am not in the computer. I'm just making things happen there" (Turkle & Papert, 1992, p. 22). In Turkle and Papert's interpretation, "[t]he remark reflects an insistence on boundaries and the development of a world view that will fall easily into line with... canonical, objective science" (p. 22).

Our evidence indicates that the *LEGO/Logo* workshops succeeding in providing girls with a safe and meaningful space for forming personal connections with technology, while at the same time expanding their knowledge and understanding of design, mechanics, and programming. Research in such settings can allow us not only to examine questions about how technology can best be utilized with girls but about how girls can "be" when working with technology. Rather than assuming, like the designers of the Barbie™ computer, that we "know" girls and what they want and need, we can utilize carefully designed learning environments to investigate how girls think, solve problems, and interact when working in supportive, technology-rich settings.

References

Bruner, J. (1960). *The process of education.* Cambridge, MA: Harvard University Press.

Burns, E. (1989). Inside the Lego house. In C. Skelton (ed.)*Whatever happens to little women?: Gender and primary schooling.* Milton Keynes, UK: Open University Press.

Collis, B. (1987). Sex differences in the association between secondary school students' attitudes toward mathematics and toward computers. *Journal of Research in Mathematics Education, 18*, 394–402.

Damarin, S. (1989). Rethinking equity: An imperative for educational computing. *The Computing Teacher, 16*, 16–18.

Edwards, L.D. (1996). Project SAME Final Report (Submitted to National Science Foundation).

Edwards, L.D., Coddington, A. & Caterina, D. (1997). Girls teach themselves, and boys too: Peer teaching in a computer-based design and construction activity. *Computers and Education, 29* (1), 33–48.

Faulkner, H. & Anderson, A. (1991). LEGO TC Logo: Gender differences in a process-learning environment. *The Computing Teacher, 18*, 34–36.

Harel, I. & Papert, S. (eds.), (1991). *Constructionism: Research reports and essays, 1985–1990.* Norwood, NJ: Ablex Publishing Corporation.

Hawkins, J. (1985). Computers and girls: Rethinking the issues. *Sex Roles, 13*, 165–180.
Latour, B. & Woolgar, S. (1986). *Laboratory life: The social construction of scientific facts.* Princeton: Princeton University Press.
Lego® Dacta (n.d.) Control Lab® and Control System® (computer software and hardware).
Matute-Bianchi, G., Stoddart, T., Edwards, L., Landesman, M. & Gaiberson, N. (1994). Project SAME: Science and math equity. An experimental program of gender equity in integrated math and science (Proposal to the National Science Foundation, Special Programs for Girls and Women).
Oakes, J. (1990). Opportunities, achievement, and choice: Women and minority students in science and mathematics. In C. Cazden (ed.), *Review of Research in Education, 16* (pp. 153–222). Washington, DC: American Educational Research Association.
Palumbo, D. & Palumbo D. (1993). A comparison of the effects of Lego TC Logo and problem-solving software on elementary students' problem-solving skills. *Journal of Computing in Childhood Education, 4* (3–4). 307–323.
Peterson, L. & Fennema E. (1985). Effective teaching, student engagement in classroom activities, and sex-related differences in learning mathematics. *American Educational Research Journal, 22*, 309–335.
Resnick, M. (1991). Xylophones, hamsters, and fireworks: The role of diversity in constructionist activities. In I. Harel and S. Papert (eds.), *Constructionism: Research reports and essays, 1985–1990* (pp. 151–158). Norwood, NJ: Ablex Publishing Corporation.
Resnick M. & Ocko S. (1991). LEGO/Logo: Learning through and about design. In I. Harel and S. Papert (eds.), *Constructionism: Research reports and essays, 1985–1990* (pp. 141–150). Norwood, NJ: Ablex Publishing Corporation.
Sadker, M. & Sadker, D. (1994). *Failing at fairness: How America's schools cheat girls.* New York: Charles Scribner's Sons.
Sutherland, R. & Hoyles C. (1988). Gender perspectives on Logo programming in the mathematics curriculum. In C. Hoyles (ed.), *Girls and computers* (pp. 40–63). London: Institute of Education, University of London (Series: Bedford Way Papers, 34).
Turkle, S. (1995). *Life on the screen: Identity in the age of the Internet.* New York: Simon and Schuster.
Turkle, S. (1984). *The second self: Computers and the human spirit.* New York: Simon and Schuster.
Turkle, S. & Papert, S. (1992). Epistemological pluralism and the revaluation of the concrete. *Journal of Mathematical Behavior, 11* (1), 3–33.
Vygotsky, L. (1978). *Mind in society* (M. Cole, V. John-Steiner, S. Scribner & E. Souberman (eds.), Cambridge, MA: Harvard University Press.
Yelland, N. J. (1994). A case study of six children learning with LEGO/Logo. *Gender and Education 6* (1) 19–33.

Endnotes

[1] The research and activities described in this paper were supported by National Science Foundation Grant No. HRD-9450077 to Principal Investigators Laurie Edwards

Learning by Design 137

and Miriam Landesman. Andrea Coddington, Deb Caterina, and Lori Felton assisted in implementing the project and in writing reports of the results. My thanks go to Seymour Papert, Mitchel Resnick, and the Epistemology and Learning Group at MIT for their hospitality during a sabbatical visit, during which I had the pleasure of learning *LEGO/Logo* and discussing ideas for Project SAME.

[2] LEGO® is a registered trademark of INTERLOGO AG.

[3] The idea of kinetic sculptures in *LEGO/Logo* was described to me by Mitchel Resnick; see Resnick (1991).

Chapter 7

Shades of Gray: Creating a Vision of Girls and Computers

Nicola Yelland

Executive: He's got the best instinct in the industry. Since he was six, he's picked the top selling game every year.
(They watch Herbert playing the prototype game.)
Roger: Well, what do you think?
Herbert: Potentially good graphics, reasonably entertaining premise, the dog's well conceived and the environment is engaging. But I'm not interested in a game that has a chubby little dog catcher as the bad boy. Even girls won't like this game. Sorry, mate.
Roger: Yeah, but wait, Herbert. What if there were a better villain; Someone you could really hate.
Herbert: It's not the hatred that's important. It's the desire to annihilate.
(101 Dalmations, Disney Film)

Introduction

This chapter proposes ways of viewing the use of computers in classrooms that go beyond the narrow descriptions that stereotype boys and girls as hard and soft masters, respectively (Turkle, 1984). It describes a more complex set of characteristics that need to be considered, especially when pairs of students collaborate on computer-based tasks. With this in mind, it discusses several examples from a research project that engaged children in mathematical thinking in a curriculum where mathematical activity incorporated the use of technology and was based in active learning, inquiry and problem solving via an investigative approach. The results from the study demonstrate the ways in which learning environments that engage children and promote such active learning, enquiry and problem solving can foster many different and effective strategies for learning with technology for *all* students, not just with girls as an afterthought as the quote from *101 Dalmatians* infers.

The study was designed to explore the ways in which young children collaborated to solve novel problems in technology-based tasks using *Geo-Logo*[1]. This version of Logo was created and embedded in the mathematics curriculum as *Investigations in Number, Data and Space*[2]. *Geo-Logo* is a computer-based environment in which children direct a turtle to complete various actions. The turtle can move distances, forward and back, with given numeric inputs in turtle steps and can be directed to turn right or left when input for angle is provided. The environment has in-built devices such as rulers and on screen protractors to facilitate engagement with mathematical ideas, and in this way *Geo-Logo* acts as a conceptual framework for the development of mathematical thinking and problem solving, particularly in geometry. Many aspects of *Geo-Logo*, and indeed mathematics, have traditionally been regarded as being more attractive to young boys rather than girls (e.g., Hoyles & Sutherland, 1989; Walkerdine, 1988). The data presented in this chapter illuminate ways in which the pairs collaborated and used problem solving strategies to complete and extend the activities that they worked on. It suggests that the ways in which teachers have traditionally regarded performance with technological tasks in terms of "hard mastery" (Turkle, 1984) need to be complemented with other descriptions so that other styles, such as "soft mastery" are recognized, together with a realization that styles may be combined and varied according the type of task being attempted. This is because new computer technologies have created contexts that enable learners to extend their repertoire of strategies to suit the needs of varied tasks and provide catalysts for higher levels of thinking and action. Research (e.g., Rogoff, 1990; Yelland, 1999) has also revealed the importance of scaffolding learners (Wood, Bruner & Ross, 1976) and indicated that children will have different learning experiences when they work individually or in pairs and that when they work in pairs the nature of collaborations and interaction may vary as a result of the gender composition of the pair.

It will be contended here that we should value and promote diversity and creativity in problem solving and the use of approaches that incorporate the use of higher-order thinking skills and innovative problem solving. Above all, the research revealed that young children, irrespective of their gender, can engage in high-level mathematical thinking at a very young age and demonstrate a passion for learning with technology.

Background

Turkle (1988) described two different styles of mastery in computer use which she labelled as "hard" and "soft". "Hard mastery" was conceptualized as:

> ...the imposition of will over the machine through the implementation of a plan. A program is the instrument of premeditated control.... The details of the specific program obviously need to be "debugged," there has to be room for change, for some degree of flexibility in order to get it right, but the goal is always getting the program to realize the plan. (p. 104)

In contrast, "soft mastery" was viewed as being:

> ...more interactive...soft mastery is the mastery of the artist; try this, wait for a response, try something else, let the overall shape emerge from an interaction with the medium...the soft master works on a problem by arranging and rearranging these element, working through new combinations. (pp. 104–105)

In her initial description Turkle was careful to illustrate both styles with male examples but then went on to state that "girls tend to be soft masters, while the hard masters are overwhelmingly male" (p. 108). One of the reasons that she posited to account for this related to the enculturation of girls into this mode of working in all aspects of their lives. Yet there is evidence that the styles of mastery are possessed by each gender (e.g., Edwards, this volume; Hoyles & Sutherland, 1989: Yelland, 1998a & b), and additionally, that the style adopted may not only be related to whether you are a boy or girl but also to other features which may be related to cultural variables like socio-economic status and/or race, or context, such as the nature and structure of the task that is being worked on. The research presented here indicates that girls can use various styles and perform and demonstrate high levels of mathematical understanding in a variety of computer-based tasks.

The other important thing to note was that in "hard mastery" mode, reaching the goal was the primary objective and thus the most efficient way of getting there was a fundamental goal of the exercise. This often involved careful plans and discussion prior to embarking on the project and a reluctance to deviate from them once the task had begun. In contrast "soft mastery" was much more of an evolutionary style yet still involved planning and executing ideas which had been thought through carefully.

Girls Like Computers

Research has shown (e.g., Yelland, 1992) that girls like to use computers just as much as boys, but often in different ways (e.g., Hoyles, Healy & Pozzi, 1992; Ching, Kafai & Marshall, this volume). Yelland (1992) reported enthusiasm for computer use by girls and noted that many of the children interviewed did not associate interest or ability to use computers with any particular gender and most regarded themselves as being good at using computers.

This has been reinforced in a number of studies (e.g., Yelland, 1995, 1998a), and further, girls who have not experienced a great deal of success in school mathematics have demonstrated high levels of competence in novel problem-solving tasks based in computer contexts. The following example (Yelland, 1998) clearly reveals the enthusiasm and confidence of two girls who were working on a computer task that required them to direct the turtle to retrieve a toy and return to their starting location. The girls had been described by their teacher as average in mathematics and having problems with number and the operations. In the task they had to realize a number of things including an awareness that too many moves would result in the turtle losing energy, which, when depleted, would mark the end of the activity. At the start of the activity it was apparent that the girls were aware of the task requirements and how they might be able to meet them:

G1 Let's try and get down there and get the train
G2 Oh so we have to go backwards
G1 No I've got a better idea—go up de, der...which is quicker?
G2 Oh yeah, Ok f..d....
G1 Which is quicker though? No, put bk I think your way might be quicker
G2 Yeah Ok

And also how confident they were:

G2 l...t...space 90
G1 Yes, yes
G2 This is going great
G1 I know we're good at this...now how many dots, let's count the dots and that might be how much each step is
G2 Yeah

The example reveals the girls' ability to recognize the task requirements and make a plan to begin the solution. They seems to blend the "hard mastery" characterized by the development of the plan with "soft mastery" of making changes in response to feedback as the implementation of the plan is enacted.

Underwood and Underwood (1999) have suggested that in relation to computer use "...boys see themselves as the rightful and superior users of the technology" (p. 14). Indeed, it would seem that this attitude is reinforced not only in popular culture (as the *101 Dalmatians* quote shows) but also by the adults who interact with children. For example, Underwood and Underwood (1999) cited a remark made by a teacher and overheard in a classroom: "After all, classroom computers are little more than extended games machines, and who has ever seen a girl out-performing a boy on *Street Fighter*?...and this is why Nintendo™ isn't making Game Girls..." (p. 14).

With respect to attitudes toward the technology, Hughes and MacLeod (1986) reported that more children in their study associated computers with boys when asked the question, "Who would like computers more? Boys or girls?" Siann and MacLeod (1986) observed gender differences in attitude whereby "girls on the whole were less interested and motivated than the boys; secondly, the girls were more disposed to turn to and seek help from the boys than the reverse; and finally, although the girls did seek help from the boys, they resented it when the help was given practically (i.e., by pressing the appropriate keys) rather than verbally" (p.137). It should be noted that the results were reported in a situation where girls were paired *with* boys. It was suggested that the boys' tendency to dominate the proceedings, as reported in four out of the five pairs of 9-year-olds in later research (Siann, MacLeod, Glissov, and Durndell, 1990) influenced the results. This later study also examined gender differences in attitude before and after children participated in computer activities. The authors found that initially boys were more confident in their own performance, showed more interest in computers, and were more likely to associate computer use with high levels of performance than girls. However, after the children participated in a computer experience (with Logo, for 12 weeks), the gender differences in attitudes to computers and their use appeared to decrease. This was despite the observation that the girls' anxiety levels relative to the boys, increased. As stated previously, when girls worked with boys in mixed gender pairs, the boys tended to dominate the sessions, but interestingly this did not result in significant attitudinal differences about computers between girls who worked with boys and girls who worked with other girls. The authors did note, however, when girls worked together in pairs they seemed to gain most cognitively.

In terms of performance, Siann and MacLeod (1986) also reported that boys in their study completed the task faster than girls, but this was not statistically significant. Other researchers (Chadwick, 1986; Gunterman and Tovar, 1987) have *not* found significant differences in performance based on gender, while the work of Hughes, Brackenridge, Bibby, and Greenhaugh, (1988) has reported significant differences in the performances in terms of expediency between girls and boys to the detriment of *all* girl pairs.

In a classroom scenario described by Smith (1999) she noted that boys were heard to denigrate the girl's interests in zoos and nature when they were working on a database project and showed little respect for their opinion and presence when they worked in mixed gender pairs. For example, they insisted that they conduct a search on motorcycles as part of a group research project despite the protestations of the girls in the group.

In fact research (e.g., Culley, 1988; Barbieri and Light, 1992; Benyon, 1993) has shown that when it comes to computer use in the classroom boys tend to dominate the computer and even resort to harassment in order to ensure that girls do not have equal access time and use of the machines. As Underwood and Underwood (1999) have observed, "...classroom observations have repeatedly reported girls sitting towards the back in computer classes, boys sitting with the right hand nearest the mouse, and girls being bullied away from control of the machine even though they express interest and then frustration at not being allowed to contribute" (p. 14).

Despite such reports it has been shown that pairs of girls can achieve success in computer-based mathematical activity (Yelland, 1998) and in fact demonstrate high levels of mathematical thinking and understanding when they are given the opportunity to do so. This includes using technological tasks embedded in computer environments which support their thinking and allow for playful exploratory behavior. This is true not only with the use of computers in school-based contexts but also in out-of-school centres as well (e.g., Kafai, 1995). Further, research (e.g., Underwood, McCaffrey & Underwood, 1990; Yelland, 1994b) has also elucidated the nature of gender differences in collaborative learning contexts. It has been noted that when girls work together on computer-based tasks, they demonstrate different forms of collaboration than either boy or boy/

Shades of Gray 145

girl pairs. This has been found to benefit the problem solving of girls in a positive way (e.g., Yelland, 1998), but some researchers have suggested that girls need boys in order to succeed in computer-based activity (Hughes et al., 1988).

Thus, research studies have tended to *compare* and contrast the attitudes, performance and interactions of boys and girls. What is intended here, however, is to illustrate the extent to which girls can engage and enjoy computer-based tasks which facilitate the understanding of complex mathematical ideas in new and dynamic ways. In this way it presents a more positive perspective of girls and technology which reveals that irrespective of gender, children can interact and use technology to explore concepts with levels of success that are conducive for active learning, inquiry and problem solving. It is also important to note that this was achieved in the context of challenging tasks which afforded the opportunity for increased conceptual understandings in mathematics.

Scenes of Girls and Computers in the Classroom

Mathematical collaborations

This section will consider data to illustrate the ways in which girls have worked on mathematical tasks, not only with enthusiasm but also with a high level of skill and demonstrated understanding. Data from the first year of a three-year project involving children in Years 3 and 4 of compulsory schooling in Queensland, Australia, will be presented. Specifically, four tasks will inform the discussion. These are *Missing Measures* and individual *Projects* from the Year 3 Investigations Unit entitled *Turtle Paths* and *Sunken Ships* and *Rectangles* from the Year 4 unit entitled *Sunken Ships and Grid Patterns*.

The sample

Two intact classes participated in the study. The children were in Year 3 and 4 of a State School in Brisbane, Australia. Each class had 28 and 26 children, respectively. The mean age of the children in Year 3 was 7 years and 9 months with a range from 7 years 1 month to 8 years 4 months. In the Year 4 class the mean was 8 years and 11 months with a range from 8 years 6 months to 9 years 7 months. The children had a computer in their classroom, and it was mainly used to play educational games related to literacy and numeracy. Some of the children had computers at home that they used for games, but mainly the machines were owned and used by either parents or older siblings. None of the children indicated that they owned the computer exclusively. Additionally, none of the children had used Logo prior to the commencement of the study.

The tasks

Missing Measures. In *Missing Measures* the children are required to complete the instructions for six items, the final one of which is a house (Figure 7.1). The task is the fifth in a sequence of eight to complete the unit.

Young children can use a variety of strategies in order to complete the drawing. For example they may guide the turtle using a series of moves, using trial and error, until the picture is complete, or they may use mathematical calculations based on deductive inferences to determine the precise number to be used for the specific side. Yelland (1992) has described such performances in terms of levels of sophistication to task solution with the intuitive strategy being considered as "naïve" while the application of prior knowledge and executive decision making demonstrated in the second example above reflected a "knowledgeable" performance. Additionally some pairs of children seemed to be in a state of "transition" whereby they showed evidence of each of the levels of performance on an inconsistent basis.

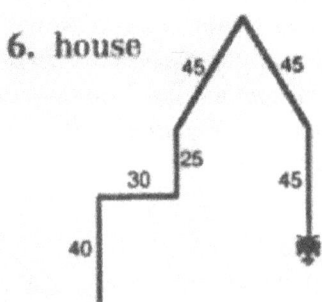

Figure 7.1: *Missing Measures*: House

In the example of the house, in order to complete the side where the turtle is located in the first instance, knowledgeable pairs were cognisant that the total length of the side had to be 65, since it was equal to the sum of the two parallel sides on the opposite side of the house, that is 40 add 25. They then needed either to find the difference between the total distance and the distance already traveled by the turtle, that is 65 subtract 45, or use a counting-on procedure from 45 to reach 65 in order to determine that the amount needed is 20. In contrast, naïve pairs would estimate a distance, either by guessing or by considering the distance in terms of the sides already drawn. In the majority of pairs such an estimation was usually short, but in some instances the pairs chose a number that resulted in a side that was too long and had to be reduced.

In order to complete the picture the base of the house had to be drawn, a knowledgeable performance would be characterized by the ability to deduce the combined lengths of the essential component parts. These were the base of the roof (45), since the roof was an equilateral triangle and even though this was not marked on the diagram, the distance at the base of the roof had to be 45, with 30, the length of the remaining (horizontal) side. Naïve pairs would again edge the turtle along until they bridged the distance between the two lines.

In this way the knowledgeable pairs demonstrated high levels of mathematical ability in using mathematical concepts in new and dynamic ways in contexts/ tasks in which they had to generate the solution to the problem. The *Missing Measures* tasks required the pairs to go beyond the ability to perform mechanical calculations which are found in traditional textbook applications and make decisions about how and when to adopt specific strategies and processes as well as perform them accurately in order to ensure that their goal is reached. Further, it also enabled them to go beyond a simple description of their performance in terms of "hard" or "soft" master.

It was evident that girls enjoyed these tasks as much as the boys irrespective of working with another girl or a boy partner. Additionally, with scaffolding, both boy and girl pairs in the study were able to demonstrate that they were *beginning* to make connections between numbers and use more sophisticated strategies in their attempts at task solution (Figure 7.2).

The graph shows that out of ten pairs of children two gave knowledgeable justifications for their strategies while five pairs did this in a transitional way. Only three pairs could not justify their strategies mathematically. Girls were also keen to continue with the drawings when the basic requirements of the task were completed. They made suggestions that they would like to include a door and some windows in order to "finish the picture." The transcripts indicated that girls not only interacted more frequently to confirm plans of action but also that their combined strategies enabled them to achieve an accurate duplication of the picture of the house in about the same time as boy and boy-girl pairs.

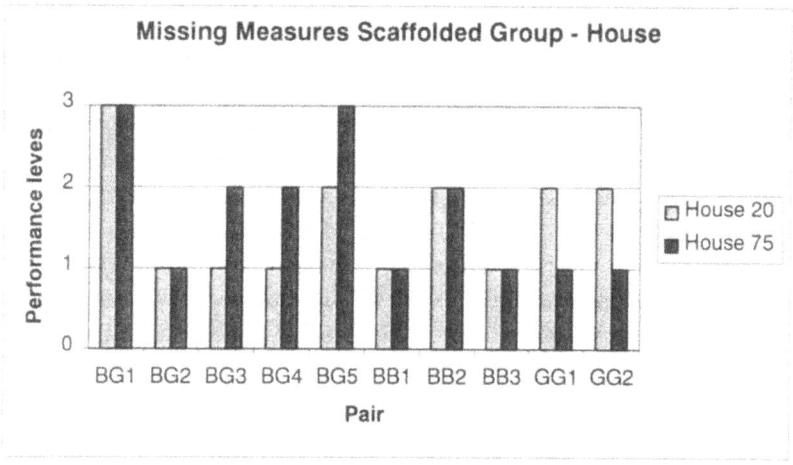

Figure 7.2: Levels of performance in *Missing Measures*

Projects. In the final task in the Turtle paths unit the children were required to create designs for a project using all the features of the *Geo-Logo* environment that they had learned. This basically involved making a picture or creating an object using plane shapes (triangles, squares and rectangles). The children had previously worked on a task called *Geo Face* in which they created a robot-like face using two-dimensional shapes and were involved in discussion about the ways in which a final product could be generated by developing procedures where the various parts were combined in sequence to produce the desired effect.

Once more it was evident that in designing and producing their projects it was evident that many children were using higher order thinking processes, on a regular basis. In one example a girl pair created a castle (Figure 7.3) that revealed a depth of knowledge about number and the ability to compare the relative sizes of number, operations with number, symmetry, spatial relationships and knowledge about two-dimensional shapes. The development of the picture was complex and consisted of six basic procedures, namely; the tower and its top (head) door, window,

Shades of Gray

dungeon and finally, castle, the procedure which generated the final product. The process took place over the period of a week in a number of sessions both off and on the computer. Two of the most striking features about the project was the commitment to completing the task even for extended periods of time (up to one hour) both on and off the computer, and the ways in which the pair seemed to combine elements of both "hard" and "soft mastery" in terms of Turkle's classification.

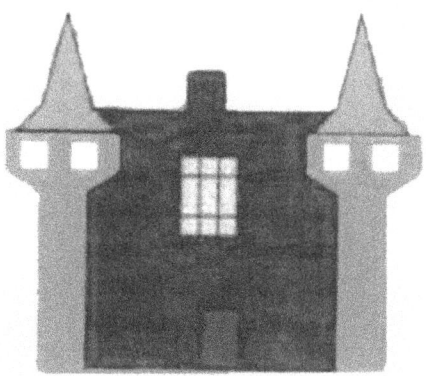

Figure 7.3: Year 3 project: Castle

The example of the sailor project (Figure 7.4a,b,c) and the associated off-computer planning, reveals the extent of the planning and implementation of ideas at the computer, required for a project. It also reflected an example of "hard" and "soft mastery" coexisting in one task. The children first drew what they wanted to create on a sheet of paper with some initial thoughts on the relative size of the various components based on their experiences in creating two-dimensional shapes in *Geo-Logo*. The pairs were then provided with another sheet so that they could plan and think about the commands/ procedures that they might use in order to create the shapes. Not all children chose to do this, but all of the girl pairs did. Yet, they did not do it for every single component part of the drawing. In the sailor, for example, the basic shapes were rectangles and squares. Once the girls figured out how to draw two rectangles and a square, they announced that they did not have to do any more as all they

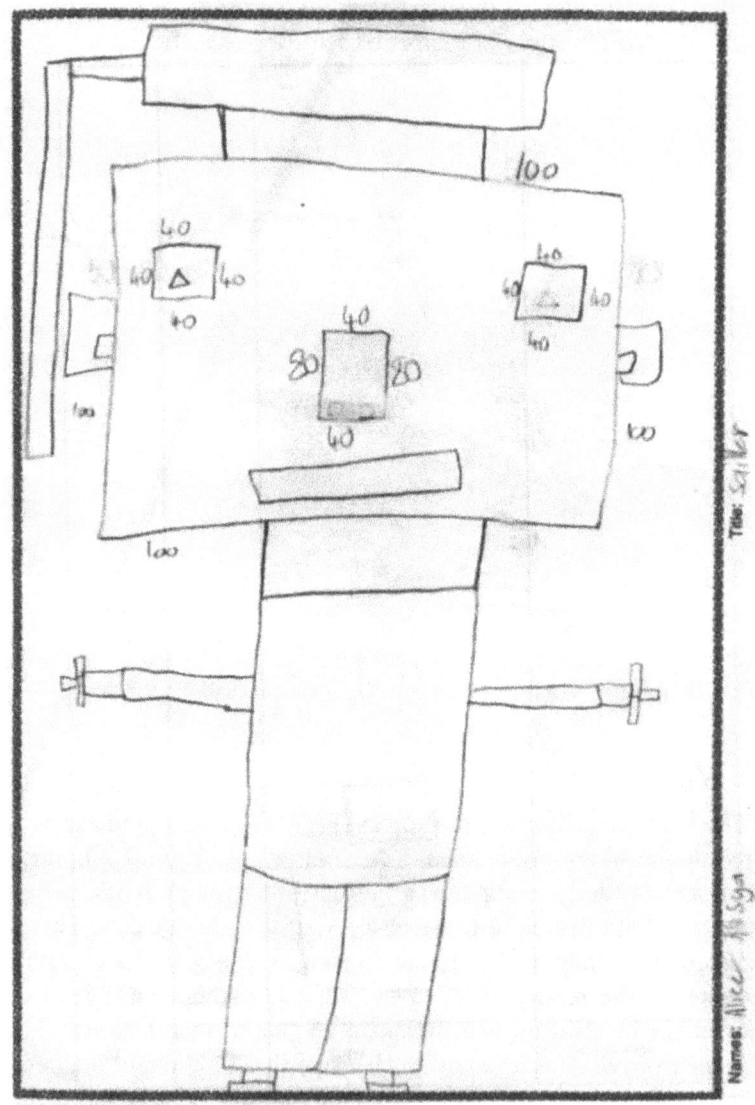

Figure 7.4a: A sailor by Alice and Alyssa (Year 3)

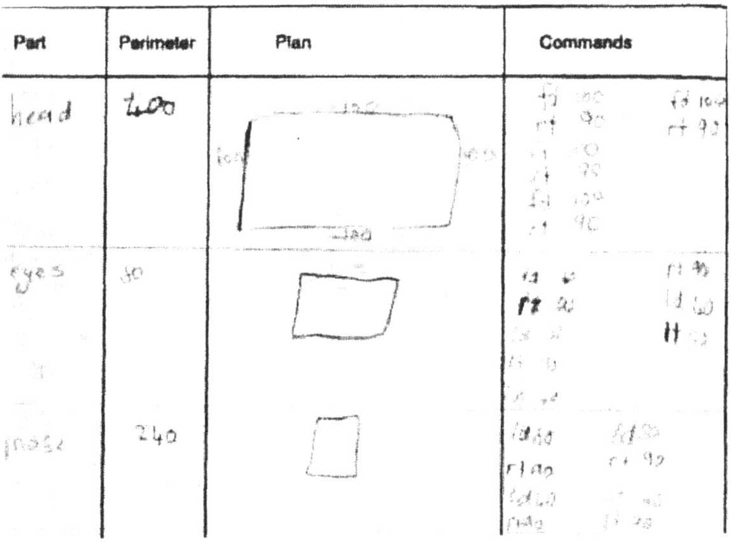

Shades of Gray 151

Part	Perimeter	Plan	Commands
head	400		
eyes	80		
nose	240		

Figure 7.4b: A sailor by Alice and Alyssa (Year 3)

had to do was change the numbers. Thus the plans served the function of creating a goal for them to work towards with some basic information but they were able to modify the plans as they went and were willing to do so. It was also apparent that some pairs were not willing to do this; they wanted to stick to their original ideas exactly. However, most pairs made changes "on the fly" as they waited to see what their commands produced. The final computer picture and commands reveal that the girls used 12 procedures to create their sailor with the final product being called sailor2 after some initial concern about the mouth of their original sailor procedure, which they were reluctant to delete while they attempted the new procedure to rectify the situation.

One of the most salient observations about the projects of the girl pairs was the nature and extent of their collaboration. It was different from that of both the boy and boy/girl pairs. Boy pairs had been found to disagree more and make more independent moves than girls in previous research (e.g., Yelland, 1992). Boy/ girl pairs did not seem to develop any specific patterns of collaboration, and variations in the nature and extent and type of interactions were thought to be based on individual characteristics of the pair, for example, in regard to their ability and personality. In each case the girls were supportive of each other's ideas and offered suggestions which were often debated extensively before a consensus was reached. Girl pairs always reached agreement about what they were doing both globally and locally in the process. They were also willing to share the keyboard, which often was viewed as the location of action.

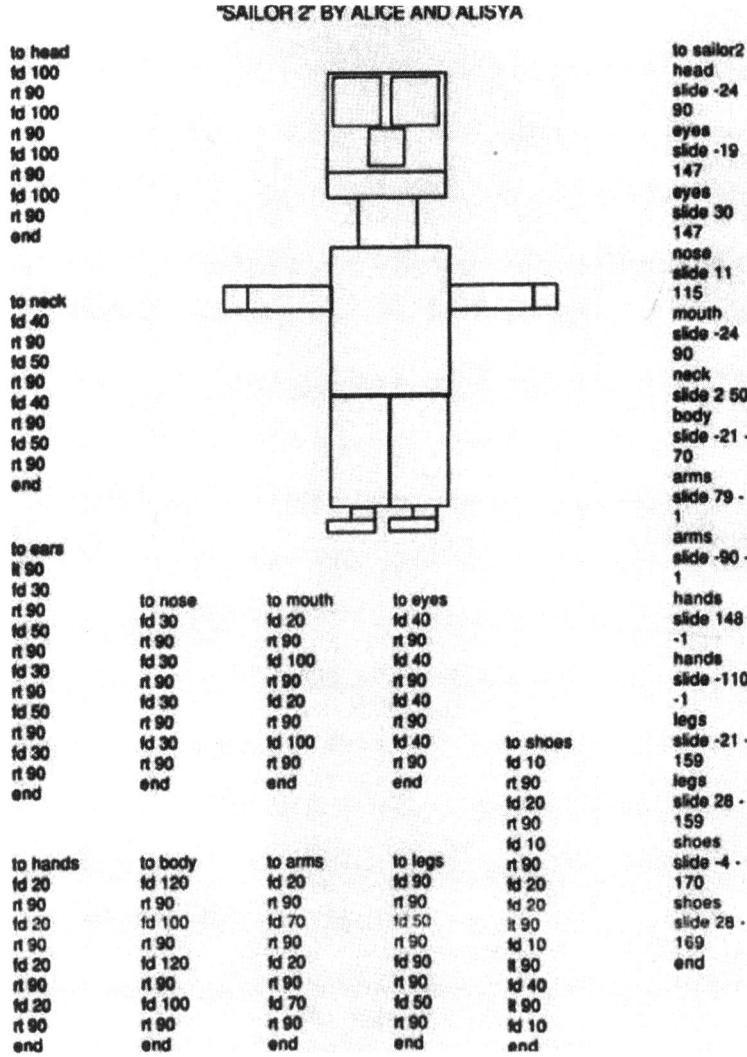

Figure 7.4c: A sailor by Alice and Alyssa (Year 3)

Shades of Gray

Sunken Ships. In the Year 4 unit *Sunken Ships and Grid Patterns* the children were engaged in some challenging tasks, which included the use of negative numbers, quadrants and the creation of computer procedures with variables. These ideas are obviously complex and usually not included in the mathematics curriculum for 9-year-olds. Yet in the context of the *Investigations* curriculum, they were encountered in an exploratory way that allowed the children to play with them and in doing so afforded them the opportunity to make sense of ideas in context (Noss, 1984). This

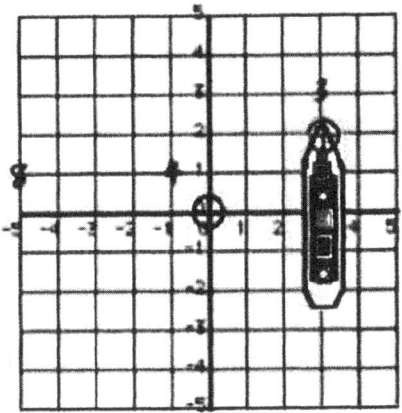

```
GG1 SS2
How far away
[-1 1] is 4
[-5 1] is 8
[3 1] is S
[3 2] is S
[3 3] is 3
[3 0] is S
[3 -1] is S
[3 -2] is S

You found the sunken ship!
You used 8 jumpto commands
```

Figure 7.5: *Sunken Ships*

opportunity would seem to not only be appropriate but also situated the complex concepts in activities that were engaging and thus facilitated understandings in ways that might not have been possible without the technology.

In the first activity in the unit, *Sunken Ships*, the girl pairs revealed as much enthusiasm as the boys in playing the game did. The activity is based on the game of *Battleships*, wherein the players have to provide coordinates in order to guess the location of a ship. They then respond to feedback in order to determine the exact location. Each time the game is played, the ship is hidden in a different random location, and the players enter their commands in the format: *Jumpto* [2 –2], where the integers pertain to coordinate positions (Figure 7.5).

In one interesting interchange, when a girl pair was playing the game next to a boy pair, the boys challenged the girls to see who could be the first to find the ship. In this instance (and others) the girl pair was able to find the ship before the boys, and the nature of their collaborations seemed to be the key to the differences between their attempts and the boys, who challenged them. All pairs realized that their first attempt was a guess, and that in some cases you could be extremely lucky! The data revealed that the girls pairs were more effective in locating the ship and usually quicker. They talked and reasoned about possible locations based on the existing information that was available to them, more than the boy pairs who often shared turns by alternating on the keyboard and did not discuss the relative merits of each other's move. The girl pairs evaluated each move as they made it and additionally explored a number of possibilities in quick succession before reaching a consensus. What was also apparent was that it did not seem to matter to the girl pairs who took on the role of operating the keyboard. In contrast the boy pairs were very adamant that each partner should have a turn entering the commands and that was viewed as "a go." As a result the girls were more likely to succeed in determining the accurate location of the ship faster and with fewer guesses, although on some occasions a lucky first guess did result in a particular boy pair locating the ship first. It was interesting to note that in a number of boy/girl pairs, the girls often tried to initiate conversation with their boy partners in an attempt to solve the problem. However, in most cases the boys ignored any suggestions, with some dominating the computer to attempt the task individually, while others let the girls have a turn and offered suggestions but basically did not listen to anything the girls had to say in the way of advice about what to try next.

Shades of Gray

Rectangles. In another activity, later in the unit, the pairs of children were required to create a procedure for a rectangle which enabled them to enter data so that a rectangle of any specification/size could be drawn. They were then asked to use the procedure to draw a rectangle in each of four quadrants so that the final product was symmetrical (Figure 7.6). This was a complex task by any criteria, but the pairs of children stated that they could easily do it! After this they had to direct the turtle to copy a picture (e.g., a cake) in a specified quadrant (Figure 7.7).

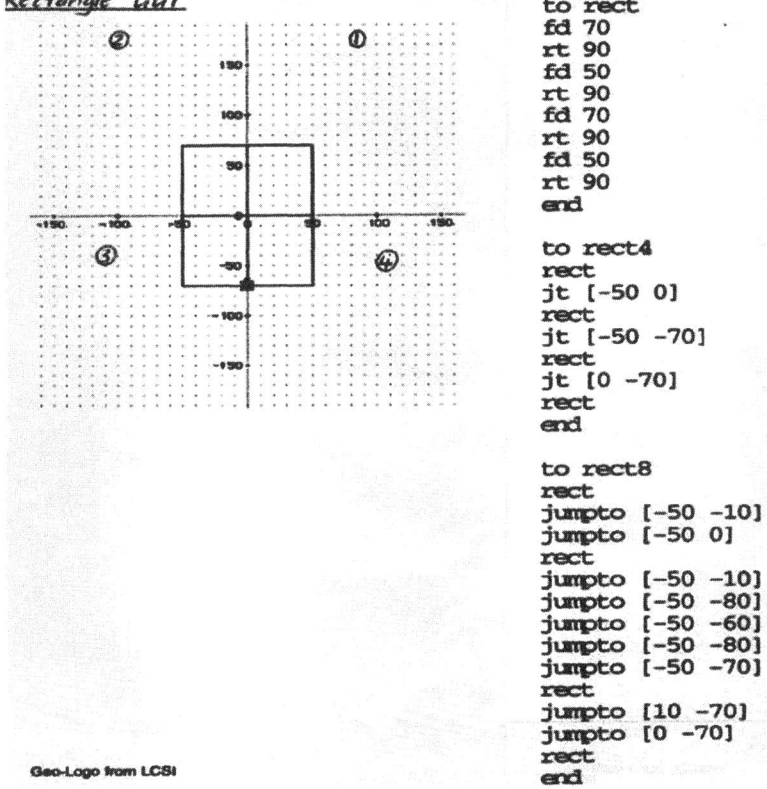

Figure 7.6: *Rectangles*

A number of complex mathematical concepts were required to successfully complete the task. They included the use of variables, negative numbers to 250 and the placement of congruent shapes in different quadrants. In Australia such concepts would not included in curricula until middle or high school, and it is not the contention here that the children in this study had a sophisticated understanding of the concepts, based solely on the activities that they participated in during the study. What was evident however, was that the children were actively engaged in the tasks and that they were able to make sense of the ideas inherent to these concepts via active exploration in the *Geo-Logo* programming environment. It was also evident that there were no gender differences in terms of levels of interest or quality of outcomes. This is especially significant for girls of this particular age, since the environment was not only a programming context, but contained artifacts that have traditionally been regarded as being located in the male domain (e.g., *Battleships*).

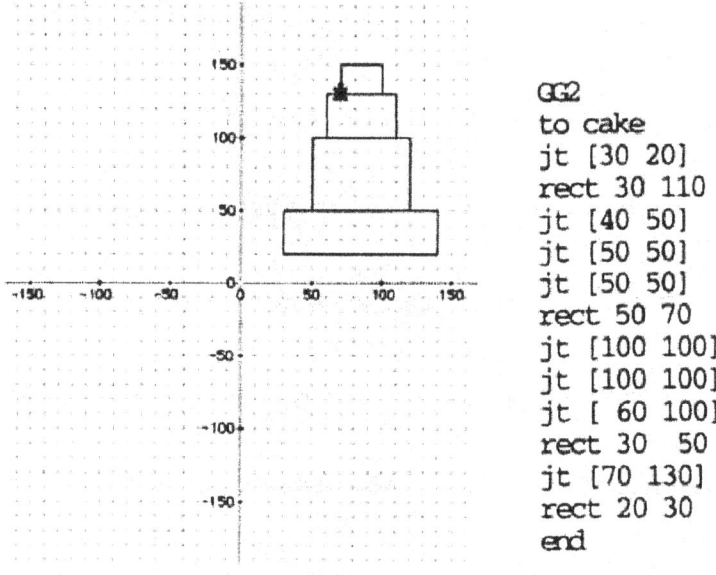

Figure 7.7: *Cakes*

It was apparent that this task appealed to all pairs, who by this stage of the research demonstrated that they enjoyed being challenged to think. There were no apparent gender differences in strategies for solution, although differences in the nature of the interactions were still apparent. All pairs, on listening to the task requirements, applied their previously generated rectangles program in a "soft mastery" style of experimentation and exploration. They did not plan this on paper first but rather preferred to estimate the coordinates of the turtle's starting point and then try the rectangle procedure with the required inputs. They often made errors of location in their attempts to create mirror images in each quadrant, but since it was easy to remove each unsatisfactory rectangle and replace it with another try, this task seemed to elicit this style of problem solving in all pairs irrespective of gender.

Interactions

The qualitative differences in the nature of interactions between gender pairs has already been alluded to in the previous section and supported in the research literature (e.g., Underwood & Underwood, 1999). Yelland, (1998) stated that the main difference in performance between boy and girl pairs was primarily related to the way in which they collaborated during problem solving. Other research has shown that girls seem to enjoy working in groups while engaged in computer tasks (e.g., Hoyles, Healy & Pozzi, 1992) and further are extremely competent at collaborating in ways that facilitate learning via a problem solving approach (e.g., Ching, Kafai & Marshall, this volume).

The following vignettes from the transcripts of the videotapes from this study offer some insight into the differences in the styles of interactions between the girl pairs and the boy pairs. In the first example, the girl pair is working together in order to complete the task. They offer suggestions to each other and in this and other episodes continually make offers of help and support each other with positive comments. In contrast the second example of a boy pair was fairly characteristic of the boy's style of interaction in pairs. The most obvious observation related to the fact that they often did not regard themselves as a pair but two separate people who were taking turns on a common task. The vignette also contains examples of recrimination which were only recorded for boy and boy/girl pairs. It is suggested here that teachers should encourage boys to interact in a more collaborative way so as to promote learning. This was demonstrated in a previous study (Yelland & Masters, 1997) when boy pairs were scaffolded both cognitively and affectively to collaborate in a technological environment, the performance level increased.

    G2:   (while looking at the screen) I know a short cut. Up there! Up there!
    G1   I'm not going that way. Oh Yeah! Good idea. What do you think...fd?
    G2:   Fd what? Let's work it out....
    G1:   Lets do 60
    G2:   OK, 60

G1: No, 50
G2 No, no, how about 20?
G1: 40, 40
G2: Oh, how about we try 40 and then we try another one if it doesn't work!

This scene was fairly typical of the interactions in girl pairs whereby they vocalized their thoughts, made suggestions, offered information and shared ideas in a spontaneous way. Another important observation was that the girl pairs always agreed on a particular command before it was entered. In contrast, the data showed that the boy pairs disagreed more frequently and in fact would often disrupt the process of solving the problem by physical intervention to take over the keyboard or by undoing their partner's previous move. For example:

B1 Types rt 90
B2 Not 90!
B1: Yes, it is. See!
B2: And we're facing that way instead (pointing)
B1: I know. I'm going to do another 90 degrees
B2: David, you're using up all my energy
B1 I haven't used up any
B2: Yes, you have. Look!
B1: Oh, Yeah! I can always delete that then it'll go back to here (pointing to start)
B2: Ok then well delete it 'cos I want to do something. Other than just being the commander. It's my go. It's my go now! Delete it!

When boy/girl pairs collaborate, the nature of the interactions was much more complex and not easily characterized. In some cases the boy or girl would simply not interact but would take turns as if they were an individual working on a task; in other instances they would collaborate successfully and share the actions and discuss their thinking and strategies. Additionally, in some pairs the boy or girl would dictate the plan and actions necessary and order their partner to complete them or do it themselves. Where one partner was extremely dominant, the research data showed that the other child might simply withdraw from participation and either just watch or walk away to another area of the classroom.

These various scenarios of interaction suggest that the quality of the learning experience very much depends on whom a child is working with and the way in which they interact. Another factor which influences the ways in which children learn in the technological contexts described here, is the nature and extent of scaffolding that they receive.

Scaffolding Children's Learning

Yelland (1999) outlined different forms of scaffolding that may be conducive for learning within technological contexts. These are "cognitive," "technical" and "affective." "Cognitive" scaffolding involves supporting children's learning with the goal of assisting conceptual development. Teachers need to develop ways to cognitively scaffold using a variety of techniques such as asking questions, modelling, providing diagrams and opportunities for brainstorming and shared problem solving. "Technical" scaffolding occurs when the teacher explains a particular feature of the computer or computer context so that problem solving is facilitated. "Affective" scaffolding is needed so that the children can develop a positive self-confidence regarding their ability to solve novel problems. Data from a number of studies have revealed that while all children benefit from all types of scaffolding, affective scaffolding was employed more often by teachers with girl pairs in initial experiences with technologically based tasks. (Yelland and Masters, unpublished manuscript). This was often necessary because girls came to the new contexts with serious misgivings about their ability to do it. Teachers often reported that such views were frequently related to their lack of interest in mathematics. In this study one scenario highlighted this situation when a pair of Year 4 girls were observed while engaged in a task called *Taxi* from the Year 4 unit, which was the next task after the *Sunken Ships* game. It was not until extended support from the teacher that they were able to comprehend the task requirements and then proceed quickly and successfully to task solution. The video data revealed that the girls were confusing the commands required to complete the task with those used in the previous activity, *Sunken Ships*. In *Sunken Ships* the commands were in the format *jumpto* [coordinates] whereas in *Taxi* they were forward/ back and left/ right, each with input numbers. At the start of *Taxi* the girls were trying to enter *jumpto* in order to move the turtle to the first house. They realized that the new commands were needed and attempted to blend them in by typing *jumpto fd 20*. When this was unsuccessful they were not only unable to articulate what they were doing wrong to each other but also could not remember what they were supposed to be doing in order to complete the task.

    G1:   What shall we do first?
    G2:   Jumpto

G1: (types jumpto as she utters jumpto forward....)
G1: I think it'll be too far!
G2: Type 90
G1: Is that what we use?
G2: (shrugs)

Teacher comes over to them:

G2: What can we use?
T: Well where are your commands? Have a look at them and see what you have got. Which ways can you move the turtle?
G1: Here they are forward and back
T: Which way do you want the turtle to go to visit each house?
G1: This way (pointing in a sweeping movement that indicates house no. 3 first)
T: Have a look at your plan (she leaves)

Then when the teacher returned after working with other pairs:

G1: We need to start again. It's still not working
T: Where are we? OK Let's start again from the beginning. You want to go from here to here (pointing from the turtle's starting position to the first house). That is forward 10,20
G1: Left
T: No think about it. It is forward 20 steps. What I want you to do is to look at where you decided to go. (She points and says...from here to here then here....) So where do you start?
G1: (points and says Here!)
T: Yes so what is the first move to make that will get you from here to here?
G1: fd 20
T: Ok, now that is fine. What next?
G1: 10,20
T: But what way do you need to face the turtle first?
G1 : Right
T: How much?
G2: 90
T: Ok rt 90
G1: (types)
T: Now what do you have to do next?
G1: 10, 20 forward
T: Yes
G1/ G2: Yes!!!
T: Now do you see the difference between the moves forward and the turns?
G1: Yes

Teacher leaves (11:00 a.m.):

G1: Ok what next? 10,20,30,40,50, 60... fd 60
G2: (as the turtle reaches the house) Now we've got it!
G1: Then turn it 90
G2: (types lt 90)

G1: Now forward 10, 20, 30, 40, 50
G1/ G2:(clap happily)
G2: Yes we got another (as they both clap excitedly)
T: Now you are going well!

Thus, it was only after the teacher stayed and scaffolded the pair to ensure that they experienced a sequence of two successful moves, re-explained the goal of the activity, and offered support in terms of encouragement to persist that the girls experienced success and then were able to continue independently with the task to conclusion. In this way, although they experienced serious confusion during their first attempts with the task, once the teacher spent time with them and supported their efforts in diverse ways, they were able to recall strategic information provided in the class lesson and apply it to the task with success. This type of cognitive, technical and affective scaffolding proved to be of particular importance to the girls, and once they were clear of it, they easily succeeded in completing the activity.

In this study it seemed that girls were initially not as confident as boys in approaching the tasks, even though on a number of occasions their performance was judged as being superior to that of the boys. However it was also apparent that once the girls received scaffolding and experienced success in meeting the goals of the various tasks that their confidence increased and then the scaffolding was removed. This observation has important implications for teaching and learning contexts with technology for girls. It suggests that in the current educational climate, there is still a need to raise the confidence levels of some girls in mathematics and technological contexts. This may be done in a variety of ways, but once achieved it is also evident as reported in the data presented here that girls are able to engage with powerful mathematical ideas at a high level when afforded the opportunity to do so.

The nature and form of scaffolding need to be flexible not only to suit the needs of the children but also according to the structure of the task. Research (Yelland, 1999) has revealed that scaffolding can be broadly considered as cognitive, technical and affective and that teachers should be sensitive to the needs of the learner in order to decide what particular form the scaffolding will take. There are many variables that will influence this decision. Effective teaching and learning contexts have many different features (Yelland, 2000) and experienced teachers are able to select and use scaffolding techniques as each situation requires.

Conclusions

The research presented here has shown the variety of ways in which girls collaborate, both with other girls and with boys, to demonstrate high levels of mathematical skills and problem-solving in computer contexts. It also demonstrates that girls may adapt their techniques and styles according to the type of task that they are working on. Children can benefit from scaffolding and will use technology in educational contexts to solve problems in novel and dynamic ways. As a result their performance in problem solving contexts is often varied and complex and needs to be described with at least the factors mentioned here included, so that we are more informed about the mechanisms that may account for learning. Research has revealed that a number of contextual features will impact on performance. These include the context in which the problem is posed, levels of engagement with the content, the resources that are available, the ways in which the children may collaborate and the nature of the scaffolding that may be provided by peers or the teacher. The gender of the problem solvers is also a factor in terms of the strategies and interactions that may be deployed in problem solving but as Hoyles and Sutherland (1989) warn, we should not arrive at quick and superficial conclusions based on short-term observations with any group of children.

Research (e.g., Hughes et al., 1988) has tended to devalue the performance of girls by contrasting it to that of boys and additionally schools have often promoted the "hard mastery" style of learning with technology which has been more closely aligned with male performance (Turkle, 1984). The data presented here have suggested that pairs of girls can collaborate effectively to solve complex problems in a novel computer context and that they may use a variety of strategies and interactions that will depend on a large array of factors. This may include both "hard" and "soft mastery" styles and variations of the two. The research results support the notion that girl pairs enjoy working with computer, and in many cases the computer context has facilitated their engagement with mathematical ideas, which was not possible without the technology. The examples presented here revealed that when computer tasks are embedded within a curriculum that also incorporates off-computer tasks and discussion times for sharing strategies, children are afforded the opportunity to collaborate to solve tasks which stimulate the use of metastrategic processes (Davidson & Sternberg, 1985). These enable them to engage with mathematical content in a context characterized by active exploration, inquiry and problem solving.

Computers have the potential to develop contexts for learning and create knowledge-building communities that will ensure that children have opportunities for learning and understanding complex mathematical ideas and working collaboratively with others. The roles of the teachers and learners in this process are critical. Teachers can support and extend children's learning with the provision of scaffolding, which will assist in the development of knowledge and the acquisition of skills for creative problem-solving as well as provide varied opportunities for shared decision making and comparison of strategies. This chapter has presented scenarios to demonstrate that children can benefit from experiences in a problem-solving context characterized by the embedded use of computers and work with powerful mathematical ideas. Furthermore, the data from the study reported here revealed that children enjoy working on computer-based tasks. They are excited about using the machines, and the activities provide opportunities for them to make sense of ideas and create their own understandings in ways that were not possible without the technology.

References

Barbieri, M. S. & Light, P. (1992). Interaction, gender and performance on a computer-based problem solving task. *Learning and Instruction, 2,* 199–213.

Benyon, J. (1993). Computers, dominant boys and invisible girls: Or Hannah, it's not a toaster, it's a computer. In J. Benyon & H. MacKay. (eds.), *Computers into classrooms* (pp. 160–189). London:Falmer Press.

Carter Ching, C., Kafai, Y. & Marshall, S. (2002). "I always get stuck with the books!" Creating space for girls to access technology in a software design project. In N. Yelland & A. Rubin (eds.), *Ghosts in the machine: Women's voices in research with technology.* New York: Peter Lang.

Chadwick, C. (1986). Differential group composition in problem solving using Logo. Unpublished doctoral thesis. Concordia University, Montreal.

Culley, L. (1988). Girls, boys and computers. *Educational Studies, 14,* 3–8.

Davidson, J. E. & Sternberg, R. J. (1985). Competence and performance in intellectual development. In E. Niemark, R. Delisi and J. L. Newman. *Moderators of competence.* (pp. 43–76). Hillsdale, NJ: Lawrence Erlbaum.

Edwards, L. D. (2002). Learning by design: Environments that support girls' learning with technology. In N. Yelland & A. Rubin (eds.), *Ghosts in the machine: Women's voices in research with technology.* New York: Peter Lang.

Gunterman, E. & Tovar, M. (1987). Collaborative problem solving with Logo: Effects of group size and group composition. *Journal of Educational Computing Research 3* (3), 313–334.

Hoyles, C., Healy, L. & Pozzi, S. (1992). Interdependence and autonomy: Aspects of groupwork with computers. *Learning and instruction 2*, 239–257.

Hoyles, C. & Sutherland, R. (1989). *Logo mathematics in the classroom.* London, R.K.P.

Hughes, M., Brackenridge, A., Bibby, A. & Greenhaugh, P. (1988). Girls, boys and turtles: Gender effects with young children learning with Logo. In C. Hoyles (ed.), *Girls and computers: General issues and case studies of Logo in the mathematics classroom.* (pp. 31–39). London: Institute of Education, University of London:

Hughes, M. & MacLeod, M. (1986). Using Logo with very young children. In R. W. Lawler, M. D. Boulay, M. Hughes & H. MacLeod. (eds.), *Cognition and computers.* (pp. 179–219) Chichester: Ellis Harwood.

Kafai, Y. (1995). *Minds in play: Computer game design as a context for children's learning.* Hillsdale, NJ: Lawrence Erlbaum.

Noss, R. (1984). *Creating a mathematical environment through programming: A study of young children learning Logo.* London: University of London Institute of Education.

Rogoff, B. (1990). *Apprenticeship in thinking: Cognitive development in social context.* New York: Oxford University Press.

Siann, G. & M. MacLeod (1986). Computers and children of primary school age: Issues and questions. *British Journal of Educational Technology 2* (17), 13–144.

Siann, G., MacLeod, H., Glissov, P. & Durndell, A. (1990). The effects of computer use on gender differences in attitudes to computers. *Computers in Education 14* (2), 183–191.

Smith, H. (1999). *Opportunities for information and communication technology in the primary school.* Stoke on Trent: Trentham.

Turkle, S. (1984). *The second self: Computers and the human spirit.* New York: Simon and Schuster.

Underwood, G., McCaffrey, M. & Underwood, J. (1990). Gender differences and effects of co-operation in a computer-based language task. *Educational Research, 36,* 63–74.

Underwood, J. & Underwood, G. (1999). Task effects on co-operative and collaborative learning with computers. In K. Littleton & P. Light (eds.), *Learning with computers: Analysing productive interactions* (pp. 10–23). London: Routledge.

Walkerdine, V. (1988). *The mastery of reason: Cognitive development and the production of reality.* London:Routledge.

Wood, D., Bruner, J. & Ross, G. (1976) The role of tutoring in problem solving. *Journal of Child Psychology and Psychiatry, 17,* 89–100.

Yelland, N. J. (1992). Young children learning with Logo: An analysis of the strategies and interactions of gender pairs. Unpublished doctoral thesis. University of Queensland.

Yelland, N. J. (1992). Introducing young children to Logo. *The Computing Teacher, 19* (10), 12–14.

Yelland, N. J. (1993). Learning with Logo: An analysis of strategies and interactions. *Journal of Educational Computing Research, 9* (4), 465–486.

Yelland, N. J. (1994a). The strategies and interactions of young children in Logo tasks. *Journal of Computer Assisted Learning, 10* (1), 33–49.

Yelland, N. J. (1994b). A case study of six children learning with Logo. *Gender and Education, 6* (1), 19–33.

Yelland, N. J. (1995). Logo experiences with young children: Describing performance, problem-solving and the social context of learning. *Early Child Development and Care, 109,* 61–74.

Yelland, N. J. (1998). Empowerment and control with technology for young children. *Educational Theory and Practice, 20* (2), 45–55.

Yelland, N. J. (1999). Reconceptualising schooling with technology for the 21st century: Images and reflections. D. D. Shade (ed.), *Information technology in childhood education annual* (pp. 39–59). Virginia: AACE.

Yelland, N. J. (2000). The importance of effective numeracy teaching and learning in the early childhood years: Issues and strategies for the information age. DETYA briefing paper.

Yelland, N. J. (2001). Girls, mathematics and technology. In W. Atweh, H. Forgasz & B. Nebres (eds.), (pp. 393–409). *Sociocultural research on mathematics education: An international perspective.* Mahwah, NJ: Lawrence Erlbaum.

Yelland, N. J. & Masters, J. E. (1994). Innovation in practice: Learning in a technological environment. In T. Killen (ed.), Educational research: Innovation in practice. Proceedings of the Australian Association for Research in Education. http://www.swin.edu.au/AARE/conf94.html File YELLN94.429

Yelland, N. J. & Masters, J. E. (1997). Learning mathematics with technology: Young children's understanding of paths and measurement. *Mathematics Education Research Journal, 9* (1), 83–99.

Yelland, N. J. & Masters, J. E. (unpublished manuscript) Rethinking scaffolding in the information age.

Endnotes

[1] D.H. Clements © (1994).

[2] *Investigations in Number, Data and Space.* Palo Alto, CA: Dale Seymour publications.

Chapter 8

"I Always Get Stuck with the Books": Creating Space for Girls to Access Technology in a Software Design Project

Cynthia Carter Ching, Yasmin B. Kafai
& Sue K. Marshall

Creating a Space for Girls in a Classroom Software Design Project

The road toward becoming technologically literate and scientifically competent has been a "leaking pipeline" for girls and women. After the elementary school years, girls feel disenfranchised in science and technology in middle and secondary schools, and at universities fewer female students choose science and engineering majors (Camp, 1997). A variety of explanations have been offered for this trend, ranging from different attitudes toward computers (Shashaani, 1994) and different levels of participation in computer and science courses (Chen, 1985; Linn, 1985), to cultural and social conditions found in science and technological domains (Provenzo, 1991; Sadker & Sadker, 1994) and different representations of women in media publications (Heller, Brade, & Branz, 1994). While each of these variables alone or in combination can influence girls' interactions with computers, we chose to examine girls' access to computer resources in classroom activities. With the increasing use of computers in classrooms, there remains the issue of whether, in fact, all students participate equally and receive equal benefits. We were particularly interested in identifying the kinds of activities and support structures that can be used in helping girls break down barriers to technological access and develop expertise in mixed-gender settings.

Toward that end, we investigated students' activities and collaborations during a three-month-long computer project. In this project mixed-gender teams of fifth and sixth graders used *Microworlds* in their classroom to design multimedia software about an astronomy unit for use by younger children. We paid particular attention to experiences of girls in these mixed-gender teams: a) their access levels to the various technologies used in the software design project at the outset, b) the change in technology access most girls experienced, and c) the factors which might have impacted these changes. In examining this last factor, we outline several support structures which emerged over the course of this project to facilitate more gender-equitable technology access. Finally, we conclude this paper with a discussion of the implications of our findings for developing and maintaining gender equity in the use of educational technology in school contexts.

Background

Many girls are not receiving the same kinds of opportunities to become technologically skilled as boys are (e.g., Wellesley College Center for Research on Women, 1994). Boys develop alliances with computers largely due to their extensive out-of-school computer experiences. Boys are also more likely to attend summer computer camps than girls; more boys than girls have their own computers at home; boys play more video and computer games than girls do, and boys are more likely than girls to see themselves depicted (as male main characters) in these games (Sadker & Sadker, 1994). All these factors relating to amount of experience with computers often have a significant effect on students' attitudes and perceptions. For example, in a survey of high school students, boys had higher ratings than girls regarding positive attitudes toward computers and perceived utility value of computers (Shashaani, 1994).

Gender differences also arise when boys and girls use computers in the school context. Studies have found that when computers are used during class time, boys are more likely to dominate available computer resources (Sadker & Sadker, 1984). In a study which observed mixed-gender dyads of students on computers, girls' attempts to request more computer access from boys often failed (Inkpen, Booth, & Klawe, 1991). Research also showed that boys were also more likely to initiate and maintain control of school computers during non-classroom hours such as lunch time and before or after school (Canada & Brusca, 1991; Kinnear, 1995).

When girls have as much exposure or interactions with computers as boys do, however, gender differences in perceived competence and access tend to disappear (Linn, 1985). In learning situations in which children can work on computers at their own pace and engage with tasks according to their interests and styles, girls tend to be as proficient as boys in programming (Harel, 1991; Kafai, 1995). Ample opportunity for access thus seems to be a crucial aspect in overcoming the disparate access and differences in levels of self-efficacy, as well as finding computational activities that appeal to both genders (Spertus, 1991).

Even when computers are not involved, putting students in mixed-gender teams for collaborative work in academic subjects can result in very different experiences for boys and girls. Research shows that gender is often a strong predictor of status in heterogeneous groups; thus, girls' contributions to group work end up being less valued than boys' (e.g., Cohen, 1994). These interaction patterns sometimes have consequences for girls' ability to make the most out of collaborative work as evidenced by subsequent knowledge assessments (Webb, 1984). Even when academic achievement is not affected by these differences in interaction, girls' self-esteem and interest in the subjects in question may suffer (Wilkinson, Lindow & Ching, 1985).

In an attempt to ensure that girls will have opportunities to become technologically proficient, some researchers and practitioners have taken the approach of providing "female only" environments. Whether this means pro-active technology intervention programs that are exclusively for girls (Martin & Heller, 1994) or forming single-gender collaborative groups in after-school computer clubs (Wood, 1996), the assumption in most cases is that girls will have a more positive experience in the absence of male computer users. While these programs represent important steps in introducing girls to technological activities, we find that eventually girls will have to learn how to negotiate access in mixed-gender settings. Our aim, in this project, was to find out how girls (and boys) might react to the challenge of working with computers and programming in mixed-gender groups in a classroom setting.

One issue we were particularly concerned about was how to measure and track changes in students' levels of participation and access to software design in their collaborative groups. In most previous studies of collaboration, groups of students are engaged in a single task such as solving mathematics problems, learning social studies facts, or learning computer skills in isolation from other subject matters (Johnson & Johnson, 1974; Slavin, 1983; Webb, 1984). In our context, however, making a multimedia encyclopedia requires many different tasks such as programming and research. In contrast to other methods which examine collaborative groups engaged in short-term, isolated tasks (Barnes & Todd, 1977; Cohen, 1982; Webb, 1984), we were interested in documenting participation patterns across multiple activities and a longer time frame.

We wanted to investigate participation in the various software design tasks over the ten-week project timeline and across the whole classroom community. The task of designing software is comprised of several interrelated activities: programming, planning, content research, collaborative team management, and graphical design. Ideally, we hoped that all students would participate in all activities equally. The fact that some of these activities are computer based (programming, graphic design) while others are not, led us to consider that gender might be a factor in students' opportunities to participate in all design components. We hypothesized that there was a distinct possibility that girls might, as in the title of this chapter, "get stuck with the books." Furthermore, as the nature of the design task changed over the course of the project (from initial planning and paper designs to computer implementation), we were also interested to see how students' participation in design would likewise change. Similar patterns of participation change have been documented in out-of-school communities (Lave & Wenger, 1991) and classrooms (Roth, 1995, 1998). These studies, however, have not focused on the important component of computer technology in the classroom, important, particularly, for issues of gender equity.

In this paper we use the metaphor of "space" to examine participation and technology access in the software design project. Here we draw on existing research which has documented how students use the physical space of their classroom while engaged in different kinds of collaborative and individual tasks (Getzels, 1974; Gump, 1974), and how the arrangement of artifacts in physical space impacts students' participation in classroom activities (Roth, 1995; Roth & Bowen, 1995). Other studies on spaces in design have looked at externalized creative spaces in architecture, such as computer-aided design programs or pencil and paper designs, and examined participant interactions around each (Hall & Stevens, 1995; Schon, 1988). In our analysis, we were interested in some similar issues: a) how boys and girls arranged themselves in different workspaces in the physical layout of the classroom, and b) how students used paper or computer-based spaces to display designs in progress. Unlike previous studies, however, we have extended the notion of space to focus not only on artifacts and the physical environment, but we also use "space" as a metaphor to integrate more intangible components of the design environment, such as student social interactions and individual or shared understandings of design plans, into our analysis. It is this integration of multiple perspectives on the design environment, plus our focus on long-term participation patterns for boys and girls, that fuels the story we have to tell.

Methods

Research participants

An integrated class of 26 fifth and sixth grade students participated in this project. There were 10 girls and 16 boys of mixed ethnic background (18 Caucasian; two Hispanic; three African/American; three Asian) ranging between 10 and 12 years of age. Nine students had previous programming experience, either from participation in another design project the previous year (n=8) or from programming at home (n=1). Seventeen students had no programming experience before the start of the project. All the students had used computers in school and were familiar with word-processing packages, graphics software, *Grolier's Multimedia Encyclopedia*, and searches on the Worldwide Web.

Heterogeneous groups of three to four students each were arranged in seven teams according to the following criteria: "experienced" designers who had participated in a previous design project, gender, grade level, and classroom leadership (as indicated by the classroom teacher). Six of these experienced students were boys and three were girls. Students received colored cards representing their particular research criteria and were told to form groups having not more than two of each color. Some students represented more than one category, so groups could not be completely matched across all variables; however, all groups contained a mix of all criteria (see Table 8.1). Our primary goal, in addition to creating mixed-gender teams, was to balance the levels of existing technological knowledge across the groups, so that each collaborative team would contain at least one student who had done some programming previously.

Table 8.1: Composition of all groups

Group 1	Group 2	Group 3	Group 4
5th grade girl 5th grade boy 6th grade boy (lead/exp.)	5th grade girl 5th grade boy 6th grade boy (lead/exp.)	5th grade girl 6th grade girl (exp.) 6th grade boy (lead) 6th grade boy	5th grade boy 5th grade boy 6th grade girl (exp.) 6th grade boy (lead/exp.)
Group 5	**Group 6**	**Group 7**	
5th grade girl 5th grade girl (lead) 5th grade boy 6th grade boy (exp.)	5th grade girl 5th grade boy 6th grade girl (lead/exp.) 6th grade boy (exp.)	5th grade girl 5th grade boy 6th grade boy 6th grade boy (lead/exp.)	

Classroom context

The software project from which our gender study comes is based on the model of 'learning through design,' in which students simultaneously learn new information and design a relevant product reflecting their knowledge (Harel, 1991; Harel & Papert, 1990; Kafai, 1995). The project took place in an urban elementary school that functions as the laboratory school site for UCLA. The participating classroom was equipped with seven computers; one was set up as a workstation at each of seven table clusters. An additional seven computers were in an adjacent room and were used for related Internet searches.

One week before the start of the project, students were given an introduction into the main features of the *Microworlds* Logo programming environment. The assignment was to build an interactive multimedia resource about astronomy for younger students. Over the course of several months students created their own research questions about astronomy, researched these questions using various sources and represented their findings in a group software product. Students worked three to four hours

"I Always Get Stuck with the Books"

per week on the project for a period of 10 weeks. Students spent a total of 46 hours in the learning by design environment, of which 23 hours were dedicated to independent work researching and creating screens in *Microworlds* representing the astronomy information they had learned. The other 23 hours were spent in whole-class activities: science instruction, class discussions about science issues and project logistics, and group presentations.

Final products

All student teams created an multimedia astronomy resource. One team included samples of different screens and animations that were created by the other teams (see Kafai, Ching & Marshall, 1997 for a more detailed analysis of students' final projects). The software for this project opens with a screen which shows three planets, Mercury, Earth, and Venus, revolving around the Sun in constant motion. Pointing and clicking on any of the three planets with the mouse will lead the user to a page showing a graphic (often downloaded from the Internet) and a summary description. Each of the pages contains a button which leads the user back to the introduction page. The introduction page also displays an arrow icon which leads to page 6, the table of contents.

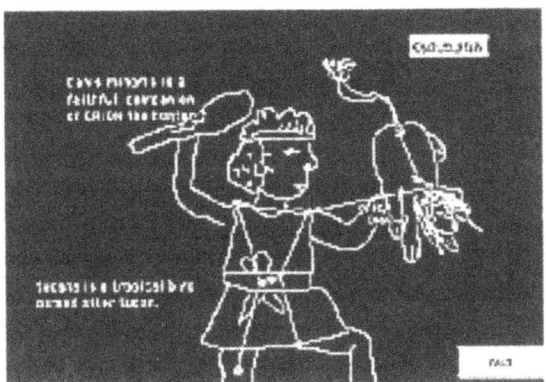

Figure 8.1: A constellation page from Team 3's final product

The table of contents provides a button that leads to a sequence of constellation pages designed by the one girl in the team. One of these is shown in Figure 8.1.

Another link from the table of contents leads to information about the

Saturn V rocket and the operation of rockets. These pages were designed by the two boys in the team. The team also created several incomplete screens about the sun, quasars, and an unfinished game. This combination of information on planets, stars or other celestial bodies and spacecraft represents the variety of knowledge represented in most teams' multimedia encyclopedias.

Student participation

Our aim was to document the developing classroom community and track students' access to the activities which constituted the practice of software design. Collaborative groups were videotaped regularly, and their activities were documented via fieldnotes on a daily basis. Student teams also kept daily reports of their progress in three-ring binders. Each day someone in the group was asked to write down in the "design folder" what each team member had accomplished during that class period. While in professional software design groups, individual activities such as coding or graphical design are usually handled by specifically designated and trained people, in educational software design groups, all students were expected to participate in all activities for their own learning benefits.

We recognized that although various activities in the classroom environment were all necessary for astronomy research and working on the multimedia encyclopedia, these activities afforded very different levels of access to one of the design project goals, one which is particularly important for girls: technological fluency. We were interested in what affordances these project activities had for the following technological fluency goals: (a) that students have access to actually designing and implementing screens in multimedia design, not just thinking about how to implement them; (b) that students experience using computers not only as consumers of software but also as producers; and (c) that students use computational media in conjunction with traditional media such as paper and pencil.

In addition to our own concerns about activities' affordances for fluency development, we found that students themselves had very definite opinions about which activities they preferred. Through observations of student arguments at the beginning of each class over whose turn it was for certain tasks and through discussions with students about access to or lack thereof of particular technologies, it became obvious to us that students viewed certain activities in the design environment as being more desirable than others. Below are two examples of student arguments, transcribed directly from videotapes of group interactions, demonstrating the perceived difference in value of working in *Microworlds* at the computer versus either (a) recording the group's daily progress or (b) researching one's individual astronomy question. The first segment shown takes place between a boy (Mel) and a girl (Christa). The second segment occurred between two boys, Joey and Lyle.

(a)   Recording versus programming

Christa: Who's recorder today? Is Fredo recorder today?
Mel: It's Fredo two times, then me two times, then Elaine.
Christa: Oh, I'm recorder tomorrow.
Mel: No, you're LAST, so you're it *today*. *I'm* programming today.
Christa: But I'm after Elaine.
Mel: Right. I just said,
Christa: Okay, fine.

(b)   Researching versus programming

Lyle: Joey, I have to finish my page.
Joey: Okay, I have to make the thing about the earth and the...moon.
Lyle: Actually you should research on comets. 'Cause that's your...question. Your question isn't, like, "how the moon goes around...the earth." It's "why comets have tails."
Joey: That's not what I'm doing right now.
Lyle: But you have to research on comets' tails!
Joey: I know!
Lyle: Well, do that today. 'Cause you haven't been doing it very...much.
Joey: I'm just pasting this on, so we have a page for all the planets.
Lyle: No, do it today!

We classified in Table 8.2 all the activities we saw students doing on a daily basis according to their affordances for access to the goals outlined above. Activities which used only traditional paper and pencil were viewed as having very little affordance for developing or enriching students' fluency with new technology. Another category was comprised of activities which used computer technology but only that with which students were already familiar. Thus participation in those activities was viewed as having affordances for maintaining a constant level of students' technological fluency but not for challenging them to develop new skills. Finally, the activities in the third group involved students working with computers in ways many had not encountered, thus having the potential to enrich their development of greater technological fluency.

Table 8.2. Activity classification

Enriching Activities	Constancy Activities	Traditional activities
Microworlds programming	*Grolier's Encyclopedia* research	Book corner research
Internet research	*Isaac Asimov* CDs research	Drawing screens on paper
Leading group demonstrations	Word processing	Team progress reports
Teaching others to program	Watching others program	

The students related "desirability" to two facets of the access afforded by the various activities. One aspect of this classification is that the undesirably perceived activities are also "low tech." As activities increase in desirability, they afford more access to computer technology, whether it be consumer applications or creative tools such as *Microworlds*. The second aspect of the classification which seemed to resonate with students was the access afforded by particular activities to "locally novel" resources. *Microworlds* programming and the Internet were the newest components of the classroom environment. They had been added only a few weeks before the start of the project. The other options, for example, books, *Grolier's Multimedia Encyclopedia*, word processing, and worksheets were very familiar to students already.

Using the scheme. In order to document changes in access over time, we selected two time points in the project: one was the third full week of *Microworlds* work, and one was the eighth week of *Microworlds* work. (Recall that the students were engaged in making their multimedia encyclopedias for a total of 10 weeks.) We determined that a week at each time point was needed for coding rather than only a few days due to a concern about all students being represented at multiple times for each data point. We wanted to record students' typical activities during those two phases, not just to document their activities on a single day, which may or may not have been reflective of their usual participation.

Results

In our presentation of results, we discuss first the outcome of descriptive analyses examining boys' and girls' levels of participation at week 3 and week 8 in project activities with varying affordances for developing tech-

technological fluency. Second, we present qualitative findings on trends in boys' and girls' participation patterns throughout the project duration, as seen through the metaphor of different "spaces" within the design environment. This second take on our results not only represents another perspective but also offers some rationales for why and how participation changes took place.

Gender and access

At the first time point, girls' average participation in traditional activities was more frequent than boys', and they were performing fewer fluency-enriching activities than boys; however, boys' and girls' participation in technological constancy activities was fairly equitable. By the eighth week, the differences between boys and girls on traditional and enriching activities appeared to even out. Additionally, the frequency of participation in constancy activities decreased across the board for boys and girls. These results seem to suggest that constancy activities somehow became obsolete or did not require as much time as the project progressed. If we consider that three of the constancy activities, word processing, *Grolier's* research, and *Asimov* CD research, all have to do with obtaining information about research questions and writing up that information in students' own words in order to design their simulations, these results make sense. Most students conducted their research during the first half of the project and spent the remaining time planning and implementing their designs and/or helping others. The change in participation we see in constancy activities, then, was most likely affected by order of events in the project progression and not gender or other collaborative dynamics.

Girls did appear to participate less in activities affording technological fluency at week 3 and participate more at week 8. The sort of changes that took place across the classroom as a whole suggests that gender played an important role in students' initial activity participation but that these gender differences did not remain constant throughout the ten weeks. There is another story to be told here, however, and that is the story of *how* these changes in participation took place. The transition from a gender-biased distribution of labor to one that was more equitable was neither easy nor spontaneous; it required significant interventions by researchers and the classroom teacher. While the absence of a control group in our design does not allow us to argue for a causal relationship between these interventions in various "spaces" within the classroom and subsequent changes in girls' activity patterns, our particular experience with attempting to alter significant design spaces for gender equity purposes provides an interesting chapter to the ongoing efforts to address gender and technology in the classroom. What those "spaces" were, how they were altered, and subsequent changes we observed will be discussed in the following sections.

Spaces for change

Our findings for the third week, that girls were typically participating in fewer programming-related activities, are reflective of several phenomena: some girls actively decided not to begin programming right away and focused more on research or graphics first, others gave in to more aggressive boys in their teams who insisted on working on the computer first, and still others seemed to wander aimlessly without a clear conception of how to approach the project. None of these things were particularly surprising, given the existing literature on gender and technology.

During the fourth and fifth weeks of the design project, however, we observed that patterns of access to particular technologies, design tasks, and group decision-making during this time seemed to be remaining fairly constant, although we had anticipated that shifts would occur gradually as more girls gained skills and knowledge of software design. Fieldnotes and video from those weeks reveal several phenomena which point to incongruity between girls' readiness and/or desire to program and their levels of access: (a) researcher conversations with girls in which girls complained of a lack of computer access; (b) group arguments over whose turn it was to work in *Microworlds* each day (see previous examples of student arguments); and (c) software demonstrations sessions in which girls revealed that despite having gathered research information, they did not have much *Microworlds* work to share due to limited programming time.

In hopes of facilitating shifts in group participation patterns, we added two features to the software design project: 1) regular group meetings mediated by the classroom teacher, and 2) a different physical configuration of computers designated for programming. We refer to the process of altering the classroom design studio as "creating spaces" on the social and physical planes of the environment. Within these "spaces," girls (and some boys as well) found contexts which were more compatible with their own ways of interacting, working, and thinking than they had encountered in the initial structure of the design environment.

Social Space. The addition of the "social space" of regular group meetings was in response to specific problems we saw happening between boys and girls in their daily interactions. We witnessed girls trying to discuss interpersonal problems within teams right away when they arose, while boys focused on getting computer work finished and would keep right on working, ignoring or not attempting to resolve personal conflicts. These findings are consistent with existing research which shows that when mixed-gender groups of students engage in collaborative computer work, boys' and girls' efforts and interest tend to be divided in favor of technology versus group orchestration, respectively (Fredricks, Blumenfeld, & Bass, 1997). After observing boys and girls having trouble communicating for several weeks, we saw a need for a specific "space" on the social plane of the design project which could be an appropriate time and place to deal with conflicts in a safe and monitored environment.

Our solution was to create group meetings which were mediated by either the classroom teacher or a researcher. These meetings occurred approximately once every 10 days. Students were told that each person in the group would have a chance to say what was bothering them, and then the whole group would address each issue. We found that while we had initially instituted the sessions to ensure that girls would be listened to by boys in airing their complaints about access, boys also had many issues they needed to address. Research suggests that when educators attend to the needs of girls in the classroom, the resulting changes are usually better for girls *and* boys (Wellesley College Center for Research on Women, 1994). The addition of an official time to talk about group conflicts seemed to make boys more comfortable and not as worried about "wasting" computer time on interpersonal issues. We observed many boys open up and discuss issues they were concerned about such as Internet use for legitimate research versus "surfing" for fun, ownership and piracy of ideas, and accusations of "goofing off." Thus, although the "social space" of group meeting time was initially created as a place to address girls' concerns, boys benefited from this development as well.

One of the outcomes of these meetings which seemed to have the strongest relation to girls' attainment of access to more advanced technologies was that all groups established a computer schedule. These schedules detailed who would work on *Microworlds* programming and research on the Internet each day. The transcript below contains an excerpt from one of these group meetings, in which Kari, the only girl in group 7, complains of a lack of access. Consequently, the classroom teacher helps the group make a computer schedule. (This is also the session that inspired the title of this chapter.)

Kari:	I need some information on planets, so I have to be on the computer.
Lyle:	It'd be better not to go through the trouble of looking on the Internet and just look in the books.
Kari:	I always get stuck with the books.
Teacher:	You know, I don't want Kari to get relegated to the books and you guys be on the computer, because that's happened a bit.
Kari:	I've never gone on the Internet.
Lyle:	Yeah, you were on the Internet yesterday.
Kari:	For the first time!
Dan:	No, you have more than that.
Teacher:	Would you guys agree that she hasn't been on the computer as much as you guys have?
Lyle:	Yeah.
Joey:	Mostly, I guess.
Teacher:	Okay, so what we need to do is make up a schedule, and Kari needs to have time. You need to keep track of who's on the computer on what day.

Video records and fieldnotes revealed that after the first round of group meetings, girls were more often working at their groups' computers. Most boys and girls also reported to researchers during the next few weeks that there were fewer conflicts in their groups after the meetings.

Physical Space. Although computer schedules created in the social space of group meetings ensured that girls received equal access to the physical artifact of the computer itself, we discovered that schedules did not ensure equal participation in programming. Students saved their work in *Microworlds* under new file names with new dates every time they worked, so researchers could keep track of how much work was accomplished on a given day. By examining students' log files, we observed that when girls had opportunities to work at the computer workstations, they often did not accomplish as much as the boys in the same amount of time.

Fieldnotes and video records from the classroom revealed that unlike boys' typically independent work styles, girls frequently shared their new work with friends and left their seats to view one another's screens. Group stations were spread throughout the classroom, making it difficult for students in different teams to communicate with one another without getting up and walking away from their own computers. Figure 8.2 shows three girls from different teams (standing) gathered around one workstation to view the animation created by another female designer (seated). Based on existing research which argues that segregated workstations tend not to appeal to girls, and they prefer a work style characterized by more social networking (Canada and Brusca, 1991), we hypothesized that girls' lack of productivity at the computer might be partially attributable to the "physical space" of the classroom workstations.

At the beginning of the project there were seven additional computers in the adjacent lab, but these were designated for Internet searches and other research only; students were supposed to program in *Microworlds* at their groups' workstations inside the classroom. During the sixth week of the project, however, four girls began "breaking the rules" and appropriating the laboratory computers for *Microworlds* work.

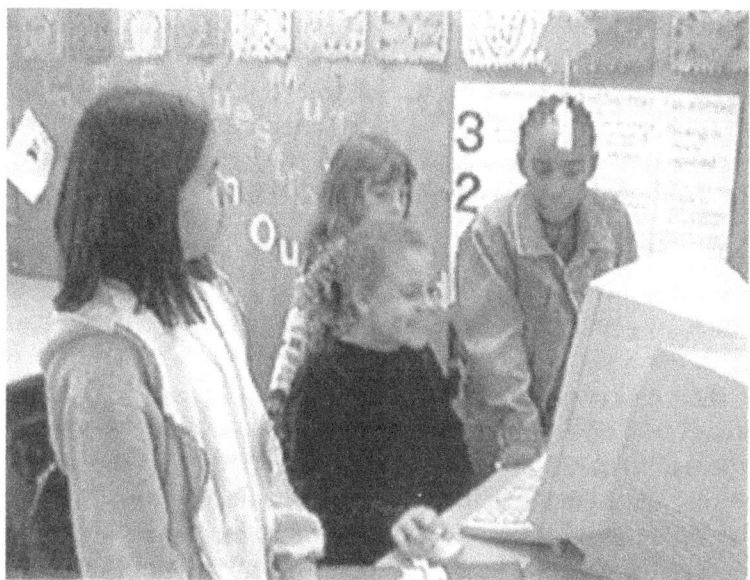

Figure 8.2: Girls from different teams examining software designs

These girls regularly moved files back and forth from lab computers to group workstations via file sharing or floppy disks. The physical space of the lab was such that computers were lined up in rows right next to each other along the walls rather than being spread out; we wondered if this arrangement made a difference. We were curious to see what effect this new physical space might have on more girls (and most students had finished the research phase of their work anyway), so we opened up the lab for regular *Microworlds* use. Changes took place almost immediately. Rather than waiting to have their activity directed by other group members, the teacher, or researchers, as was often previously the case, many girls grabbed their floppy disks and headed off to the lab on a daily basis with a long list of things they wanted to accomplish on their own.

Creating a new "space" on the physical plane of the design environment in which to do programming afforded boys and girls different options for how to work and help one another. Most boys worked at the isolated group workstations, which were spread out across the classroom and would call one another over for help with specific problems. All but two girls and two boys, on the other hand, worked collaboratively and used the space in the adjacent computer lab. We observed these students talking and giving programming/design advice by glancing over at one another's screens while they were all working together. This arrangement seemed to encourage those involved to stay on-task longer and develop innovative ideas to be shared with the rest of the community. These findings are consistent with existing research which shows that motivation and achievement are higher among girls in peer groups with similar mindsets and goals (Fredricks & Alfeld-Lo, 1997).

Cognitive Space. Finally, another space in the design project environment is "cognitive space." The cognitive arena of the project refers to two kinds of planning, one shared and one individual. Shared planning refers to the ways in which student teams negotiated how they would make their multimedia software. We provided students with a space in which to make their shared plans explicit and a team notebook containing the daily reports described earlier and space for other plans. We found that the contents of these shared planning notebooks were very similar across groups. For the most part, student teams did not include anything in the way of screen designs, astronomy notes, or Logo ideas in these notebooks. In fact, they usually did not contain anything other than an archive of the teams' daily reports, and plans recorded here mostly related to division of labor and allocation of technology resources within groups. We had hoped that the group notebooks could be a place for groups to document and deal with issues of astronomy research, screen ideas, and programming hints as well as division of labor. Interestingly, once group meetings were established, these issues were dealt with in that social space instead. Thus the most effective shared cognitive space seemed to be "in the air" during students' structured conversations rather than on paper.

The individual level of planning involves the students' cognitive negotiation between their own ideas for contributions to their team's multimedia product and their conceptions of project parameters, deadlines, and available resources. The space provided for individual planning took the form of individual "designer's notebooks" where students could record their ideas, plans, and progress, thus making that negotiation explicit. The notebooks were designated for individual use and were in addition to the shared team notebooks discussed above. Planning within the cognitive space of the designer's notebook did not take into account issues of access and management of limited technological resources; it was only focused on the individual designer's ideas and goals. Contents of the individual notebooks varied widely among students. Some of the kinds of planning students documented in their individual notebooks included notes from science instruction, screen designs, Logo code ideas and helpful hints, project calendars with important deadlines, and printouts from information resources about particular astronomy topics. Other students, however, did not seem to use their individual notebooks very much. Interestingly, we found that some girls used their individual notebooks a great deal during the time when they were accumulating ideas for screens but not implementing them for whatever reason. Thus, when they obtained *Microworlds* access, either through negotiating turns at group workstations or programming in the lab, they drew more heavily on the plans contained in the cognitive space of their individual notebooks.

Discussion and Implications

In our discussion of results, we will address several issues which arise from the findings. First, what is the significance of the "spaces" that were created? Why were they effective? And second, what suggestions do our findings offer in terms of directions for future research? Finally, what are the implications of our findings for the ways we think about current trends in educational technology and research on gender and computers? Each of these questions will be addressed in turn in the following sections.

Negotiating "spaces" in multimedia design

In our view, the spaces that we examined in the classroom environment are more than interventions to increase girls' access; they represent a way of conceptualizing three kinds of negotiation that occur in the multimedia design process. In the social arena of collaborative teams, designers attempt to create shared understanding within their groups. Designers must negotiate between their own goals and ideas for the astronomy software and those of their team members, which is not an easy task. The addition of a specific space designated for conflict resolution moved this negotiation from being an implicit necessity to being an explicit goal. In the physical space of the classroom and its computer configurations, designers negotiate between their preferences and ideal working conditions, whether they be collaborative or independent, and the options afforded them by the physical environment. Adding another computer configuration allowed some girls a "better fit" between their apparent preferences and the available options. And finally, the cognitive space of the individual and team design notebooks allowed students to draw a line separating their planning negotiations with team members from their own individual plans for multimedia pages, a division which may have been helpful in compensating for initial gender differences in access to programming. Looking at the project environment through the lenses of cognitive, physical, and social spaces proved to be a useful exercise for thinking about activity in these arenas. We did not actually *create* the cognitive, physical, and social "spaces" in the design project; they were present from the outset. We merely altered the configuration of two of these spaces to allow for different ways of negotiating the terrain of software design than were afforded previously.

Directions for Future Research

One of the most important points emphasized in this study deals with accounting of how students work in collaborative groups in actual classroom environments when there is more than one activity going on at the same time. In the design project discussed here, it was important to examine all the activities students could be engaged with according to their affordances: affordances for novel technology use, affordances for fun and interest as reflected in student desirability, and affordances for access to the practice of software design. This study represents an important step in going beyond the typical computer/no-computer distinctions in gender and technology research to look at what different computer applications girls and boys were using in a multi-task environment. Our future research will take the next step and look at *how* boys and girls are using the resources they have at their disposal, not just which resources they are using. For example, it would be interesting to know what sorts of programming girls and boys are doing in *Microworlds* on a daily basis, not just whether or not they are using *Microworlds* at all. Additionally, efforts are currently underway to look at the division of labor in creating final multimedia products and the different tasks (for example, when creating graphics, animation, sound, and audio) that boys and girls may undertake in their groups when working with *Microworlds* of other software design tools.

Implications

In talking about the implications our findings have for gender and technology research, we want to return to two of the driving forces behind our investigation: 1) the low level of women's participation in computer science and related fields and 2) the issue of girls' access to technology in classroom communities. The extent to which girls learn to use cutting-edge technology and become participants in software design, or other computer communities will be influenced by experiences that they have had early in their school lives.

Lave and Wenger (1991) argue that, "understanding the technology of a practice is more than learning to use tools; it is a way to connect with the history of the practice and to participate more directly in its cultural life" (p. 101). Girls' access to full participation in software design or other similar activities is thus important not so much because they learn isolated computer skills (which may or may not become obsolete eventually) but rather because participation affords girls a way to connect with the male-dominated practice of software design. Previous intervention models such as science and technology after-school programs and summer camps that reach out to females in high schools and colleges, while important, may be situated too late in development, considering that girls form many beliefs about themselves and their relationship to science and technology at a much younger age (Kahle & Meece, 1992). For that reason we propose to provide younger girls with opportunities to interact with advanced technologies and science in substantial ways.

A related issue is the emphasis we place on children as producers, rather than strictly consumers of computer software (Kafai, 1995). Our findings suggest that while the software industry is beginning to create products for girls as software consumers, the idea of girls aged 10 to 12, as software *designers* is still unusual and/or unexpected. The fact that gender was so strongly related to initial participation in fluency enriching (or "high tech") activities in our study is of particular interest, because it suggests that even at a young age, children's actions with respect to classroom technology are very gender biased, another argument for the early positioning of interventions mentioned above. The change in access most girls experienced, however, shows that these behavior patterns are not immutable in a supportive environment.

We need to examine new developments in education and technology and consider their implications for how we think about gender and computer use. Computers no longer reside solely in a distant laboratory with few if any ties to other classroom activities (Kafai, 1995). Recent developments in technology and education include computers as vital components of long-term, multifaceted projects in the classroom (Blumenfeld, Soloway, Marx, Krajcik, Guzdial, & Palincsar, 1991). If girls have limited access to computer resources in integrated classroom settings, they not only miss out on the opportunity to develop technological fluency, but they also risk missing out on learning other subject matters mediated by computer use as well. In our project, which was designed to provide students with creative and innovative opportunities, girls' initial computer work consisted mostly of word processing and consumer-based use of software encyclopedias. But observing the initial inequality in technology access per se is not the surprising issue; given that some boys in our project had different technology experience to begin with, one would expect such differences. What is important is that these inequalities did not persist throughout the project. Organizers of technology-rich activities such as software design in classrooms need to recognize that individual students, boys and girls, may have different levels of access to and interactions with technology. What is important to realize is that participation patterns can and should change as the project moves toward completion. Project-based collaborative groups have the potential to be adaptive, dynamic systems; our study demonstrates that researchers and teachers need to take an active role in helping students realize that potential.

Finally, our research provides support for the argument that we are reaching a point in gender and technology research where the issue may no longer be about *if* girls are using the computer but rather *how* are they using it. Through creating new spaces in the design environment, we were able to provide opportunities for girls to gain technology access. We argue that such measures are necessary to facilitate girls' development of their own identities as participant members not only in the classroom computer community, but also in the technological community at large.

Acknowledgments

The research reported here was supported by grants from the Urban Education Studies Center at UCLA and the National Science Foundation (REC-9632695) to the second author. Manuscript preparation was partially supported by a pre-doctoral research fellowship from the National Institute of Mental Health. We thank the teacher, Cathie Galas, and her science class at Corrine Seeds University Elementary School for their participation. We also thank Aimee Dorr, Noreen Webb, Sherry Hsi, Wolff-Michael Roth, and the editors, Nicola Yelland and Andee Rubin, for their helpful and insightful comments. An earlier version of this chapter appeared as an article in *Journal of Science, Education, and Technology*.

References

Barnes, D. & Todd, F. (1977). *Communication and learning in small groups.* London: Routledge & Kegan Paul.
Blumenfeld, P., Soloway, E., Marx, R., Krajcik, J., Guzdial, M. & Palincsar, A. (1991). Motivating project-based learning: Sustaining the doing, supporting the learning. *Educational Psychologist, 26,* 369–398.
Camp, T. (1997). The incredible shrinking pipeline. *Communications of the ACM, 40* (10).
Canada, K. & Brusca, F. (1991). The technological gender gap: Evidence and recommendations for educators and computer-based instruction designers. *Educational Technology Research & Development, 39* (2), 43–51.
Chen, M. (1985). Gender differences in adolescents' uses of and attitudes toward computers. In M. L. McLaughlin (ed.), *Communication Yearbook 10* (pp. 200–216). Beverly Hills, CA: Sage.
Cohen, E. G. (1994). Restructuring the classroom: Conditions for productive small groups. *Review of Educational Research, 64,* 1–35.

Cohen, E. G. (1982). Expectation states and interracial interaction in school settings. *Annual Review of Sociology, 8,* 109–235.

Fredricks, J. & Alfeld-Lo, C. (1997). The right kind of socialization goes a long way with girls: Path analyses of gender differences in tenth grade science learning. Paper presented at the annual meeting of the American Educational Research Association, Chicago, IL., 1997.

Fredricks, J., Blumenfeld, P., & Bass, K. (1997). The relationship between motivation, thoughtfulness, and group processes: An exploration of gender in project based science classrooms. Paper presented at the annual meeting of the American Educational Research Association, Chicago, IL.

Getzels, J. W. (1974). Images of the classroom and visions of the learner. *School Review, 82* (4), 527–540.

Gump, P. V. (1974). Operating environments in schools of open and traditional design. *School Review, 82* (4), 575–594.

Hall, R. & Stevens, R. (1995). Making space: A comparison of mathematical work in school and professional design practices. In S. L. Starr (ed.), *The cultures of computing.* (pp.118–145). Oxford, UK: Blackwell Publishers.

Harel, I. (1991). *Children designers.* Norwood, NJ: Ablex.

Harel, I. & Papert, S. (1991). Software design as a learning environment. In I. Harel & S. Papert (eds.), *Constructionism.* (pp. 42–84). Norwood, NJ: Ablex.

Heller, R. S., Brade, K., & Branz, C. (1994). The representation of women and minorities in print media. *GATES, 1*(2), 1–8.

Inkpen, K., Booth, K., & Klawe, M. (1991). *Cooperative learning in the classroom: The importance of a collaborative environment for computer-based education.* EGEMS Technical Report. University of British Columbia.

Johnson, D. & Johnson, R. (1974). Instructional goal structure: cooperative, competitive, or individualistic. *Review of Educational Research, 44,* 337–343.

Kafai, Y. (1995). *Minds in play: Computer game design as a context for children's learning.* Hillsdale, NJ: Erlbaum.

Kafai, Y. B., Ching, C. C., & Marshall, S. (1997). Children as designers of educational multimedia software. *Computers & Education, 29,* 117–126.

Kahle, J. B. & Meece, J. (1994) Research on gender issues in the classroom. In Gabel, D. (ed.) *Handbook of research on science teaching and learning.* New York: Macmillan.

Kinnear, A. (1995). Introduction of microcomputers: A case study of patterns of use and children's perceptions. *Journal of Educational Computing Research, 13,* 27–40.

Lave, J. & Wenger, E. (1991). *Situated learning: Legitimate peripheral participation.* New York: Cambridge University Press.

Linn, M. C. (1985). Fostering equitable consequences from computer learning environments. *Sex Roles, 13* (3/4), 229–240.

Marshall, S. & Kafai, Y. B. (1997). Children's conceptions of project management: Issues of change and transfer over time. Poster presented at the annual meeting of the American Educational Research Association, Chicago, IL.

Martin, D. & Heller, R. (1994). Bringing young minority women to computers and science: Developing intervention programmes that work. *Gates, 1,* 4–13.

Provenzo, L. (1991). *Videokids.* Cambridge, MA: Harvard University Press.

Roth, W. M. (1995). Inventors, copycats, and everyone else: The emergence of shared resources and practices as defining aspects of classroom communities. *Science Education, 79,* 475–502.

Roth, W. M. (1998). *Designing Community.* Kluwer Academic Press.

Roth, W. M. & Bowen, G. M. (1995). Knowing and interacting: A study of culture, practices, and resources in a grade 8 open-inquiry science classroom guided by a cognitive apprenticeship metaphor. *Cognition and Instruction, 13,* 73–128.

Sadker, M. & Sadker, D. (1984). *Year 3: Final report, Promoting effectiveness in classroom instruction.* Washington, DC: National Institute of Education.

Sadker, M. & Sadker, D. (1994). *Failing at fairness: How our schools cheat girls.* New York: Touchstone Press.

Sanders, J. (1988). Computer equity for girls. In A. Carelli (ed.), *Sex equity in education: Readings and strategies.* Springfield, IL: Charles C. Thomas.

Schon, D. (1988). Towards a marriage of artistry & applied science in the architectural design studio. *Journal of Architecture and Education, 41* (4), 4–10.

Shashaani, L. (1994). Gender differences in computer experience and its influence on computer attitudes. *Journal of Educational Computing Research, 11* (4), 347–367.

Slavin, R. (1983). When does cooperative learning increase student achievement? *Psychological Bulletin, 94,* 429–445.

Spertus, E. (1991). *Why are there so few female computer scientists?* MIT Artificial Intelligence Laboratory, Technical Report #1315, Cambridge, MA.

Webb, N. (1984). Sex differences in interaction and achievement in cooperative small groups. *Journal of Educational Psychology, 76,* 33–44.

Webb, N. (1984). Microcomputer learning in small groups: Cognitive requirements and group processes. *Journal of Educational Psychology, 76,* 1076–1088.

Wellesley College Center for Research on Women. (1994). *How schools shortchange girls: The AAUW report.* New York: Marlow & Company.

Wilkinson, L. C., Lindow, J., & Chaing, C. (1985). Sex differences and sex segregation in students' small-group communication. In L. C. Wilkinson & C. B. Marret (eds.), *Gender influences in classroom interaction.* New York: Academic Press.

Wood, J. (1996). *Adolescent girls, creative expression, and technology: Lessons from Boston's Computer Clubhouse.* Paper presented at the annual meeting of the American Educational Research Association, New York, 1994.

Chapter 9

Tia and the Virtual Expert

Michele Evard

Traditionally, elementary school classroom activities do not encourage or support collaboration (e.g., Webb, 1985). Children tend to work individually on assignments, tasks that have been designed to assess the students' mastery of predefined material. In such a context, the teacher is the source of all knowledge, and controls if and when information is transmitted to students. Students are allowed to ask questions of the teacher, but rarely are they allowed to obtain task-related information from their peers. Students who choose to talk to one another during freer periods generally confine their interactions to a small group of friends of the same gender (AAUW, 1992). When allowed to ask a question of other students, boys restrict themselves to male friends, and girls to female friends, severely limiting the possible exchanges (Evard, 1996a; Webb & Palincsar, 1995).

This research project to be described in this chapter studied the impact of a local school network on fifth-grade students' learning and interactions when they were allowed to use it to seek out and contribute information for their own purposes. I designed an online system (Evard, 1998; Kortekaas, 1994) that provided opportunities for fourth- and fifth-grade children to ask questions and share ideas in a publically accessible computerized arena. The students could use the system to read and write messages at any time when they had computer access. At no time were they *required* to read or write anything. Over the course of the project, the online system became a *Virtual Expert* for the classroom, as the group of students was transformed from a collection of individuals into an entity that served as "resident experts" for the group. This transformation happened through use of the online system that made each message available to all the participants. It was more than another way of connecting students directly to one another. Instead, each person was connected to the new entity and could choose how and when to interact with other students through the system.

Students could ask questions of the *Virtual Expert* at any time and could contribute information when they had time and knowledge. Additionally, each student had some connection with each question that was asked. Students working on similar projects are likely to face similar problems at different times and therefore frequently have information that could help others. Several students could also be thinking about related issues and could provide multiple perspectives for their peers. In this respect, each child knew that the questions had been asked because the questioner wanted to *use* the answer. Responses were thus of practical use to other students. This is very different from a traditional school activity in which children often answer questions devoid of context, on a worksheet that is only seen by the teacher.

As students interacted with and through the *Virtual Expert*, they learned about seeking and providing help to and from each other. They also had the opportunity to volunteer their assistance to classmates, going beyond the limits of their previous classroom roles. In this way, students could view themselves and their classmates as experts. This chapter recounts the story of a girl named Tia and her interactions in the *Virtual Expert* community to illustrate some of the possibilities for growth as an individual within a learning community.

A Theoretical Framework

The theory of constructionism builds on Piaget's theory of constructivism (Papert, 1980, 1993). In constructivism, Piaget asserts that a learner builds knowledge: rather than passively receiving information, each learner constructs his own intellectual structures. Constructionism further states that the creation of personal knowledge structures is facilitated by construction of an object that can be shared with others. While creating an object of her own design, a child will frequently need new information and will therefore seek knowledge "for a recognizable personal purpose" (Papert, 1980). According to the theory, a significant portion of the value of making external objects is due to the opportunity for sharing such public creations. Things "in the world" can be "shown, discussed, examined, probed, and admired" (Papert, 1993). A learner who shows her creation to others can obtain a deeper understanding of it through other people's perspectives on the object and on the ideas to which it is related. Further refinement of the object may then be desirable.

The focus of this research was on interactions between children who are engaged in constructionist projects of their own design. Other learning theorists and educators have dealt with interactions between students and experts; their ideas have been applied in various and different ways.

Vygotsky (1978) concentrated his studies of cognitive development on the effects of social interaction. He defined the zone of proximal development as "the distance between the actual developmental level as determined by independent problem solving and the level of potential development as determined through problem solving under adult guidance or in collaboration with more capable peers" (p. 86). According to his theory, learning occurs when a person does something that is in this zone just beyond her actual developmental level. Rogoff (1990) described this view of learning by saying that when a learner is aided by an expert to do something slightly beyond his competence, the joint activity allows the learner to internalize the processes the expert has shared with him. The learner can then use these processes independently.

Educators who have used Vygotsky's constructs speak about the expert's assistance as scaffolding: the expert provides support for the learner to reach a goal that she could not attain without aid but does not entirely take over for the learner.

The idea of Vygotskian scaffolding fits well into a school model of learning in which children are working on projects or solving problems. The teacher can be the expert and aid students when they need assistance. Each child's zone of proximal development is different, however, so each one needs individualized attention and information. This can often require a significant amount of time on the part of the teacher.

Although scaffolding is most often spoken of as occurring between an expert and a novice, there is no reason why peers cannot provide this form of support for each other. No two people have exactly the same knowledge at any point in time; it is logical, then, that one child might know something which another child needs to know and vice versa.

Other research projects (e.g., Daiute & Dalton, 1993; Kafai & Harel, 1991) have had similar goals. For example, in order to allow students to act as resources for one another, some teachers and researchers have grouped students in peer teaching and collaborative learning projects in the classes. However, due to a number of varied factors, such as the gender composition of the group, the extent to which these assigned groups can facilitate problem solving is often limited. The goal of the *Virtual Expert* project was to allow all students to participate as they deemed appropriate rather than assigning them to groups. To achieve this, a computer-based system was used.

A broadcast-based communications environment on a computer network allows everyone involved to read all messages, including statements, questions, and answers. The nature of the environment can help eliminate redundancy of topics since all messages can be read, and students are aware of what has previously been discussed. People with similar problems or concerns are able to locate each other through online messages, and if desired and appropriate, they can then speak face to face. Multiple responses to a message can provide disparate viewpoints or problem-solving strategies; the different perspectives can also be discussed in this environment of collaboration around ideas. Participants in such an environment have the opportunity to share their expertise in particular areas, gaining a measure of appreciation in the community.

The Hennigan School, a public elementary school located in one of Boston's lower socioeconomic neighborhoods, hosts Project Headlight (Papert, 1993), where constructionist projects can be studied. In Project Headlight, there are approximately one hundred IBM personal computers available to students in fifteen classrooms. There are two computers in each classroom, but most of the computers are located in four circles in the common area shared by all the classrooms. Computer time is scheduled so that each class has access to the machines for at least four 50-minute sessions per week. Most teachers assign the students programming projects in Logo; these projects are often connected to topics being studied in the classroom and last from four to six weeks. At times, a teacher will conduct a Game Design Project (Kafai, 1995), in which fourth- or fifth-grade students spend four months or more designing and implementing educational video games for younger students. On occasions, word processing assignments are given.

In one study a group of 19 children in an advanced fifth grade class were observed over the course of their five-month Game Design project. The length of this study was critical for understanding how the students interacted with the online system and how its use affected their interactions with one another.

Each of the nineteen students in this classroom chose to participate in the online environment. Every child in the class wrote at least one message and connected to the online system on at least three occasions. All together, they wrote 164 messages during 51 programming sessions (50-minute class periods). Their messages fell into six broad categories: questions about Logo and their projects (52); restated questions, which a student felt had not been answered sufficiently (15); answers to questions (73); informative posts that were not direct replies to online questions (2); miscellaneous messages, including empty messages and other errors (18) and test messages that the students posted while learning about the online system (4). Of the messages written by students, 87% were directly about the game design projects. In addition to the students' messages, the teacher and I wrote twenty messages: fifteen answers, four informational messages, and one miscellaneous message.

The students were allowed to use the *Virtual Expert* at any time they wished. Often they chose to do so when they had questions or when they wanted to take a short break from their current programming. Most of the questions happened early in the projects or when a student was beginning a new section of her program. On many occasions, a child would refer back to the answer someone else had received instead of posting a new question. During the course of such a project, there are lulls in the number of questions asked, and thus there were lulls in the amount of time spent with the *Virtual Expert*. There were times when a student knew how to do what s/he needed to do and spent many sessions doing so. This was not a failure of the *Virtual Expert* system but the nature of a long-term project. Indeed, the pattern of activity in a *Virtual Expert* can help a teacher identify times when students are simply implementing or repeating things they already know how to do. There were also fewer questions about new information addressed to the teacher at such times, although there were more questions about how to fix problems in programs. This type of question generally required in-person assistance from an adult and were hard to ask online.

During the course of this project, an important change in behavior was observed in many of the students: instead of behaving online as they did in the classroom, they were able to break out of those roles. In particular, some children who were generally considered not helpful, either due to attitude or ability, chose to answer many questions that their peers asked in the online environment. The case of one girl in particular illustrates how the *Virtual Expert* system provided an opportunity for children to break out of prior roles.

Tia's Story

Tia was a loud and independent girl in her advanced-work fifth-grade classroom. Although she was in the middle of the age range, she was taller than most of her classmates and stood out in the crowd. The students had been together since the beginning of fourth grade, but Tia did not have any particular friends or followers. She told me that she did not interact with many children her age outside of school hours. At home with her Jamaican father and her stepmother, Tia was not allowed out of their apartment on her own due to problems in their neighborhood. She spent many weekends with her African-American mother, who was recovering from a drug addiction. While at her mother's apartment, Tia was very happy to have access to a computer with an encyclopedia software package.

According to her teacher, Tia was intelligent but had been diagnosed with a learning disability. Her reading skills were tested as being at the third-grade level, and she seemed uninterested in writing. When she did write, her teachers felt that even though her writing skills were improving, her ideas would benefit from elaboration and clarification. Her math skills were more advanced than her reading skills; she scored at the sixth-grade level in math, and she participated more actively in math class than in other curriculum areas. Her observed computer skills were not as advanced as those of most of the other students' in her class.

As the students began their fifth-grade year, their teacher felt that Tia would not be very active in a community of learners who assisted one another. In the classroom, Tia did not request help from other students, and they in turn did not approach her for aid either. One reason for the lack of interaction might have been that Tia appeared disinterested in school activities and distant from the other students. The teacher believed that Tia's independent attitude would make her uninterested in asking or answering questions, while at the same time her lack of skills might cause her to be afraid to participate in a collaborative environment.

A few weeks after the online system was made available, however, Tia was observed spending a significant amount of time reading messages and replying to them online or in person. Tia had sufficient skills to read the online messages, and although she was not always able to understand or answer the questions, she chose to reply to many of them. Other students recognized that she was answering questions, and many of them reported that she had helped them. Thus Tia was able to take advantage of certain aspects of the online system to shed her previous role and become a helpful member of her classroom community. Although she was not the only student to undergo such a change, she provided a most striking case due to her low initial communication skills.

Tia over time

Tia originally intended to create a math game about mathematics that would consist of 3 levels each for questions about addition, subtraction, multiplication, and division (Table 9.1). Her plans were characteristic of what is often called a top-down or planner's approach (Turkle & Papert, 1991). She detailed the entire project, dividing tasks into modules. She followed her plan throughout her project, making some changes as necessary but still working on one section at a time. Other students took the opposite approach, referred to as bottom-up or bricolage (Turkle & Papert, 1991), and allowed their projects to emerge; they, too, might have begun with their title screens. They did not restrict themselves to writing pre-planned sub-tasks. Instead, they would see how they liked what they tried out and follow what was most interesting from their own work or others. A mixture of these two approaches can be seen in some students to varying degrees (Kafai, 1995).

Tia's participation in the group was closely related to her progress in her game. She had no questions during the first two phases, since she was using knowledge she had learned during previous projects. During Phase 2, when the online system was first available, Tia read messages but did not reply or send her own. The first few sessions she logged in once, read several messages, and logged out. From then on, she chose to sit at a pair of computers each day so that she would have one for programming and one for the online system. When I asked her why, she said that way she could always have the online system ready if she needed it or had time to read messages.

Tia's third game phase involved designing and implementing a mechanism for selecting a level and took place during Sessions 8 through 16. The method Tia chose required that she learn several new concepts at this time. Once she decided what she needed to learn about, Tia turned to the online system and began asking questions; she did not ask an adult or classmate for help. She knew that she could use something called "colorunder" but was uncertain how to do so, so she posted her first question during Session 8.

> Subject: Color Under
> Does anybody know how to use Color Under?
> Tia J.

Table 9.1: Tia's main game phases. Sessions are numbered from the first day of the Game Design project. The online system became available during session 4.

Phase	Session #s	Game Content
1	1–4	Title screen, graphics.
2	4–8	Main screen, layout and graphics.
3	8–16	Main screen, selection mechanism for type of questions.
4	16–33	Addition questions: graphics then response selection mechanism, four sets of 4 problems; difficulty increasing from set to set.
5	34–40	Subtraction questions.
6	41–46	Multiplication questions.
7	47–49	Division questions.
8	49–50	Design and implementation of the beginning of a new game.
9	51–53	Completion of her original game, fixing bugs.

Obviously Tia left out many details that readers would want to know. Her writing skills allowed her to ask a question, but she did not have sophisticated questioning skills. Her second posted question was a clarification of her first. In this message, written during Session 11, she explained what she had already learned and what she wanted to know.

> Subject: More help on Colorunder
> No one has really answered my question on colorunder. I understand that I have to press if Colorunder = Number of Color and type what I want it to do. But what if you do to start how does that fit in?
> Tia J.

This question was more detailed than the first and included more context. She realized that her question needed to be more direct if she was to get helpful replies.

Phase 3/Session 8 was the beginning of Tia's most active online period. When she needed information, she searched old messages for it or introduced new questions into the system. This was the first time she deviated at all from her planner's approach. As she learned what she could do, she was able to modify her plans accordingly.

Tia's first reply to a question occurred only one week after her own first question was posed, when she responded with instructions about the command that she herself was still learning about.

> Subject: Re: Using Colorunder
> I don't know how to use Colorunder. Can anybody teach me how to do it?
> Mara
>
> Type if Colorunder = number of color color and what you want it to do
> Tia J.

Although Tia did not completely understand how to use colorunder, she decided to share with Mara what she had learned. Perhaps she thought this was the only part Mara needed to know or that this would help Mara get started. In any case, this message provided a striking example of a student who had incomplete knowledge yet who was willing to share what she did know with others. The information she shared was correct and helpful to Maria as an introduction. Maria's subsequent questions online or in person therefore were more detailed, and the answerer could address them more specifically.

Tia's ability to write questions increased somewhat over time. During Session 19, for example, she asked another question.

> Subject: How to make another answer?
> I already know how to tell another people to answer a problem but what if they get the wrong answer how can they change there [sic] answer?
> Tia.

In this message, Tia began by telling the reader what she already knew and then a problem she thought might occur (the person might answer incorrectly); her actual question requests details on the solution she has chosen (allowing the player to offer another answer). This message contained more details than her previous questions, even though it was the first time she had asked it.

Tia also continued to reply to other students' online questions. She went on to help other students with online questions in person. During Session 25, when she obviously had a solution to her previous question, she decided to write a new message that would be a reference for other students who wanted to have multiple-choice questions in their games.

While programming the later phases of her game, Tia did not need new information since she was reusing procedures she had already written. She did continue to log in, however, and answered questions from her peers. She also spent time helping other students in person.

In the end Tia was somewhat disappointed with her game. She realized that it was not entirely as she had planned and wished it were more interesting. She said that her favorite part was the level selection page. This was not surprising, since once Tia completed phase four, the addition level, there were no new programming problems; she just had to copy previous levels and fill in the new type of questions. This was not very interesting to her, and she thought going through the entire game would not be very interesting for other people. She received positive reactions from younger students who came to the game fair, but she stated that she still preferred Emma's game to her own.

Tia's role in her classroom changed significantly during the course of this project. She was one of the most active girls in the online environment: she asked seven questions of her peers and replied online to six of their questions. In addition to providing answers online, Tia went in person to help several students whose messages she read online. She decided, without adult prompting, to post an informational message about how to program multiple choice questions even though none of the students had asked a related question online.

There was evidence that other students' perceptions of Tia seemed to change as a result of her online messages and in-person responses to their questions. In addition to broadcasting their questions to the group, some students sought Tia out directly when they knew she had programmed something they wanted to include in their games. She became a member of the group of friends formed initially of Megan, Cathy, Yolanda, and Tammy and occasionally chose to sit at a computer near Oriel, Mara, or Emma so they could play and test each other's games.

Lessons from Tia

Tia was a solid example of a student whose behavior changed in conjunction with her interactions through the *Virtual Expert*. The online environment provided her with an opportunity that she used effectively. She was not the only student who participated throughout the project, nor was she the most prolific message writer. Her experience was exceptional because she was considered to have both low skills and poor socialization abilities before this project. Other students who had one of these two difficulties also chose to help their peers in similar ways.

Tia wrote a moderate number of messages, both as questions and as answers. She also chose to help several students directly, without the computer as an interface. The change in her participation occurred over time and persisted throughout the project. She did not become more isolated as she increased her online interaction; instead, the opposite occurred: she formed connections with other students and became an active part of the classroom community both on line and in person. As she obtained new knowledge, she willingly shared what she had recently learned with her peers.

Her participation in the online environment also changed over time, depending on where she was in her game. She began her project by programming the things she already knew how to do; when she finished those sections, she sought new information because she needed it. After spending several sessions learning about commands and how to integrate them into her program, she used her new knowledge throughout the rest of the project. Once she decided to do something new again, she returned to the online environment for assistance.

Because all of the students' questions were available for any of them to read, Tia was able to identify those questions that she felt she could answer. She had the opportunity to behave as an expert, and she chose to assist her peers on a number of occasions. This was a new role for Tia, and one that she had not previously had in the classroom. In this environment, she did not need to wait for another student to address a question to her directly; instead, she had control over when she would answer. Thus, interactions through the *Virtual Expert* enabled Tia to construct a view of herself as an expert in certain situations.

The record of Tia's use of online information revealed a period when she was able to use what she already knew rather than seek out new techniques or knowledge. This period was not caused by a weakness in the *Virtual Expert*. It was a natural aspect of doing a long-term project. The system helped reveal this period and its length, providing what could be valuable knowledge for a teacher. Thus, if students become stuck, their teacher could intervene.

Girls and Boys Online

One of the goals of this work was to provide an environment in which students would feel comfortable altering their previous classroom discourse. A primary aim in designing the system was to afford the opportunity for children to realize that each one of them had valuable knowledge that could help their peers in the completion of the project. For this recognition to occur, the students had to communicate with one another in ways that were atypical in their classroom. One of the most obvious changes was related to gender. Boys and girls answered each other in the online environment whereas in class they seldom interacted.

The number of messages posted demonstrates that the girls in this classroom participated in the online environment as much as boys did. Eight of the nineteen students in this classroom were girls; they wrote 43% of the students' messages. This is an average of 8.9 messages each. The eleven boys averaged 8.5 messages apiece. This is a clear contrast to computer critics' expectations that boys will monopolize school computers and online activities.

During the first few sessions that the online system was available, the boys wrote many more messages online than the girls did. After the first session, during which boys posted 25 messages and girls only posted four, participation was more balanced; the girls wrote a total of 67 messages and the boys wrote 68.

This study has shown that the girls in this classroom participated in the online environment as much as the boys did. Indeed, five of the girls each wrote more messages than most of the boys did. The other three girls wrote only a few messages, but each indicated that they used the online environment when she felt it was appropriate.

Other differences become evident by comparing the number of messages in each category. Only girls replied to responses they had received to their questions, asking for more information or providing more specific details; the boys who received answers that they did not consider helpful did not reply to the responses they received. Several girls wrote new messages, instead of replying to responses, and referred to their previous questions, explaining that they did not understand information given in response to their questions or it was not what they needed. Three boys also restated their questions in new messages, but none of them responded, or referred to, the replies their initial questions had received. It was as if they felt the unhelpful messages were not worth acknowledging.

The four public test messages were all from boys. Some of the girls did try writing messages to try the online system, but they did not post their test messages. For example, Oriel composed a test message her first time online but then asked how to avoid making it public. She said she wanted to know how to post a message but did not feel the need to complete the action. Tia also wrote a test message and canceled it rather than posting it. Other students may have done similar tests without being observed. The boys who posted their messages may have felt that they were testing an impersonal software system rather than affecting other students. Tia and Oriel, on the other hand, wanted to be sure their messages did not appear in public because they said others would not want to read them. They were considering the reaction from the community rather than to the technology.

These two girls, Tia and Oriel, were the students who wrote the only informational posts that were not replies to online questions. They took the initiative to introduce their newly obtained knowledge to the group.

A stereotypical view of boys might be that they will answer questions in public (if they know a plausible answer), but they are unwilling to show ignorance and therefore will rarely ask questions. On average in this online setting, boys did answer more questions than girls did, but this was due to the four boys who posted significantly more answers than questions. All of the boys asked at least one question online.

It has been noted that in classroom situations, boys are often called upon much more frequently than girls are, and boys are much more likely to volunteer information (Sadker & Sadker, 1994; AAUW, 1992). This is clearly not caused by girls having much less to contribute than the boys do. Given this online environment, the girls asked and answered many questions. Some of them also provided information that had not been requested online. Thus, an online environment can help girls to participate more fully in classroom communities.

Girls and Boys in Person

It is certainly important that the quantity and quality of messages written by girls were similar to those of the boys, but another gender-related topic was perhaps even more significant. In this environment, girls and boys did not limit their replies to peers of their own gender.

During prior observations of this fifth-grade class and others, it was observed that boys would initiate face-to-face interactions with other boys and girls with other girls.

It was rare to observe a school-related conversation between a boy and a girl, and usually if one did occur, the teacher initiated it. These observations are consistent with studies of voluntary segregation by gender in other elementary schools (AAUW, 1992).

In a previous study (Evard, 1998), several fifth-grade girls reported quite plainly that if a girl approached a boy, even during class time, it would appear that she might be interested in him romantically and her friends would tease her. The boys were not as forthcoming about their reasons. Their attitudes implied they had no reason to talk to a girl about their work, and if they did have questions, they would appear stupid if they asked for help from a girl.

Even so, in this study, boys answered girls' messages and girls answered boys' messages from the very first session. Each message had its author's real name at the top, so the students knew exactly to whom they were replying. Gender was not a barrier in this environment. In fact, most of the online replies were to classmates of the opposite gender: 64% of the boys' replies were addressed to girls, and 62% of the girls' replies were to boys. Researchers who studied small cooperative learning groups have found that girls tended to help both boys and girls in person, but the boys primarily assisted other boys (Sadker & Sadker, 1994).

When a conversation between a boy and girl is online in a public space, all of the other students can see what the topic is, and there is no longer any possibility of teasing the boy and girl about what they might have been saying. The broadcast nature of the online system also meant that a girl was not asking a boy a question, she was asking anyone who knew the answer. Similarly, a boy who received an online answer from a girl had not sought her out in particular. This may have eliminated some of the potential stress from the situation.

There were many instances during this study in which a girl would learn that a particular boy had information that would help in her game or vice versa. Some of the students even became more comfortable speaking to peers of the opposite gender in person as a result of this. In particular, Oriel interacted with several of the boys. When Shane had a question about some information online and asked Oriel for help in person, she told him to sit next to her so she could help him. Later in the project, Oriel knew that Dennis had used a particular technique that she needed because he had asked about it on the online system. When she needed that information, she went and asked him for help in person.

There were also occasions during which social pressures inhibited in-person interactions between girls and boys. During one session, Emma asked me a question, and I told her that Pascal had done something related to it, so she should see his game to decide if that was what she wanted to do. She immediately said "okay," but then turned to Mara who was giggling. Mara said she was laughing at Emma and whispered something to Emma about Pascal. Emma then decided that she would not go talk to Pascal alone but that she would go with me. When Pascal showed us his game, Emma did not speak to him but addressed all her questions to me. The comments Mara had made clearly affected her willingness to speak with Pascal in public.

Thus in the online environment, the gender of a message's author was not a barrier to positive interactions, even though gender had been an inhibitor in face-to-face discussions.

Concluding Words

The students in this project used an online discussion system to help them build a community in which they supported each other's learning. I formed the idea of a *Virtual Expert* to help understand this phenomenon. I define a *Virtual Expert* as an online entity, created by a group, of which every participant can ask questions as they would of an individual expert, to which each student can contribute and that provides a community memory. I chose the name *"Virtual Expert"* to indicate that the group creates a new entity, not a typical individual expert, and an online system provides the environment.

An expert can help a novice learn. Some educational thinkers have studied this relationship. For example, Vygotsky hypothesized that learning occurs during "problem solving under adult guidance or in collaboration with more capable peers" (1978). Theorists who have built upon his work have focused on adult guidance, particularly the assistance of an expert. They define scaffolding as the support provided by an expert that enables a learner to reach a goal that she could not attain without aid.

My concept of having the students as a group act as an expert was based on two ideas: a group of people has more knowledge than any one of its members, and a group can serve as an expert for each of its members when it has a suitable communication mechanism.

The first idea is obvious. People have different experiences. Even when a group of children are sitting in the same room, listening to the same teacher, they do not necessarily learn the same things. Each student constructs his own understanding of what the teacher presents, based on his past experiences.

The second idea is more complex. What does it mean for a group of people to serve as an expert for all of its members? According to the

American Heritage Dictionary, an expert is "a person with a high degree of skill in or knowledge of a certain subject." The definition only indicates what the expert has, not what he provides for others: there is no sense of whether an expert is helpful to other people. Experts who are willing to help others may not always be available, they may not understand questions they are asked, and they might not know appropriate solutions. Experts might not remember previous interactions with the people they help.

This *Virtual Expert* had less severe versions of these limitations. A student could ask a question at any time and learn more about the problem by articulating it. Then he would have to wait for someone to answer him. Questions were not always understood, but a child who wrote an ambiguous message could clarify it. The students were sometimes unable to answer a question even once they understood it. At those times, an adult could step in and try to provide a solution. Finally, the online environment did have a type of memory, since all the messages were always available. All the students did not read all the messages, however, so when a child asked a second question, there was no guarantee that the classmates who read it had read the first question.

A *Virtual Expert* such as this one has several strengths that a single person is less likely to have. Because the primary contributors were students who were involved with similar projects, answers were very likely to be in the appropriate context and understandable by those who read them. Multiple perspectives on any question were possible. Sometimes conflicting or complementary advice was given. All the messages that had been written were available throughout the project, so that a student with a question could look at previously written similar questions and the answers those messages had received. Perhaps most importantly, the *Virtual Expert* was an entity to which each child could contribute, so there was not the feeling that the students knew nothing and the expert knew everything.

Social dynamics inhibit some students from speaking out in the classroom. The fear of looking stupid, for example, can hinder students from asking questions. Additional barriers exist if students can ask questions of each other directly. For example, other children can observe who approaches whom and speculate on the nature of interactions. The *Virtual Expert* changed the social environment of the particular class in this study. It provided privacy by allowing students to articulate their questions without interruptions or immediate reactions. Privacy was also important when students who were considered to have low skills wanted to read questions, they had the opportunity to search for questions that they could answer and act as experts when they chose. At the same time, it was also public, so that the topic of each interaction was obvious; this was particularly important when a conversation was between a girl and a boy. Communication was not limited to online interactions; once a connection was made, students could speak to one another in person if they felt it was necessary or appropriate. Their interactions with and through the *Virtual Expert* altered the roles they had previously established for themselves.

The *Virtual Expert* provided a context in which these fifth-grade children were able to discuss projects via an online network in their school. The primary hypothesis was that once children were given the opportunity to communicate online about projects which were personally meaningful, they would form a community in which they could support each other's learning and in doing so enhance their own problem-solving and design skills and processes. This they did. In addition, their communication was viewed as a valuable experience in and of itself.

Tia was one of several children who took advantage of the *Virtual Expert* system to explore how she could help her classmates. With the aid of their online discussions, students changed their community from one in which only a few members were considered helpful to one in which any member could help one another. Through their online exchanges, students gained programming skills and knowledge from their peers, a different view of their own communication, and new perspectives on each other as individuals.

The *Virtual Expert* system enabled both individual and community developments. It allowed students to share their knowledge with their peers and without many of the difficulties inherent in face-to-face interactions. The *Virtual Expert* gave these children the ability to ask questions of their peers to learn from their peers, and to experience the role of an expert.

References

AAUW (1992). *How schools shortchange girls.* Washington, D.C.: The American Association of University Women Educational Foundation.
Daiute, Collette & Bridget Dalton (1993). Collaboration between children learning to write: Can novices be masters? *Cognition and Instruction, 10,* 281–333.

Evard, Michele (1998). Twenty heads are better than one: Communities of children as virtual experts. Doctoral dissertation, Massachusetts Institute of Technology, Department of Media Arts and Sciences, Cambridge, MA.

Evard, Michele (1996a). A community of designers: Learning through exchanging questions and answers. In Yasmin Kafai & Mitchel Resnick (eds.), *Constructionism in practice: Designing, thinking, and learning in a digital world.* Hillsdale, NJ: Lawrence Erlbaum Associates.

Evard, Michele (1996b). So please stop, thank you: Girls online. In L. Cherney & E. Weise (eds.), Wired women: Gender and new realities in cyberspace. Seattle: The Seal Press.

Kafai, Yasmin B. (1995). *Minds in play: Computer game design as a context for children's learning.* Hillsdale, NJ: Lawrence Erlbaum Associates.

Kafai, Yasmin B. & Idit Harel (1991). Children's learning through consulting: When mathematical ideas, software design, and playful discourse are intertwined. In I. Harel & S. Papert (eds.), *Constructionism.* Norwood, NJ: Ablex.

Kortekaas, Mark (1994). News and education: Creation of "The Classroom Chronicle." Master's thesis, MIT Media Arts and Sciences Program, Cambridge, MA.

Papert, Seymour (1993). *The children's machine.* New York: Basic Books.

Papert, Seymour (1980). *Mindstorms.* New York: Basic Books.

Rogoff, Barbara (1990). *Apprenticeship in thinking: Cognitive development in social context.* New York: Oxford University Press.

Sadker, Myra & David Sadker (1994). *Failing at fairness.* New York: Charles Scribner's Sons.

Shaw, Alan (1995). Social constructionism and the inner city: Designing environments for social development and urban renewal. Doctoral dissertation, Massachusetts Institute of Technology, Department of Media Arts and Sciences, Cambridge, MA.

Turkle, Sherry & Seymour Papert (1991). Epistemological pluralism and the revaluation of the concrete. In Idit Harel & Seymour Papert (eds.), *Constructionism.* Norwood, NJ: Ablex.

Vygotsky, L. S. (1978). *Mind in society: The development of higher psychological processes.* Cambridge, MA: Harvard University Press.

Webb, Noreen (1985). Verbal interaction and learning in peer-directed groups. *Theory into Practice, 24,* 32–39.

Webb, Noreen M. & Annemarie S. Palincsar (1995). Group processes in the classroom. In David Berliner & Robert Calfee (eds.), *Handbook of educational psychology.* New York: Macmillan.

Chapter 10

E-GEMS: A Project on Computer Games, Mathematics and Gender

Maria Klawe, Kori Inkpen, Eileen Phillips,
Rena Upitis & Andee Rubin

In this chapter, we describe the work of an interdisciplinary team of researchers, teachers, and computer game designers involved in the development of electronic games for education in math and science. The first four authors have all been members of this team, known as E-GEMS: Electronic Games for Education in Math and Science, since its inception. The primary goal in creating E-GEMS was to explore the possibilities of using specially designed computer and video games to increase learning and appreciation of mathematics and science by children aged 10–14, with a particular focus on girls. This age range was chosen because research has indicated that this is when most children, especially girls, lose interest in these subjects (Bendixen-Noe & Hall, 1996; Hanna, 1996; Rosser, 1995). We were interested in electronic games because of their appeal to children and because they offered excellent opportunities for visualization and exploration of complex mathematical concepts.

On the other hand, we had serious concerns about using electronic games to interest girls in mathematics. Most girls, especially aged 10 and older, seemed to be less interested in playing electronic games than boys and less interested in using computers in general. Thus the question of whether it was possible to create electronic games that would be attractive to most girls in this age range was an issue for E-GEMS researchers from the start. Over the last five years, the topic of girls and computer games has received a great deal of attention in the popular media, but the number of successful commercial games that strongly appeal to girls remains small.

In this chapter, we describe the evolution of the E-GEMS work, beginning with the development of an understanding of the gender issues involved in the design and use of educational electronic games. We then show how this understanding resulted in design decisions affecting two pieces of educational software: *Counting on Frank,* a piece of commercial software on which we consulted, and *Phoenix Quest,* which we designed and built ourselves, based on our research. The chapter is organized in three parts. First we present the results of our initial studies of the ways in which girls interact with computer and video games. We next describe our experiences in designing and developing two mathematical computer games that were designed to appeal to girls (as well as boys). Finally we discuss the interactions of girls with computer games that we have observed in E-GEMS classroom studies over a six-year period.

Girls' Interactions in Electronic Game Environments

Our project began in 1993 with an intensive two-month study that explored children's interactions while they played commercial video and computer games in an informal setting. The research took place at Science World in Vancouver, British Columbia, in an exhibit called the Electronic Games Research Laboratory. Science World is an interactive science museum, where children and adults can explore various science concepts through hands-on activities and experimentation.

The exhibit was designed to create an informal learning environment for children of all ages and was developed and staffed by E-GEMS researchers. The study area included two video game units, a Sega Genesis and a Super Nintendo Entertainment System, and two computers, a Macintosh and an IBM-compatible PC. The children who visited the exhibit made a clear distinction between the video games and the computer games and often had different reactions to the two categories of games. A design station was also constructed where children were encouraged to explore their own ideas for creating electronic games. This area included a Velcro-covered box and a wide variety of objects (e.g., blocks, pieces of fabric, small dolls and animals and other non-computer artifacts), many of which could be attached directly to the walls of the box. Clipboards, paper, pencils, and colored markers were also available for writing and drawing. A final station housed a Macintosh-based survey on electronic games.

During the two-month period of the study we observed over 10,000 children playing the various video and computer games. Our study revealed substantial gender differences concerning children's preferences and attitudes towards electronic games (Inkpen, Upitis, Klawe, Hsu, Leroux, Lawry, Anderson, Ndunda & Sedighian, 1994; Lawry, Inkpen, Upitis, Klawe, Hsu, Leroux, Anderson, Ndunda & Sedighian, 1995).

Among the girls who enjoyed playing electronic games, there was strong interest in the numerous social aspects of the games: these girls could name a myriad of characters, describe story lines, and describe the relationships between characters in the games (Inkpen et al., 1994). Girls stated that they liked games with worthwhile goals, creative activities, challenge, and aspects they could personalize, such as being able to choose their own character. They reported that they did not feel that "shooting bad guys and monsters" was a particularly worthwhile goal. Girls appeared less interested in the minute details of the secret clues in the game and the obstacles that needed to be overcome.

While they enjoyed playing electronic games alone at times, for many girls the games were only one aspect of a rich social environment. Most girls played the games with friends, family members or other visitors to the exhibit and often engaged in other social activities while playing. For example, three girls played a video game called *Sonic the Hedgehog* for over an hour and a half (the longest period of time any group of girls were observed to play a game during the study). These girls sat on the floor with a female researcher and took turns playing the video game, drew pictures, and talked about friends, school, and sports. Without the additional off-computer activities to provide a social context for the games, it is unlikely that the girls would have been motivated to play the game for as long a stretch of time.

While the interest level varied between individual girls, several trends emerged:

1. Many girls visiting the exhibit were more interested in computer games than in video games.
2. Some girls indicated that they felt playing computer games was a more "worthwhile" activity than playing video games.
3. Many girls enjoyed playing at the design station, drawing game

characters and interacting with others at the station.
4. Ease of access was an issue; many girls entered the exhibit area, but left immediately if others were already playing.

Children played collaboratively in the exhibit much of the time. Both girls and boys enjoyed playing games with others and often appeared to be more successful as a result of this collaboration. Based on these observations, a number of E-GEMS studies were designed to further investigate children's collaboration in electronic learning environments. The initial investigation explored the benefit of having children play together on a single computer. In this study, we found that girls were able to solve more puzzles on average when they played together on a single computer than when they played side by side, on separate computers (Inkpen, Booth, Klawe & Upitis, 1995). We noticed, however, that while the girls often wanted to work collaboratively, contention frequently arose over sharing the mouse.

As a result, we turned our research to hardware designs that could support collaboration. We explored two multiple-mice systems to find out if they could provide children with better access to the computer environment (Inkpen, McGrenere, Booth & Klawe, 1997; Inkpen, Ho-Ching, Kuederle, Scott & Shoemaker, 1999; Scott, Shoemaker & Inkpen, 2000). The first system enabled each child to have possession of a mouse while utilizing a turn-taking strategy to transfer control between the two mice. Two different strategies were explored, a "give" protocol and a "take" protocol. A "give" protocol required one child to press her right mouse button to transfer control to the other player's mouse. A "take" protocol allowed either child to "take" control of the game at any time by pressing her right mouse button. The results showed that pairs of girls were able to solve more puzzles on average when provided with two mice, utilizing a "give" protocol, than when they tried to share a single mouse (Inkpen et al., 1997).

A second system enabled children to use multiple cursors as well as multiple mice, allowing the children to interact simultaneously with the computer if desired. Girls, in particular, were extremely excited by the notion that they could both play at the same time. As one of the girls said, "This is fun. We're all best friends and we're all playing!" Seventy percent of the children in a recent study stated a preference for playing the game if they had multiple mice and multiple cursors rather than being forced to share one mouse and one cursor (Inkpen et al., 1999).

This research provided E-GEMS with insights for the design of electronic learning environments for girls as well as strong evidence for the academic and social benefits that can result from supporting children's collaboration in interactive learning environments.

Creating Mathematical Computer Games to Engage Girls

Learning from *Counting on Frank*

The first significant experience in game development for the E-GEMS team arose from our involvement in 1994 with *Counting on Frank*, a commercial game developed for EA*Kids, the division of Electronic Arts that published their "edutainment" products at that time. The game is based on a popular children's picture book of the same name. In *Counting on Frank* the player's goal is to help a boy, Henry, and his dog Frank, win a contest by guessing the number of jellybeans in a jar (a different number each time the game is played) and by collecting clues they receive as rewards for solving mathematical word problems. The main educational activities in *Counting on Frank* were solving word problems, using the clues to determine the number of jellybeans, and playing four other mathematical strategy games, each with several variations. Figuring out the number of jellybeans from the clues required reasoning about number patterns, inequalities and modular equivalences. The primary entertainment elements were the "click-ons" in each of the eight main scenes in *Counting on Frank*, objects which, when clicked, create a humorous animation generally unrelated to the educational activities.

EA*Kids asked E-GEMS to assist with the development of *Counting on Frank* because they were concerned about both the pedagogical and entertainment values of the mathematical activities. At the time, the media was full of stories about the Barbie™ doll who said "Math class is tough," and EA*Kids were concerned about the way in which two of the main female characters in the game, Henry's mother and his best friend, Ginger, were portrayed. In the book, Ginger did not exist and Henry's mother was a minor character, who had no particular attitude toward math. In the first version of the game, however, both females made comments about how "bad they [were] at math," and "how smart Henry [was]." In fact, both mathematics and females were portrayed in a variety of other undesirable ways throughout the game as well. These aspects of the story had been added by a pair of female writers commissioned to create the script for *Counting on Frank*. Although the book had no negative images of either mathematics or females, the writers, neither of whom had liked math in school, had subconsciously introduced many traditional biases and stereotypes.

By the time E-GEMS joined the development effort, most of the character animation sequences had already been finished. Since this animation was the most expensive component in the development, our ability to make major changes to the design of the main part of the game was limited. We were, however, able to remove or replace all the negative characterizations of females and mathematics and to give Ginger a larger and more positive role in the game, though her role remained small in comparison to those of Henry and Frank.

The development of the math games in *Counting on Frank* was less advanced so we had more freedom to apply the findings from our Science World and classroom studies to improve their design. For example, because girls particularly like creative design activities and the ability to customize their play, the planned traditional "dots and boxes" game was extended to a large collection of tessellation patterns, and players were allowed to choose their own colors and playing characters. Because multi-player games appeal to both girls and boys, two-player versions were added for as many of the math games as possible. Several levels of play were added to some games to increase the challenge as well as mathematical scope of the games. To increase the likelihood of repeated play, the variety of problems was significantly increased and randomness was introduced to the problem definition and reward schemes.

Counting on Frank was published in late 1994 and was successful in most respects. It was nominated for the Software Publishers Association best home product award and selected by PC Magazine as one of its top ten educational CD-ROMs in 1995. While not a runaway commercial success story, *Counting on Frank* sold reasonably well in the home and school markets, and continues to be popular with children (especially girls), teachers, and parents.

E-GEMS conducted several studies on school and home use of *Counting on Frank* (e.g., Klawe, Super & Westrom, 1996) using a specially constructed version that allowed us to collect log file data from students playing the game. We found that *Counting on Frank* was attractive to most girls and boys in the 8–12 age range. Next the game exposed children to a wide range of content that was recognizable to them as mathematics. Additionally, children playing *Counting on Frank* balanced their time between the education and entertainment aspects of the game.

From the patterns of play obtained from the log files, we believe the attractiveness of *Counting on Frank* was related to its wide range of activities and the freedom to move among them at will.

In terms of the mathematics learning goals of the software, the clue design functioned particularly well. The EA*Kids development team was at first skeptical about clues that required 8 to 12-year-old students to use sophisticated mathematical knowledge, such as deciding which numbers "have a remainder of 5 when divided by 7." However, several design elements made the mathematics accessible to a wide range of students, including providing redundant clues and providing a number line visualization tool on which players could keep track of the numbers they had eliminated and those that were still possible (Super, Westrom & Klawe, 1995). Interestingly, many students actually chose to stop collecting clues when they didn't have enough information to specify the number of jellybeans and just guess; it seemed they wanted the game to have an element of luck as well as skill.

We also found that the math games provided excellent contexts for classroom projects that engaged children in deep mathematical thinking (Klawe, Westrom, Super & Davidson, 1996). In spite of these positive outcomes, our research demonstrated that playing *Counting on Frank* in isolation (i.e. without other related math activities) did not result in gains in performance in the kinds of word problems contained in *Counting on Frank*. Our studies indicated some of the design elements that may have limited its effectiveness in this respect. These included:

- the limited number and variety of word problems to solve,
- the lack of incentives to move on to the harder levels of the game,
- the lack of informative help when errors were made,
- the absence of activities that would engage children in a more thoughtful and thorough exploration of word problems.

Creating *Phoenix Quest*

Design criteria. Based on what we learned through the Science World studies and as a result of the development work and research on *Counting on Frank*, the E-GEMS team decided to develop a prototype computer game from scratch, which came to be called *Phoenix Quest*. Our goal was to create a mathematical computer game that took into account the preferences expressed by girls: a story with a strong narrative component, a major female character, opportunities to collaborate, and opportunities to play a significant positive role in the narrative of the game. The design of *Phoenix Quest*, therefore, emphasizes story line and interaction with the story's characters. In addition, the mathematical activities are portrayed as difficulties that the player helps the characters overcome.

In order to provide the desired depth of story and characterization, the game is played in the context of a 65-chapter novel written by a prize-winning Canadian children's author. The story begins with Julie, an adolescent girl and the primary protagonist, trapped in the Phoenix Archipelago, a mythical set of islands off the coast of Hong Kong. Julie can communicate with the player via postcards; as the game begins, she has sent the player a desperate postcard asking for help escaping from the Archipelago. Getting more information about Julie's dilemma requires the player to write back to her, asking for details. The player learns that Julie's quest is to escape from the Archipelago and prevent the world from turning dark by finding the stolen Phoenix feather. She is joined in her adventures by Darien, a trapped boy of similar age. Together, they embark on a long and arduous road that leads, in the end, to a final confrontation with the mastermind of the story, the mysterious Keeper, who has the stolen feather. As they solve a variety of mathematical and language problems (with help from the player), additional aspects of the adventure are revealed, through chapters in a magic journal kept by Saffron, one of the other characters. The story is long and complex, with many close-call-disasters that the player must avert.

The communication theme continues throughout the game. The player receives periodic mail from Julie or Saffron providing a clue to the next step in the puzzle and is encouraged to continue exchanging email with Julie, in particular, as the adventure proceeds. When the player writes to a character, the computer responds with a return postcard written in the voice of the appropriate character. Primarily, this is accomplished by matching keywords and, although it works in many cases, non sequiturs are common. The player is cast primarily as Julie's savior or guide. Email addressed to Julie is answered in the first person, with the player referred to in the second person ("You should help me out of the maze"). Mail from other characters is answered similarly, consistent with the role of the player as a helper from "outside" the game world.

E-GEMS 217

The game takes place on a map of the Archipelago, each island of which is the scene of several puzzles. At first, there is only one island and one puzzle, a geometric maze. As the player solves puzzles, more islands and more puzzles are added to the map and more of the story is revealed (See Figure 10.1). There are 65 chapters in all; to get them all (which is necessary to go on to the final stage of the game), the player must solve all of the puzzles, at least at several levels of difficulty. Besides revealing a new puzzle or a chapter of the story, solving a puzzle may add a *Strife* card to the player's deck. These *Strife* cards play a large role in the endgame, in which the player matches wits with the Keeper in a game of *Strife*, a card game akin to *Magic the Gathering*, which was popular at the time. Assembling a deck capable of winning at *Strife* requires the completion of a wide variety of activities, and thus *Strife* provides powerful motivation for engaging in all aspects of the game.

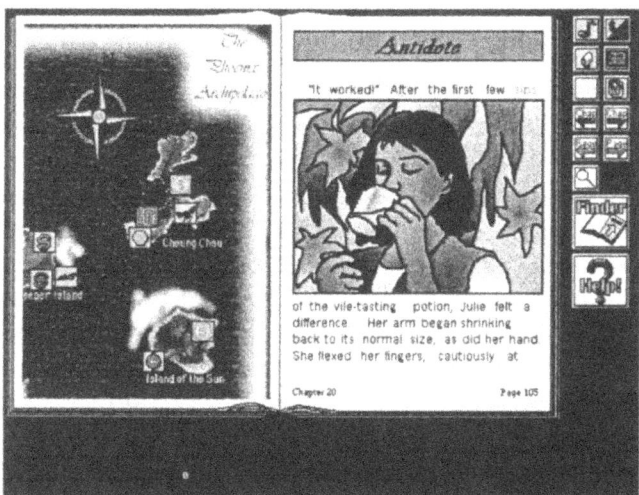

Figure 10.1: Example of a "cloze" passage screen

In addition to the math puzzles described below, there are two language activities in *Phoenix Quest*. In each chapter, there are power words, each of which has a definitional clue, which is usually given by Saffron. When each power word is discovered, either another chapter or another illustration is revealed. There are also "cloze" passages at the end of several chapters (which some players called "white pages"). These are texts describing the action of the chapter with many of the letters missing; the task is to fill in the missing letters with as few errors as possible.

In designing the game, we had to keep a careful balance between the puzzles and the story. If the puzzles are too engaging, the story tends to fade into the background, and eventually its power to engage is lost. On the other hand, it was important to make the puzzles integral enough to the story that players were motivated to tackle them because of their role in the narrative rather than finding them a nuisance.

In terms of the puzzles themselves, one of our design goals was to provide multiple entry points and paths through the game for players at different levels of mathematical sophistication. Thus, each puzzle can be played at multiple levels, but it is not necessary for a player to complete the difficult levels of any puzzle to continue in the game. Our observations of *Phoenix Quest* being played have led us to add easier levels to some of the puzzles so that younger children will be able to play.

Many of our design decisions were based on our own research experiences with children. For example, "collecting" plays a major role in *Phoenix Quest*; players collect chapters, puzzles and *Strife* cards. This design is based on our observation that children in the 10–14 age range enjoy creating their own collections (even though boys and girls generally collect different things). In *Phoenix Quest*, while the sequence of islands and chapters is similar from game to game, the *Strife* cards are dealt out randomly. The suspense and excitement of "turning over" an unknown card are quite motivating. (The appeal of this role of chance is reminiscent of the desire of children playing *Counting on Frank* to add an element of chance to their game.) To support the players' sense of collecting, they are provided with an album in which to keep and organize their *Strife* cards.

The game of *Strife*, in particular, was based on the game of *Magic the Gathering* which many children were playing while *Phoenix Quest* was being designed. *Magic the Gathering* however, with its emphasis on strength, power and weapons, was more popular with boys. Girls, we thought, would be more interested in a game where winning had to do with being nice or nasty to their competitor. Once the basic structure of the cards was set up—there are character, action, and gear cards we invited some 10-year-old girls to come up with the names and activities that each represented. The "Lost Puppy" card, for example, is an action card with which a character rescues a puppy and gains more karma. Similarly the "Healer" character raises other characters' strength, while the "Tent" gear card prevents the loss of gear cards when a "Thunder Storm" (or other inclement weather) card is played.

We designed *Phoenix Quest* explicitly to support collaboration. Most of the puzzles are not timed, so there are many opportunities for players to discuss a puzzle before trying a solution. We believed that because the game incorporates (simulated) conversation, players would tend to talk out loud while they were playing and, thus, end up talking to one another as well as to Julie.

Another design criterion was not explicit at the beginning but emerged through the design process. This has to do with the mathematical tools the game provides—and those that it doesn't provide. We believe it is important for students to use real mathematical tools in a motivating context in such a game. Thus, there is no calculator capability built into *Phoenix Quest*; if players need to use a calculator, they must use a physical one. Similarly, for puzzles that require players to specify angles or lengths, we have not provided electronic rules or protractors; again, players must find and use tools that are not on the computer.

Based on research indicating that girls are mostly not interested in games in which the character dies and they need to start the game over (as is the case in many video games), in *Phoenix Quest*, there is no ultimate negative feedback: there is no way the player can cause the ultimate tragedy of Julie's death. Rather, failing at individual puzzles prevents Julie from progressing toward the final goal of retrieving the Phoenix feather. In addition, a player can never lose chapters or *Strife* cards that have already been obtained; there is no way to "go backward" in *Phoenix Quest*. There *are* certain puzzles in which Julie (or Darien) "dies" after a certain amount of time or a certain number of wrong guesses. Negative feedback in these cases is sometimes a spoken or written, "Julie dies." However, in these puzzles, the player can play again without any penalty.

Observations. As designers, we have observed *Phoenix Quest* being used in over 20 Grade 4–7 classrooms in Canada; Andee Rubin and colleagues at TERC carried out a more focused study of five girls ages 11–13 who played in teams of two or three persons once or twice a week for over a month in a laboratory setting with two computers. The discussion below is based on both of these experiences, with specific attribution when the observations were carried out in only one place. Many of our observations supported our design principles, while others challenged some of our decisions. In general, the girls we watched remained interested in the game over a large number of sessions, became invested in their progress and played in general collaboratively, with personal dialogue mixed freely with discussions of the game. There was enough variability in the difficulty level of the puzzles to provide different players with an appropriate challenge.

In particular, the first puzzle, *Hexagons* (See Figure 10.2), proved to be effective in "hooking" players. In the story, Julie has to traverse a deep chasm across a bridge tiled with hexagons, each of which contains a number. There is a path through the hexagons that follows a mathematical rule e.g., all primes, all perfect squares, all multiples of 6, etc.

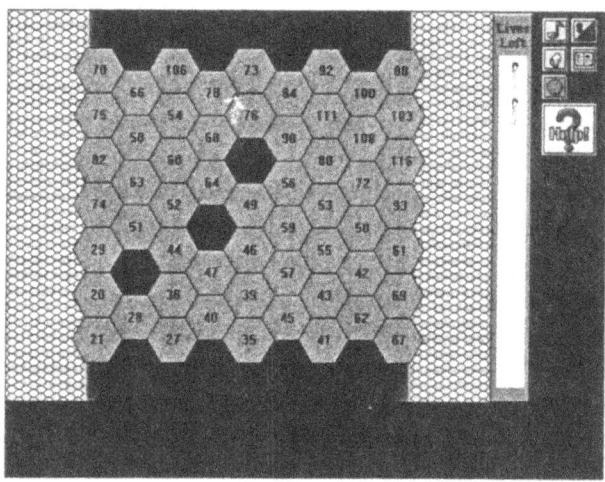

Figure 10.2: *Fibonnaci* game

The task is to get Julie across without making too many wrong guesses; for each wrong guess, a monster (e.g., fire-breathing dragon, giant Venus fly-trap, etc.,) appears and creates a pit which obliterates the number on that hexagon, using up one of Julie's lives. After all of Julie's lives are used up, (the number of lives she has depends on the level of the puzzle), Julie "dies," and the player can start over, playing either the same level or another (higher or lower) level or move on to another puzzle. There is no real penalty for causing Julie's demise. If the player is unsuccessful in helping Julie cross to safety, the correct path is highlighted on the maze. If Julie crosses safely, the player must identify from four choices what the pattern was. Choosing incorrectly also causes Julie to "die," but the correct choice is not indicated.

Because players can make some progress with a limited guessing strategy, *Hexagons* is a good place for them to start. Yet it is difficult enough that there is a sense of challenge and satisfaction in being successful. It is also relatively easy to get better at the puzzle, since the basic forms of the puzzles (e.g., sequences of primes, perfect squares, multiples of a single number, modular equivalences) remain the same, while the numbers become more difficult. At TERC, the *Hexagons* puzzle also provided us with some interesting insight into how powerful mathematical knowledge and language can be. One of the possible patterns is a Fibonnaci series (one in which each number is the sum of the previous two). The term (which the girls pronounced "Fibonucci") came to be a subject of conversation outside of their game play time. We hypothesize that the girls prized this piece of knowledge, since so few other children of their age knew what it meant.

Phoenix Quest engendered a certain amount of light-hearted competition among players and/or teams. Players could compete with themselves, with a predetermined goal, with others on their "team" and with other teams. At TERC, we saw few instances of players competing with themselves, although that possibility exists in several of the puzzles, particularly in a bee puzzle (how many stings?) and two mazes (how many rotations?). We observed players competing with a predetermined goal in the cloze passages, where they tried hard to miss the fewest possible letters and, thus, to get the "Awesome" rating (which is downgraded to "pretty good," etc., as you miss more letters). Competition within a team often took the form of "scuffling" for the mouse or deprecating one another's performance. Competition between teams was made possible by the ways in which progress could be reported, e.g., "we got chapter 10" or "we beat level 5 of the coins puzzle" or, ultimately, "we got to *Strife*." We judged competition to be a major motivating factor in the group we watched, as each team kept track of the other's progress, both explicitly by asking and quietly, by sneaking a peek. One player's mother observed that her daughter,who was "not a math kid,"was excited about her opportunities to play *Phoenix Quest*, a fact that she attributed partly to the gentle (or, as we have called it, "benign") competition that had emerged among the players.

One of our design features met with different responses in different settings. At TERC, the postcard communication feature got negative reviews. Because Julie answers email through key words and phrases, her responses are sometimes nonsensical; in these cases, the player's relationship to her may be closer to "disgusted friend" than "benevolent guide." Several of the players we interviewed vehemently described Julie as "stupid" because she never answered their questions about the puzzles. While they gave up on her after a while, except for the game of trying to get her to say dumb things, it is interesting that she evoked such a strong response. In some of the E-GEMS classrooms, however, many girls developed what seemed to be genuine relationships with Julie and Darien. They devoted great energy to trying to find out everything possible about their likes and dislikes and wrote them long personal letters about their lives.

In the TERC study, Julie as a character seemed to fade over the course of the game. Rather than referring to Julie's progress ("Julie got through the maze" or "we got Julie through the maze"), players described their progress as if they were actually the participants in the puzzles: "We got through the maze." In some of the puzzles, in fact, Julie had only a tenuous relationship to the action (it is hard to see why Julie would need to catch some fish). Consistent with this was the players' general lack of interest in the story (perhaps because it was presented out of chronological order), which would have offered more details about Julie's personality and predicament. Even for the players who seemed least involved with the story, however, it was clear that the game and narrative structure enhanced the appeal of the puzzles; the same set of puzzles without the surrounding story and characters and sense of progress would have never held their attention for so long.

Finally, observing girls playing *Phoenix Quest* allowed us to see several kinds of collaboration. The structure of many of the *Phoenix Quest* puzzles makes cooperation easy; there are few puzzles where hand-eye coordination is important or where there is pressure to get a puzzle done in a particular amount of time. Where there is pressure, it is usually to make as few mistakes as possible, since in many puzzles, you can make only so many mistakes before Julie "dies." Thus, we observed many examples of players hypothesizing about answers and evaluating evidence with the rest of their team, of one person figuring on paper or with a calculator while the other handled the mouse, and of spirited discussions (which might also be considered arguments of a sort) about next moves. In several of the puzzles there was an obvious division of labor, most notably in stepping stones (where one player would count on the screen and the other would enter numbers) and bees (where one player would figure out the angle and the other would type or lob the honey).

Several "helper" roles also grew out of the game play. One team would often ask the other for help, particularly if they knew that the other team had already "beaten" a particular puzzle. Within a team, one player was often known to be the one "good with fractions" or the one who could type best (for the "white pages"). Sometimes the helpers explained what they were doing; at other times, they just gave the answers.

Even though our emphasis was on meeting girls' preferences, *Phoenix Quest* has been highly popular with both girls and boys (and adults) throughout the various phases of its evolution (Young & Upitis, 1999). However, we also observed that boys and girls are initially attracted to different parts of *Phoenix Quest*, and that they approach the game with markedly different styles (DeJean, Upitis, Koch & Young, 1999). Although girls and boys spent similar amounts of time on the math and language aspects of *Phoenix Quest*, our data indicated that the nature of the time spent on these aspects of the game varied by gender. For example, in one of the Grade 4 classrooms, boys acquired an average of 7 puzzles, compared to an average of 4 puzzles acquired by girls over a period of two months. However, in other classrooms, when students had a chance to play for a more extended period and when the teacher encouraged class discussions and girls-only play times, both boys and girls had collected all of the puzzles. The differences in the numbers of puzzles acquired by boys and girls in the initial phases of play might be attributed to the different ways in which boys and girls approached *Phoenix Quest*. It was common during initial explorations for girls to spend more time on the story and postcard writing while boys raced to find and complete the puzzles. In the long run, however, boys and girls spent equal amounts of time on the language and mathematics aspects of the game.

Boys seemed to be interested in completing or "winning" the game, and therefore concentrated on completing activities in the shortest time possible. As a result, they shared information with one another in the way of "tips" and "shortcuts" in order to help each other advance in the game. Often, boys talked about *Phoenix Quest* when they were sitting at their seats away from the computer as well as in the hallways and on the playground. Girls, on the other hand, tended to limit their conversations about *Phoenix Quest* to their assigned computer time and with their assigned computer partners. As well, they took a more exploratory approach to the game rather than one that was focused on completing the game. However, while boys were interested in winning, they too became absorbed in the activities of the game. For example, boys were interested in understanding the functionality of the *Strife* cards and played the *Strife* game not only to win but for the pleasure of the game itself.

Girls, Computers, and Classroom Culture

In studying a game like *Phoenix Quest* in a classroom, we were immediately confronted by the classroom culture surrounding computers. In one particular Grade 4 classroom in Canada where we tested *Phoenix Quest*, we observed the following progression of student use of computers. This sequence of events is not all unique to this classroom; rather, it is a common way that computers eventually get to be used by most of the students in a class. In describing the evolution of her classroom, this teacher wrote:

> In September..., there is immediate talk about the computers. Usually, the boys are the first to ask if they can play. It is apparent, however, that the girls are waiting to hear the answer. Once the teacher establishes that the computers are accessible, generally it is the boys who seek to play the games, while the girls seem happier watching, playing the games "in their heads." At times, it appears as if the girls are uninterested, but this is not the case; they are getting ready to play. Although there are exceptions to this pattern of play (in both sexes), it does seem as if the girls build in a "readiness" stage for themselves. They stand in a group and watch, talk and ask questions. Why is there a reluctance to sit down and play?

Many reasons have been offered for this difference in boys' and girls' use of computers in classrooms. For some girls, it is a lack of experience with computers that keeps them from approaching. For others it may be shyness; for still others it is the fact that it is the beginning of the year, and girls start the process of getting to know the others in the class differently from boys. Many girls prefer to sit together and talk as they establish new friendships and rekindle old ones. Some girls also prefer working on a class project with the other girls rather than sitting at a "machine" and playing by themselves. Before computer research periods are introduced into the classroom schedule, most students see the computer as a single-user unit. Perhaps this is the way computers are traditionally used both at home and in school computer labs. In any case, the girl who initially chooses to sit and play at the computer is often a risk-taker and willing to isolate herself from the socializing activities of those other girls who stand talking and watching.

We have also observed that it is usually not long before the other girls want to play as well, although there is often a problem of access. In this particular classroom, typical of several others we observed, a small group of girls approached the teacher to explain the problem. "We can never get on the computers," "The boys are hogging the computers," "The boys won't let us play." When these statements were verified by the teacher, however, it turned out that the boys had not even been asked to let the girls have some playing time. So, the teacher told the girls that a schedule was going to be made and suggested that in the meantime they negotiate some playing time with the boys. Grudgingly, the boys freed up less than half of the computers for the girls and, perhaps out of necessity and perhaps out of choice, the girls who were interested in playing usually approached these computers in a group. Of course, this is not "fair" allocation of time or resources, and once the girls started playing (and enjoying the game) they were quick to point this out.

In one of our other research classrooms, the teacher developed an unusual strategy to equalize boys' and girls' access to computers. In collaboration with her Grade 7 students, she developed a strategy referred to as "any two, any time," which was designed to create equal opportunities for computer use for girls and boys. Instead of designating two computers as "girls only," a strategy that some other teachers have used, the teacher allowed all four classroom computers to be used either by boys or girls. Generally, the boys would claim the computers at the first available opportunity, and within the first few minutes the computers would be occupied only by boys. However, when a girl had completed her work or wanted to complete class-related work on the computer, she had the option of "bumping" any one of the four boys off of the computer—a ritual often performed with great relish. Girls were given equal ownership of the computers as they owned the rights to any two computers in the classroom at any time. In this way, the girls who were intent on finishing their assignments could still do so but not at the expense of "losing" their computer time.

Summary

Trying to describe and influence the role of computer games in girls' lives is a complex and sometimes discouraging task. In 2001, the gap between men and women in computer science and engineering is still significantly wider than it is in the biological sciences and the trends are not particularly encouraging. The majority of games on the market are still designed with boys' interests in mind. The work before us is twofold. Our research has asked as many questions as it has answered and there is much to be studied. But we must also find ways to enlist the publishers of computer games in the quest of providing opportunities for all children to engage in mathematics and science through computers.

References

Bendixen-Noe, M. & Hall, L. D. (1996) The quest for gender equity in America's schools: from preschool and beyond. *Journal of Early Childhood Teacher Education, 17* (2), 50–57.

DeJean, J., Upitis, R., Koch, C. & Young, J. (1999). The story of Phoenix Quest: How girls respond to a prototype language and mathematics computer game. *Gender and Education, 11* (2), 207–223.

Hanna, G. (1996). *Towards gender equity in mathematics education.* New York: Kluwer.

Inkpen, K., Booth, K. S. Klawe, M. M. & Upitis, R. (1995). Playing together beats playing apart, especially for girls. *Proceedings of Computer Supported Collaborative Learning (CSCL) '95*, 177–181. Hillsdale, NJ: Lawrence Erlbaum Associates.

Inkpen, K., Ho-Ching, W., Kuederle, O., Scott, S.D., Shoemaker, G.B.D. (1999). This is fun! We're all best friends and we're all playing: Supporting children's synchronous collaboration. *Proceedings of Computer Supported Collaborative Learning (CSCL) '99*, December 1999, Stanford, CA.

Inkpen, K., McGrenere, J., Booth, K.S. & Klawe, M. (1997). Turn-taking protocols for mouse-driven collaborative environments. *Proceedings of Graphics Interface '97*, Kelowna, BC.

Inkpen, K., Upitis, R., Klawe, M., Hsu, D., Leroux, S., Lawry, J., Anderson, A., Ndunda, M. & Sedighian, K. (1994). We never have forgetful flowers in our garden: Girls' responses to electronic games. *Journal of Computers in Mathematics and Science Teaching, 13* (4), 383–403.

Klawe, M. M., Westrom, M., Super, D. & Davidson, K. (1996). *Phoenix Quest*: Lessons from developing an educational computer game. *Proceedings of the International Conference on Multimedia Technology and Management,* (CD ROM). Hong Kong: ICMTM.

Klawe, M. M. & Phillips, E. (1995). A classroom study: Electronic games engage children as researchers. *Proceedings of CSCL '95*, (Bloomington IN, October 1995).

Klawe, M., Super, D., and Westrom, M. (1996) *Counting on Frank*™: Postmortem of an edutainment product. Available from http://taz.cs.ubc.ca /egems.

Lawry, J., Inkpen, K., Upitis, R., Klawe, M., Hsu, D., Leroux, S., Anderson, A., Ndunda, M. & Sedighian, K. (1995). Exploring common conceptions about boys and electronic games. *Journal of Computers in Mathematics and Science Teaching, 14* (4), 439–460.

Rosser, S. V. (ed.), (1995). *Teaching the majority: Breaking the gender barrier in science, mathematics, and engineering.* New York: Teachers College Press.

Scott, S. D., Shoemaker, G. B. D. & Inkpen, K. M. (2000). Towards seamless support of natural collaborative interactions. *Proceedings of Graphics Interface* (Montreal, PQ, May 2000), 103–110.

Super, D., Westrom, M. & Klawe, M. (1995). Design issues involving entertainment click-ons. In *CHI '96, Conference Companion*, 177–178.

Upitis, R. (1998). From hackers to luddites, game players to game creators: Profiles of adolescent students using technology. *Journal of Curriculum Studies, 30* (3) 293–318.

Upitis, R. & Koch, C. (1996). Is equal computer time fair for girls? Potential Internet inequities. *Proceedings of the 6th annual conference of the Internet Society,* (CD ROM). Montréal, Québec: INET.

Young, J. & Upitis, R. (1999). The microworld of *Phoenix Quest*: Social and cognitive considerations. *Education and Information Technologies 4* (4), 1–18.

Contributors

Dorothy Bennett is a Senior Project Director at EDC's Center for Children and Technology. She has had 15 years of experience in the research and development of educational media in mathematics and science education. She has also served as Co-Principal Investigator on the nationally recognized NSF-funded Telementoring Project, a telecommunications-based mentoring program for high school girls in project-based science and engineering programs and continues to consult on numerous projects nationwide.

Cornelia Brunner has been involved in the research, production, and teaching of educational technology in a variety of subject areas for thirty years. In addition to conducting research projects about the relationship between learning, teaching, and technology, she has designed and implemented educational materials incorporating technologies to support inquiry-based learning and teaching in science, social studies, media literacy, and the arts. She has taught experimental courses at Bank Street College and the Media Workshop New York, in which teachers are introduced to new technologies and learn how to integrate technology into their curriculum.

Elizabeth Bullen has a background in the humanities. Her doctoral thesis explored representations of masculinities in recent Australian fiction. She has taught literature and English at the Flinders University of South Australia. In 2000, she published several articles written with Jane Kenway in British education journals. She currently works as a Research Associate in the Centre for Studies in Literacy, Policy and Learning Cultures at the University of South Australia. Her research interests include gender, postmodernity, postcoloniality, and popular culture.

Cynthia Carter Ching is an Assistant Professor of Educational Psychology at UCLA. Cynthia's research focuses on learning through design, gender and technology, and apprenticeship patterns among children with different levels of technological expertize.

Laurie Edwards is an Associate Professor of Education at St. Mary's College of California. She holds a Ph.D. in science and mathematics education from the University of California at Berkeley (1989) and has carried out research into students' learning with a variety of open-ended computational environments, including mathematical microworlds, dynamic geometry software, and Logo and Logo-like languages. She is interested in designing effective activities and settings to support learners' construction of new understandings in such environments and in promoting equity in mathematics and technology.

Michele Evard received her doctorate from MIT, where she worked with Seymour Papert in the Media Laboratory. Her thesis was entitled "Twenty Heads Are Better Than One: Communities of Children as Virtual Experts." Since that time, Michele has been focused on the learning of her own three children, André, born in 1998, and Rose and Joelle, born in 2001. She plans to continue to learn about learning from them.

Margaret Honey, Vice President and Director of EDC's Center for Children and Technology, has worked in the field of educational technology since 1981. Her primary research interests include the role of technology in school reform, the use of telecommunications technology to support online learning communities, and gender and technology, including issues of equity and access. Dr. Honey's studies include the first national survey to look at K-12 educators' use of telecommunications. This was one of the first development projects to cultivate the Internet as an environment in which to conduct teachers' professional development (http://www.edc.org/CCT/mlf/MLF.html) and the nationally recognized Union City Online project, investigating the educational potential of networked technologies when coupled with district-wide systemic reform (http://www.union-city.k12.nj.us).

Celia Hoyles has been the Professor of Mathematics at the University of London, Institute of Education since 1984. Professor Hoyles is interested in the design of computational environments that offer new representational forms to assist students from diverse backgrounds in expressing and communicating their ideas and strategies. She is co-author of *Windows on Mathematical Meanings, Learning Cultures and Computers,* and she co-edited *Computers and Exploratory Learning* and *Rethinking the Mathematics Curriculum,* which debated the place of mathematics in the new millennium. She is an executive editor of the journal, *The International Journal of Computers for Mathematical Learning*. She was invited to serve as consultant and commentator in the United States for the new *NCTM Standards 2000* Writing Group on the role of technology and in 2000 served on the review panel of the *National Science Foundation* in the United States to evaluate research proposals in mathematics and science.

Kori Inkpen is an Associate Professor in the Faculty of Computer Science at Dalhousie University. Her research interests involve exploring ways to utilize computer technology to effectively support face-to-face collaboration, particularly in the areas of education, entertainment, and business.

Yasmin Kafai is an Associate Professor of Psychological Studies in Education at UCLA. Associate Professor Kafai is a widely recognized expert in educational technology. Her pioneering work in learning through design at MIT investigated children's conceptions of computer games by allowing them to create their own. Currently her research focuses on creating sustainable cultures of learning through design in both K-12 and teacher education. Yasmin is a recipient of the NSF Early Career Award and serves on the national committee on gender and technology.

Jane Kenway was the Foundation Director of the Deakin Center for Education and Change from 1993 to July 1999, when she took up a chair in the School of Education at the University of South Australia. She teaches Educational Policy and Administration, and her research expertize is in education policy with reference to schools and education systems in the context of wider social and cultural change. Within this focus she has a specific interest in issues of justice, gender, locality, and technology. She has published widely in international journals, in books, and in professional journals for an educational audience.

Maria Klawe is the Founder and Director of the E-GEMS project, a collaborative research project on the design and use of computer games for mathematics education (Grades 4 to 9). She is also known for her research in discrete mathematics and theoretical computer science. Maria is currently the Dean of Science at the University of British Columbia in Vancouver, the Vice-President of the Association for Computing Machinery, and holds the NSERC-IBM Chair for Women in Science and Engineering.

Karen Littleton is a Lecturer in Developmental Psychology at The Open University. Her research interests focus on the social processes of children's learning. Her previous publications include *Cultural Worlds of Early Childhood* (1998); *Learning Relationships in the Classroom* (1998); *Making Sense of Social Development* (1998) (all edited with Martin Woodhead and Dorothy Faulkner); *Learning with Computers* (1999) (edited with Paul Light); *Social Processes in Children's Learning* (with Paul Light); *Rethinking Collaborative Learning* (2000) (edited with Richard Joiner, Dorothy Faulkner, and Dorothy Miell).

Sue Marshall is a Project Director in the School of Education at The University of California, Irvine. She has managed numerous projects involving technological innovations in K-12 schools, both at UC Irvine and in her previous position as a post-doctoral fellow at Northwestern University.

Katie McMillan Culp is the Assistant Director for Research at the Education Development Center's Center for Children & Technology. She has conducted a series of evaluations of programs seeking to improve uses of technology in K-12 classrooms, including studies of teachers' and students' use of modeling and simulation tools in science classrooms. She has also led qualitative studies of technology integration at both the classroom and district level. She is a graduate of Amherst College and holds a Ph.D. in developmental psychology from Teachers College, Columbia University.

Eileen Phillips has taught elementary school for thirty years and is currently a Vice-Principal in Vancouver, Canada. She has been a teacher-researcher since 1992, and has published a number of articles on mathematics education and is a co-author of *Creative Mathematics: Exploring Children's Understanding (1997)* (with Upitis, R. et al.,). Ms Phillips is currently completing her Ph.D. with research on an exploration of children's mathematical writing at grade four.

Andee Rubin is a Senior Scientist at TERC in Cambridge, Massachusetts. Her research focuses on mathematics teaching and learning, the role of technology in supporting mathematical thinking, and the role of gender in both.

Zoë Sofia (who also publishes as Zoë Sofoulis) is Senior Lecturer in Feminist and Cultural Studies at the University of Western Sydney and has a long-standing interest in the irrational and corporeal dimensions of our relations to high technology. Her publications include *Whose Second Self? Gender and (Ir)rationality in Computer Culture* (1993), and *Planet Diana: Cultural Studies and Global Mourning,* for which she was a contributing co-editor, and various papers on feminism, technology, and contemporary art. She is currently researching and writing a book about different kinds of container technologies.

Rena Upitis, former Dean of Education at Queen's University in Canada and presently a Professor of Arts Education, has conducted research on children's use of technology in exploring music, mathematics, science, and language for the past two decades. She is currently directing a national Canadian longitudinal research study on the effects of the arts on student attitudes towards learning, student achievement, and teacher beliefs and practices.

Nicola Yelland is Professor and Head of the Department of School and Early Childhood at the RMIT University in Melbourne, Australia. Her research interests center on the use of information and communications technologies (ICT) by teachers and children in a variety of contexts. Nicola teaches undergraduate and graduate classes in mathematics education and ICT and works with teachers in professional development activities.

Index

A

Ability, 9, 11–12, 15, 40, 44–47, 66, 93, 112, 142–143, 147–148, 152, 160, 169, 196, 199, 207, 214
Access, xiii, xix, 3, 4, 8, 12–13, 15, 24, 33, 36, 56–62, 74, 77, 88, 92, 97–98, 101, 109, 114, 144, 167–170, 174–180, 183–187, 191, 194, 196, 212, 225, 230
Aesthetic, 59, 102, 107
Aggression, 38–40, 60
Alterity, 103
Animation, 18, 83, 86–87, 102, 104, 181, 185, 213–214
Assessment, xviii, 11, 24
Attitudes, 8–9, 11, 71, 80, 101, 114, 126, 143, 145, 167–168, 204, 211, 233
　　positive, 8–9, 168

B

Barbie™, 17, 34–36, 50, 119–121, 128, 135, 213
Barratt, 97, 114
Barthes, 57, 64
Bottom-up, 14, 130, 197
Binary relations, 35
Bricolage, 130, 134, 197
Brunner, Bennett & Honey, 34, 71–73
Butler, 60

C

Choices, 34, 37, 56, 60, 80–81, 221
Cognitive space, 182
Collaborative, 12–13, 16, 67, 131, 134, 144, 158, 169–170, 172, 177, 179, 184, 186, 194, 196, 231
Computer
　　culture, 14, 18, 25, 63
　　games, 16, 60
　　use in school, 6
Constructionism, 123, 192
Constructionist, 13–18, 124, 193–194
Conventional, 34, 57, 65
Conversation, 71, 76–83, 155, 204, 207, 219, 221
Culture, xviii, 10, 13–14, 16, 24, 33, 49, 58–61, 63, 65–67, 99, 143, 224, 229
Curriculum, xviii, 5, 10–11, 13–14, 24, 56–57, 59–60, 62–63, 67, 83–84, 98, 139–140, 153, 163, 196, 229
Cyberfeminism, xviii, 56, 67
Cyberfeminist, 57, 60, 62–64
Cybertechnology, 63

D

Design, xiv, xviii–xx, 23, 72, 82, 99, 106, 109, 119–122, 124, 126–127, 129–134, 174, 177, 207, 210, 214–215, 218, 230

classroom, 178, 182
computer, 168
criteria, 48, 76, 82, 85, 123, 126, 133, 135, 215, 219, 221
differences, 37
environment, 187, 213, 230
fashion, 120
game, 23–24, 35–36, 49, 87, 194, 198, 210, 214, 216, 231
graphic, 170
hardware, 212
multimedia, 184
of tasks, 12, 83, 174
online, 83, 87
project, 171, 173–174, 177–179, 182, 184, 192–193, 195
research, 25, 34, 93, 171, 177, 218
software, xiv, 167–168, 170, 172, 174, 178, 184–186
station, 212
Dialogue, 76, 112–113, 130–131, 220
Dungeons and Dragons, 38, 41

E

EA*Kids, 213, 215
E-GEMS, 209, 210, 212–215, 222, 231
Embedded, 14, 140, 144, 163–164
Enrolments, 56, 62
Epistemological pluralism, 13–14, 16
Equipment, 3, 97, 99–102, 106–109, 111–114
Equity project, 121
Expenditure, 3
Expertise, 5, 8, 36, 132, 168, 194

F

Forces, 34–35, 185

G

Game-playing, 17
Gender paradox, 34–35
Generativity, 44–45

Girl-oriented websites, 64
Globalization, 59

H

Hard mastery, 122, 126, 134, 140–141, 143, 163
Hawkins, Honey, Brunner, & Moeller, 33
Hennigan School, 194
Home, xviii, 4, 7, 16–17, 24, 60–62, 72, 77, 89–90, 104, 109–110, 128, 133, 146, 168, 171, 196, 214, 224
Hot Wheels™, 119–121
Hoyles, xviii, 3–7, 12–14, 17, 126, 131, 140–142, 158, 163, 230

I

Integrated Learning Systems, 16
Interactions, 12, 16, 20, 24, 56, 145, 151, 157–159, 163, 167, 169, 171, 175, 179, 186, 191–193, 195, 200–201, 204–207, 210
Interface, 17, 43, 66, 82–84, 88–89, 91–92, 104–106, 113, 133, 201

L

Lave and Wenger, 185
Learning, xiv–xv, xviii, xix,
gender &, 4, 12–14, 16–17, 24, 42, 48, 57, 67, 83, 87, 97–98, 101–102, 108–110
ICT &, 120–132, 134–135, 139–141, 144–145, 158–159, 162–163, 169–170, 172–174, 185–186, 191–196, 199, 201, 204–205, 207, 209–210, 212–213, 215, 229–233
LEGO/Logo, 123–128, 130–132, 134–135
Littleton, xviii, 3–4, 6, 11–13, 17, 25, 232

Index

M

Mathematical thinking, 139–141, 144, 215, 232
McKenzie & Company, 37
Messages, 39, 77–78, 82, 191, 194–195, 197, 199–204, 206
Microworld, 99, 103, 107–108
Microworlds, 168, 172, 175–176, 178–183, 185
Missing Measures, 145–148
Mortal Kombat, 37
Myst, 37, 43–44, 46–50, 89, 120

N

Narrative, 17, 19, 37, 42, 45, 47–48, 86–87, 91, 113, 216, 218, 222
National Grid for Learning, 4
National Science Foundation, 121, 187, 231, 233
New learning, 4
Nintendo generation, 55

P

Papert, 4, 13–14, 16–17, 33, 55, 98, 122–123, 126, 130, 134–135, 172, 192, 194, 197, 230
Parents, 7, 57–58, 61–62, 80, 122, 133, 146, 214
Participation, xiv, xviii, 4–6, 9–10, 24, 35, 56–57, 59–63, 79, 109, 159, 167, 170–171, 174–178, 180, 185–187, 197, 201–202
Phallic content, 40–41, 50
Phallic universe, 39–40, 48
Phoenix Quest, 210, 215, 217–219, 221–224
Physical space, 170, 181, 184
Playground Project, 17, 233
Playground team, 18
Pleasure, xviii, 39, 51, 57–60, 64–65, 67, 110, 224
Power Rangers™, 35–36
President's Committee of Advisors on Science and Technology, 33
Programming, xix, 14, 18–19, 21, 33, 113, 121–123, 126–128, 131–135, 156, 169–172, 175–176, 178–180, 182–185, 194–195, 197, 200–201, 207
Project Headlight, 194
Project SAME, 121–124, 126, 129, 132–134
Projects, 127, 145, 148
Puzzles, 212, 217–223

Q

Questions, 35, 56, 77–79, 81, 89–93, 97–98, 101, 103, 106, 109, 114–115, 135, 159, 172, 177, 184, 191–192, 194–208, 222, 224, 226

R

Rectangles, 145, 155–156
Risk-taking, 38
Role models, 10, 65

S

Scaffold, 129
  affective, 160
  cognitive, 159
  technical, 159
Scaffolded, 124, 127–130, 134, 158, 161
Scaffolding, 140, 147, 159, 162–163, 193, 205
Second self, 99, 103, 105
Secondary education, 6
Social space, 179–180, 183
Soft mastery, 122, 126, 134, 140–143, 149, 157, 163
Stereotyping, 24, 120–121
Strategy, 11, 40–42, 50, 66, 120, 133, 146, 212–213, 221, 225
Sunken Ships, 145, 153–154, 160

T

Task Force on Education Network Technology, 33
Teams, 23, 38, 168–169, 171, 173–174, 178–179, 181–182, 184, 219, 221
Technologic, 67
Technology and Design Fair, 133
Technophilia, 97, 100, 114
Telementoring, 76–77, 80, 82, 229
Technology and Design Fair, 133
TERC, xvii, xx, 219, 221–222, 232
Top-down, 14, 122, 126, 129, 134, 197
Toontalk, 18–19, 21
Transitional objects, 44, 110
Turkle, 14, 33, 63, 98–99, 103, 111, 122, 124, 126, 130, 134–135, 139–141, 149, 163, 197
Turtle paths, 145

U

University entry, 7

V

Virtual Expert, xix, 191–192, 194–196, 200–201, 205–207
Vygotsky, 128, 193, 205

W

Wellesley College, 168, 179
Wizardry, 37–38, 41–43, 48–49

Y

Y Generation, 57–60, 64–67

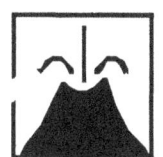 # ERUPTIONS
New Thinking across the Disciplines

Erica McWilliam
General Editor

This is a series of red-hot women's writing after the "isms." It focuses on new cultural assemblages that are emerging from the de-formation, breakout, ebullience, and discomfort of postmodern feminism. The series brings together a post-foundational generation of women's writing that, while still respectful of the idea of situated knowledge, does not rely on neat disciplinary distinctions and stable political coalitions. This writing transcends some of the more awkward textual performances of a first generation of "feminism-meets-postmodernism" scholarship. It has come to terms with its own body of knowledge as shifty, inflammatory, and ungovernable.

The aim of the series is to make this cutting edge thinking more readily available to undergraduate and postgraduate students, researchers and new academics, and professional bodies and practitioners. Thus, we seek contributions from writers whose unruly scholastic projects are expressed in texts that are accessible and seductive to a wider academic readership.

Proposals and/or manuscripts are invited from the domains of: "post" humanities, human movement studies, sexualities, media studies, literary criticism, information technologies, history of ideas, performing arts, gay and lesbian studies, cultural studies, post-colonial studies, pedagogics, social psychology, and the philosophy of science. We are particularly interested in publishing research and scholarship with international appeal from Australia, New Zealand, and the United Kingdom.

For further information about the series and for the submission of manuscripts, please contact:

        Erica McWilliam
        Faculty of Education
        Queensland University of Technology
        Victoria Park Rd., Kelvin Grove Q 4059
        Australia

To order other books in this series, please contact our Customer Service Department at:

        (800) 770-LANG (within the U.S.)
        (212) 647-7706 (outside the U.S.)
        (212) 647-7707 FAX

Or browse online by series at:

        www.peterlangusa.com